ROBERT BYRON
LETTERS HOME

ROBERT BYRON
LETTERS HOME

Edited by
LUCY BUTLER

JOHN MURRAY

To my Helpmate

Introduction and compilation © Lucy Butler 1991
Letters © The Estate of Robert Byron and Lucy Butler 1991

First published in 1991 by
John Murray (Publishers) Ltd
50 Albemarle Street, London W1X 4BD

The right of Lucy Butler to be identified as the author of this work
has been asserted by her in accordance with the Copyright, Designs
and Patents Act, 1988

British Library Cataloguing in Publication Data
Byron, Robert 1905–1941
Letters home.
1. Travel – Biographies
I. Title   II. Butler, Lucy
910.4092
ISBN 0-7195-4921-3

Photoset by Rowland Phototypesetting Ltd
Bury St Edmunds, Suffolk
Printed by The Cambridge University Press
Cambridge

Contents

Editorial Note   vi

Introduction   1
 1. Eton and Oxford, 1922–1925   7
 2. Greece, 1926–1927   57
 3. England and Austria, 1928–1929   95
 4. India and Tibet, 1929–1930   120
 5. Russia, 1932   177
 6. Persia, 1933–1934   188
 7. America, 1935   226
 8. Russia, 1935   236
 9. China, 1935–1936   256
10. Last Letters, 1939–1941   288

Index   306

Editorial Note

Of Robert Byron's letters to his mother, the main part, some 175, are first published here from the originals in family possession. Nearly as many again have been omitted as not being of sufficient interest, including as they do juvenilia from Eton and Oxford and letters dealing with family affairs or workaday procedures with his publishers and the press. In the letters here printed, editorial cuts made for the same reasons have been indicated thus: [. . .]; I have also cut out repetitious instructions as to where to write next or when to expect Robert home. Obvious misspellings and oddities of punctuation have been silently corrected but some of Robert's idiosyncratic forms of spelling have been retained. It has not been possible to ascertain the date of every letter; where there is any doubt merely the month and year have been given.

Introduction

Robert Byron was born on 26 February 1905 and lived thirty-five years. In them he achieved his aim of acquiring before he was thirty such a comprehension of the world as to make him a connoisseur of civilizations. An astringent protagonist of artistic truth, he sought to understand each country he visited from studying the origins of its art and architecture. In penetrating the mysteries of Greek fresco painting he advanced the then novel challenge of the Byzantine heritage as a creative force. Further east, Robert's great inspiration came from the revelation of the masterpieces of Timurid brickwork found in Persia. He wrote of them in his best-known work, *The Road to Oxiana*: 'Seven minarets and a broken mausoleum are all my portrait of an age. . . . Even in ruin such architecture tells of a golden age.'

The first of Robert's journeys to Greece made him aware of the Byronic significance of his name there. In researching into his ancestors he failed, as had other members of his family before him, to establish the missing link between them and the line of Lord Byron the poet – though both came from Lancashire and bore the same crest, a mermaid, and motto, *Crede Byron*. Robert's branch of the Byrons was first recorded at Newchurch Pendle in Lancashire in 1599. The first direct ancestor on record was Edmund (born 1634) who seems to have been a man of some means, having acquired property around Rochdale. He sent his son, another Edmund, to Corpus Christi College, Oxford. This Edmund became a Prebend of Bath and Wells, much respected for his saintly life, and was buried at Glastonbury. His son, yet another Edmund, made for London where he managed to secure the affection of Elizabeth Green, heiress, by gazing at her across the pews of St Anne's, Soho. His love letters, diligently copied out and preserved, are no less boring than most others.

Their elder son Thomas became quite a blood: sent to Eton, member of the Whig Club, a Colonel in the Guards, he married Lucy Anne

Whetham, a long-nosed lady of 34 who had just inherited a fortune on the death of her brother John. The Whethams were first cousins of General Wolfe, the victor of Quebec. The nice little slice of money bought the newly-marrieds the estate of Coulsdon near Croydon, where they moved into the old manor. In 1850 their great-nephew pulled the old house down and built Coulsdon Court, a substantial gabled pile of bright red brick standing in bright yellow gravel punctuated by flower-beds of bright red geraniums. This imposing property was inherited in 1863 by Robert's grandfather, Edmund Byron, who had not long left Oxford. Having married his first cousin, Julia Jeffreys, Edmund proceeded to lead the life of a country gentleman, devoted to hunting (as Master of the Old Surrey foxhounds for twenty-five years), to shooting, to being a JP and to running his estate in masterful fashion. The schoolmistress, whose house was half a mile away, was not allowed to keep a dog lest its barking disturb him. The voices of his own hounds were of course music. Edmund and Julia, a cold, unloving mother, had three sons, of whom the first two went to live in Canada. The youngest, Eric, was Robert's father.

Never strong, Eric must have been stricken with polio when a boy, whence his hunched appearance and nickname Punch. He nearly died of pneumonia at Marlborough College; overcoats were not allowed against the biting east winds off the downs. After school Eric was launched with £100 a year to make his way as an engineer. Apprenticed near Chesterfield, he shared digs with Norman Robinson, an exuberant and brilliant young man (later an inventor at Vickers) and eldest son of a large family of which Robert's mother Margaret (known as Daisy) was the second daughter of five. The Robinsons, who had changed their name from Robertson after the '45, never soiled their hands by making any money but William, Daisy's father, who bore a striking likeness to the Duke of Connaught, had had the good fortune to marry 18-year-old Alice Chater, from a family of Huguenots who had both brains and money. William seemed quite content to live off his wife's family and share jokes with his children. All the daughters painted, delicate studies of flowers in art nouveau patterns then fashionable, lilies and poppies entwined, reminiscent of 'The Blessed Damozel', as were their names. Daisy was bold enough to study at the South Kensington Art School, though she refused to adopt the 'greenery-yallery' draperies of the other students. She was thoroughly grounded in the Italian masters; the Pre-Raphaelites however she found faintly ridiculous.

Margaret Robinson and Eric Byron were married in St James's, Piccadilly, in 1903 and set up house on £150 a year and a minor engineering practice. They lived in lodgings in various places such as Wembley, where Robert was born, before moving to Bolton, then on to Anglesey and back to

Charlton and Blackheath. This peripatetic life round the suburbs meant that, for Robert, Coulsdon, always there in the background, was the one place that never changed. In describing it later he wrote: 'Looking back I shall never forget the joy of the country and the beautiful gardens, clouded as it was by a grim shadow, my grandfather.'

Mrs Byron, bored by her unrewarding existence, took to copying old masters in oils in the National Gallery and spent hours teaching her small son. She used to read him Shakespeare, and Robert distinctly remembered reciting 'All the world's a stage' at the age of 3: perhaps provoking then and there his lifelong animosity towards the Bard. He learned to read from Beatrix Potter's books, his mother spelling out the last word of each sentence. 'Thus,' wrote Robert, 'I was fitted for my struggle in the great world by learning that Jeremy Fisher fell into the P O N D.'

Robert had two sisters, Anne born at Charlton in 1910, and Lucy at Blackheath in 1912. During the First World War the Byron family moved to Chesterfield where Eric, unable to fight owing to his early neglect, became an Inspector for the Ministry of Munitions. On the outskirts of the town they leased from friends a house with a fine view of a railway viaduct and miners' begrimed cottages. From there Robert went to his preparatory school at Abberly, evacuated from Blackheath. Robert's name was put down for L. Todd's house at Eton but was withdrawn in 1918 when he won a scholarship to College. With the Armistice in November, however, Collegers who would have gone off to fight stayed on. Robert was without a place. The headmaster, Alington, could not interfere. Mrs Byron, hurrying down to Eton, sat outside the Provost's Lodgings until she had wrung a place out of him, in F. E. Robeson's not very distinguished establishment.

So in the spring of 1919 Robert went to Eton. He wrote: 'It was there I discovered how to use my mind and thus won the title of a man.' He freely acknowledged that his eyes had been opened by his friendship with Lord Clonmore (Cecil, only son of the Earl of Wicklow). Snub-nosed, and with a helpless giggle, Clonmore had been brought up by his Hamilton grandmother. He was used, wrote Robert, to 'a society still buoyed up, despite the war, on the power and prosperity of late Victorian England . . . naturally prolific of sardonic disdain for the unimportant which destroys the canting phrase or the pretentious attitude as the sun destroys the snow. Clonmore looked at Eton as Voltaire looked at France. We railed at the school while we were there, pitying the masters as being outside the pale of normal intelligence and looking forward to the time, now abundantly realized, when the captains and athletes who imposed on us should have sunk into the limbo we so confidently reserved for them' (Robert's early memoir, 'Remember the Morning'). This aristocratic facility to stand back and weigh up gave Robert at least two years' advantage over the more conventional public school types when he arrived at Oxford. It nourished his enquiring and combative attitude of mind. Being with Robert was never dull.

In 1922 Edmund Byron died. Instead of leaving his estate to Eric, as was his intention, he had been overpersuaded by his daughters to share it out among them all. They in their rapacity insisted on the estate being rapidly sold off in small lots, thereby forfeiting a gold mine; situated as it was twelve miles from Charing Cross.

In 1919 Eric, no longer obliged to live in Chesterfield, decided to move to Wiltshire to be near Savernake Forest, in which he used to wander as a boy out from Marlborough. The family settled in a small Georgian farmhouse perched on a hill overlooking the Bath Road. With the advent of his share of the capital from the Coulsdon estate Eric was prepared to launch out, having his eye on Savernake Lodge situated in the middle of the forest and inhabited by a relict of Lord Brownlow. She was assiduously cultivated and, in 1923, was persuaded to agree to a Byron take-over of the rest of her lease from the Ailesbury estate. So in the hot June, with the poppies and borage blazing their colours up the border of the garden within the forest, the family moved in.

Savernake Lodge, known locally as The Ruins, was the converted stables of a dower house burned down in the 1860s. The stables had been converted into a house featuring a long passage with rooms leading off it and ending in a large drawing-room. Above were bedrooms of the same layout and the slated roof was finished off at the southern end by a louvered tower. At right-angles to the drawing-room a wide passage led to another bedroom and study appropriated by Robert. The house ended in a large raftered room known as the nursery where the children spent hours by the open log fire reading Baroness Orczy, kicking the dogs out of the way, playing the piano or keeping the gramophone going with records of Brahms or Liszt, while Robert wrote. A window in this room became an escape route for them all. When unwanted callers were imminent they would leap out and into the forest, leaving a furious Mrs Byron trapped in the drawing-room. The garden led through a wilderness of rhododendrons up to the deer fence and in the autumn stags could be heard roaring as they defended their territory against one another. And an occasional fox might be barking at the moon.

For the Byron children the weeks of winter were marked off by hunting days. Robert and his father shared horses until Robert bought his own in Ireland, the beloved Aubrey. Robert's affection for his father, not an intellectual man, was enhanced by all the country interests which they both enjoyed. Mr Byron, no longer earning his living, was always busy about the place, cutting down trees, making a tennis court, a member of the local hunt committee, manager of the forest school. Mrs Byron, though lacking a formal education, had an integrity of mind that never allowed Robert to get away with the slipshod or the unconvincing. Her love of truth had been transmitted to her son and at times she carried it to lengths beyond the border of politeness, to the embarrassment of her family. Once when at her lunch table Sachie Sitwell lamented to her how difficult it was to find subjects about which to write, she enquired: 'Mr Sitwell, why do you write at all?', a question his friends had long refrained from asking.

Mrs Byron loved entertaining and was only happy when the house was full; and full it often was. When at Oxford Robert would collect up his friends, pile into any handy car, and drive over to Savernake. Then the nursery would echo with Victorian ditties. At weekends neighbours such as Bryan and Diana Guinness would come over from Biddesdon bringing perhaps Nancy Mitford, Hamish Erskine, Oswald Mosley or Johnnie Churchill in tow. Friends like Olivia Greene and Oliver Messel were asked for hunt balls. Henry Yorke brought his beautiful fiancée Dig down from London. Young Derek Hill came up from his hated school at Marlborough for reassurance. Violet Wyndham was always arriving with her house party – somewhere to go on Sunday afternoons. In the semi-darkness, the house being lit only by oil lamps, such figures as Alice Keppel, Lord Berners, Hermione Baddeley would appear out of the gloom watched by G. M. Young and literary Mona Wilson, who had walked over from Oare. Among this crowd wandered Robert's two sisters. Beautiful Anne with her talent for design, which she never fulfilled, was dabbing at an art career but preferred her hunting and the young men who flocked around her; Lucy, of the same greenish fair hair as Robert, was too shy to say much, though occasionally coming out with an acceptable contribution to the brilliance around her.

Such was the home to which Robert returned time after time. He described it as a home 'which I loved more than anything I knew and an upbringing which had implanted – though I did not understand this at the time, certain ineradicable standards, standards I could no more tamper with than my own face'.

The letters published here abound with references to home. They confirm that Robert was a traveller who loved England. He had written elsewhere: 'If I love my country for the sake of the familiar scene, of the people and the objects that speak to me of my childhood and shaped me into a man, it is because these things are the symbol of my life's pursuit, of freedom, justice, truth, of the desires cherished in common by the inhabitants of the earth.'

These letters of Robert's were not carefully composed. They were dashed off in his horrid handwriting and old-fashioned spelling to his mother to share with her his immediate impressions and feelings at each new experience he encountered. When absent from her there was not a week in his life, unless he warned her beforehand, in which he did not write to her once if not twice. His whereabouts seemed to be no deterrent. Whether on Mount Athos with its mule post, or in a rest-house in Tibet, or a filthy caravanserai in Persia, he wrote as usual and somehow the letters arrived at home, often sent across Siberia as being the fastest route. Unlike his travel books, so painstakingly distilled from his diaries and notebooks, in which Robert aimed to share his pleasure with the reader, these letters give occasional glimpses of the purpose which held his life together. They remain an expression of a humanist ideal in which Robert viewed the world from his own perspective, a perspective lovingly inculated in him by his mother.

I

Eton and Oxford
1922–1925

My Darling Mother

I have little doubt that Psalm 90 is the most beautiful thing in the English Language. We had it at Grandpa's funeral, do you remember?

Poor Robeson is in a frenzied calm: he either thinks I have had a mental relapse and that my mind is at last really unhinged *or* that I have started on such an unprecedented course of vice, that he is quite unable to check it: Henry[1] had told me stories of a fabulous antique shop where the man was half-witted and overflowed with priceless rarities. So on Friday afternoon, we were walking very slowly in the most middle-aged way in the depths of Windsor, two miles out of bounds, calmly discussing Lady Cardigan's Memoirs – how she poor woman has been completely overshadowed by Mrs Asquith whom of course Henry knows and *hates*.

Well we were walking along between rows of aspidistra-covered villas, when one Slater, a master, came along in a car driven by a Hogarth-like ruffian – Slater put on his best glare – with superb nonchalance we continued our conversation – Slater drove wildly on and stopped about 500 yds up the street where he thought we couldn't see him. Nevertheless we walked straight on, gave names and addresses with supreme disdain, continued our discussion, entered several other antique shops and went home. I am up to Robeson for German and forgot to do five things for him. Of course he never gets angry with me –

---

1. Henry Yorke, later the novelist Henry Green, author of *Blindness*, *Living*, *Pack my Bag*, etc.

he can't for some extraordinary reason – but I know the symptoms. Anyway Alington was *quite* delighted about it all and flung his usual cheap sarcasm over us like lumps of dough. We eventually had to write out the Bounds rules six times. But I think it has endangered Robeson's health. Robeson knows the Yorkes, they both live at Tewkesbury: can't you see him telling Mrs Yorke I am really not a suitable companion for her son! How I should love it. Henry assures me his people will hate me – so of course I am quite prepared. Of course Henry is very accomplished in his way: he can talk like no other person I've ever met. It is a talent I have never seen so exaggerated. He is also very funny. He makes great friends with such people as Lord Dunsany and Leo Maxse[1] who are reputed to be the cleverest people in England – especially the latter. May I ask him out to lunch on Saturday? I think you would love him! I really must go to bed now – if Robeson found me with the light on, he would wire for the Lunacy Commissioners.

You know I told you I was going to have lessons in lacquering, well I went down to Haliday and he said he could do it – that it was very easy and also he would teach me how to model in plaster of Paris and glue – so at last I shall be able to carry out my mad designs and make candlesticks covered with fruit and flowers exquisitely lacquered. [. . .] What a wicked man Alington is. Bell has set us an essay on 'going out in the rain' – original in a cheap way. History is rather dull, but so is everything. For heaven's sake see that I leave at the end of the summer – I mean this middle-aged stagnation with occasional fits of suicidal depression *cannot* be good for me. Still there is Henry and letter-writing. Cecil[2] is clamouring for me to go over there and stay – his description of Shelton in the spring is too enticing – I can imagine it. I am longing for leave. The Yorkes belong to the extremist class of English intellectuals – people who cherish the memories of conversationalists and who know everyone with a mind in England. I know you think I am on the brink of destruction, but wait till you meet Henry – may I ask him out to lunch?

Love to Papa and sisters
so looking forward to Saturday
Bobs

---

1. Leading literary figures of the day.
2. Cecil (Billy), Lord Clonmore, later 8th Earl of Wicklow. He became friends with Robert when they were both in Robeson's house at Eton.

February 1922   Eton

Dear Mother

Thank you so very much for your charming long letter and the plate marks. I enclose what information I can find. I should say that the Robinson sugar-sifter is far more valuable than anything in the Coulsdon collection, but I don't know. I may be quite wrong: but it is one of the earliest ones made as they started quite late in the history of plate.

The other day I bought the most charming lamp of *very old* wood carved richly into flowers – about a yard long – so pretty, I think – everyone so far has laughed when they see it – most ridiculously rough and *very* old I should say. I am pursuing my search for church candlesticks, but I have just heard from a Roman Catholic place and the only passable ones are sixty pounds each – no good, do you think? I *do* wish this frost would stop. If it goes on there will be skating and I shall have to buy some skates. It will then thaw at once.

I am staying out: not because I am ill but because of the draught in chapel. Alington and I had an argument yesterday because I persisted in huddling myself in that huge striped scarf of yours when one is not allowed in chapel. However I am waiting for my letter to appear in the *Chronicle* on Thursday. [. . .]

Drawing extras with Evans are a farce. I wish I could go to the Slade for a while. My whole life is made up of a craving for beautiful things.

I went beagling with Henry Yorke yesterday: I do love him. He talks in a very affected delightful voice: he isn't affected not in his voice but it sounds it – d'you know what I mean.

I started explaining that as I had quarrelled with all my relations perhaps I shouldn't be able to come to London. Henry said 'Oh do come to us – please – we've got a very large house – not the least inconvenience – bring your people too (!) you may be rather frightened of my Father – just like a large negro – he will shake [you] by the hand and run away – my mother will quarrel with you at once and then be charming – do come etc.'

They have got a very large House, Adam from top to bottom. Then he began again 'My Father, you must know makes baths – has the most delightful showroom also the most bewitching typist: he has taken to choosing the parlourmaid lately and in consequence we are surrounded by a perfect bevy of beauty: my mother outwardly fumes but is inwardly delighted.' I then told him you were on the lookout for a bath and he started the most captivating description of a black marble one made for the King of Siam to bathe his ladies in etc. His uncle designs the baths and they make the most immense profits, and did all through the war. He is so amusing. He said 'I have firmly convinced half the school that I am penniless: they believe that my existence depends on the charity of M'Tutor' (notoriously stingy!).

He told me all about his uncle Lord Leconfield's enormous collection of china, pictures etc. at Petworth: and *how he absolutely refuses* to let anyone see it ever – so sensible, I think. Dear Henry I wish he was in M'Tutor's. I think I shall try to go down to Coulsdon with him and Rudolph[1] on the Sunday of Leave. [. . .] I think I shall end now. So looking forward to you all coming – I am bored stiff with History and my life is made up of writing dull essays. Going mad by degrees

Love
Bobs

March 1922   Eton

My dearest Mother

Let me first warn you I have an immense amount to say and feel that I shall have to do it in serials: everything has been crammed with incident. [. . .]

To begin my tale.

I am very tired. Social activity for three whole days is racking but interesting. So lucky I get a certain amount of capability from you: otherwise the labour would be appalling. Also of course, I have had nothing to eat. Not that there wasn't profusion, but you know what it is. M'Tutor is too pleasant for words: he begged me some time ago to tell him what the Yorkes said about him. They *did* say a lot but all I shall tell him is 'violent militarist'!! Henry was going to bring back the carriage

---

1. Rudolph Messel, son of Harold George Messel and Leonora Gibson of New York, first cousin of Oliver Messel and Anne, Countess of Rosse. In the same house at Eton as Robert and Cecil Clonmore.

umbrella for the same exploit![1] His father delighted at the idea! But his mother wanted it.

Well to the 'incident'. Next door to the Yorkes live the Whitbreads, bulti-billionaires (beer) and Lord-Lieutenants. We were met at Paddington by a palace that drove us to the house. Junior Whitbread is quite insignificant: but it was so pleasant.

Then the most astounding thing happened. There was an immense crush coming out of Paddington and we were crawling slowly along between a crush of cars, when we suddenly came abreast with a large blatant mermaid – behold! Grandpa's old car, driven by two Red Cross nurses with some Etonians inside! An extraordinary combination – very odd! We got to the door and entered. Mrs Yorke, short and dark, could I have no doubt be the most terrifying woman – worse than you – deliciously sarcastic and with the Wyndham facility for Johnsonian English, which of course Henry has inherited.

I am afraid I can't go on now – the letter will become duller than otherwise as I am so tired. Wait till tomorrow.

Tuesday

I have got your letter. I am sorry if mine was unkind – I was so angry and wretched that you should have got hold of the wrong end of the stick. And you still have rather. Don't you see that the umbrella incident coincides with every *convention* Etonians have ever had: that when Etonians hear of it, they puff out their chests with pride and go one better: this is the worst of it. No, it was not unconventional, I assure you. At least I suppose by convention here, one means the traditions of boys and not a *few* militarist masters. I'm afraid there was nothing unconventional in it, so sorry. Shall we close the subject? Even M'dame says she thinks M'Tutor's had to make such a fuss over nothing. I put it down to spite, but may be wrong. As for risks, I assure you I never take them: my nerve is that of a middle-aged stockbroker.

Now let me go on with my story. Yes, Mrs Yorke – very charming. We had lunch and then rushed to the cinema. Henry goes *every* day in the holidays – he is a connoisseur. Lord Leconfield complained to *The Times* about it once. I've forgotten the film but we saw Princess May's wedding *twice*. We then came back and had tea. Mrs Yorke and I

---

1. This refers to Robert opening up an umbrella while on OTC parade at the onset of rain.

discovered a common bond: *Decoration*, we talked for a long time: she became so excited over my lacquering she shewed me round the house. It was too lovely, *all* Adam from garret to kitchen with Angelica Kauffmann ceilings. We talked incessantly, got on to the subject of Grinling Gibbons and there she said she must take me to Petworth, her brother Lord Leconfield's place, which contains one of the finest collections of works of art in England, doesn't it? Anyway nobody has ever been allowed to see over it yet, not even well-known artists. In fact he has given terrible offence in several quarters I believe so I shall be too delighted to go and Henry assures me that it will come off at the end of next holidays, when his mother's car is all right again. I should feel immensely privileged. [. . .] Then Gerald Yorke, the elder brother arrived from Cambridge. Very handsome and *very* amusing. Then Mr Yorke arrived ditto, ditto. Sarcasm flew. Mrs Yorke of course knew the Bevans[1] in a business way and described Mrs Bevan as Birmingham middle-class. Then we got into a taxi and went to *The Bat*. We had Lady Evelyn Cotterell's stalls as she had just died: otherwise we shouldn't have got in. Mrs Yorke in a striped gold and black very long and tight-fitting gown. Wonderful dresses and lots of men in swallow-tails: stiff with Etonians. The King and Queen were in a box and appeared to be enjoying themselves. Lady Dalhousie was opposite them, her neck and bosom *literally blazing* with diamonds. Mrs Day scowled at me from the dress circle, she was very ugly in white of all things. In the play crime followed crime: lights went on and off. Gerald Yorke terrified two rows of the stalls by a bloodcurdly whisper 'There's a man under the sofa!' There wasn't. The King is said to have gone to Revilles[2] and asked if the waist might not be a little more defined in the royal wedding dress. 'Impossible' he was told and retired abashed!

Yes how *The Bat* would have bored you! But I enjoyed it very much. Quite the thing to see!! Mrs Yorke said apropos of Adam that Americans pay millions for any panelling or dadoing in wood so of course you might sell the drawing-room panelling for a few thousands. [. . .]

Then we went to bed. Sunday morning we spent at the Zoo – so trying, but the Yorkes would make anything amusing. [. . .]

1. G. L. Bevan had been arrested in Vienna in June 1921 and was condemned at the Old Bailey for unscrupulous financial dealings.
2. Court Dressmaker.

Mrs Yorke's brother, a handsome full Colonel and wife Muriel, came to dinner. 'Muriel' and Mrs Yorke hate [each other], so I was informed. After dinner we played bridge. As they had been asked especially to play with Henry and me, I really didn't see how to refuse. I hadn't the face to be thought one who thinks it wrong to play cards on Sundays. I really don't see what I could have done without being rude. 'When one is in Rome . . .' Colonel Yorke was an exceedingly bad player and Henry won 7/- off me. Mrs Yorke was furious. But Henry begs me not to pay. I hope this Sabbath debauchery doesn't make you squirm. But what would you have done under the circumstances? It isn't as if I was grown up or knew them. And as you often say 'Convention!' and if I had refused they could have looked on me as a Presbyterian aesthete, a pose which I do not try to attain to. Then we went to bed.

On Monday we went out. Mrs Yorke took us to look at her hat shop windows. She has very good taste. Her family are very frightened of her. I think she liked my contradicting her. [. . .]

Then we wandered round the other side into the National Gallery. The pictures are all rearranged and the place re-done up. Awfully well done. I revelled in it. Henry, brought up on Turner who spent most of his life at Petworth, gazed enthralled at Turner. I quoted Frith at him which drove him mad. [. . .] Then we left and Henry took me to lunch with his grandmother Lady Leconfield, a sister of Lord Rosebery: very witty and over seventy. She had the most exquisite dinner service, dark cream with little flowers all over it. Dear old lady. Henry is so fond of her.

Then we went to the cinema and saw the Royal wedding three times with the same march each time. [. . .] Then we went back to tea. Mrs Yorke gave me a pound; should I have accepted? I don't know. Luckily the footman and servants had all departed to Tewkesbury for a large house party on Wednesday and so there was only the butler to tip – such interesting details!! Then we returned here: oh how blank. Beagling this afternoon. [. . .] Henry with my assistance persuaded his people to let him resign from the Corps. Will you write to Robeson about me? [. . .] Half mile on Friday – oh! Hell!!

Love Bobs

November 1922   Windsor

Dearest Mother

I hope you will forgive the horrid little postcard but I really haven't had a moment's spare time today till now – eight o'clock. Let me explain why.

Directly after chapel Howard[1] and I went up to the station to meet Rothenstein[2] who was coming down to lecture to the Eton Society of Arts: that is to say that the Eton Society of Arts got him down themselves, which is in itself a triumph. Rothenstein is, though you probably don't know it, a very well-known personality in intellectual London, having been established for over thirty years, a friend of Beardsley, and the intimate contemporary of Augustus John, MacEvoy, Clutton Brock etc.

He was a charming little man, about 5 foot 2 inches high, hideously ugly rather like a Japanese, with a funny round Homburg, a thick blue woollen scarf, black overcoat and a funny little very dark speckly double-breasted suit. Black oily hair – not bald, but not long.

A perfectly *charming* little man – we talked to him all the way down from the station and round the buildings, a real knowledge of old masters [. . .] but not tiresomely abstracted. Howard tried to talk High Art and explain how we had changed the attitude of Eton towards ART. I spragged this by saying we had done it by shewing them that Art wasn't necessarily serious (this is entirely true and due to me and Henry; we *have* had an influence I think). Then to lunch. [. . .]

After luncheon to his lecture – luckily (again through my efforts) a good number of just plain commonsense people turned up, besides masters, Mrs Alington, children, Henry with his Aunt, Miss Yorke, the lady-in-waiting, who is staying with the Alingtons.

Then he spoke: extraordinary. His theory was this: (I should remember it, as you can see at once it is the right one – the only one that covers the facts) In the old days artists were *given* their subjects. They painted to order more or less – set subjects – crucifixions or battle scenes

---

1. Brian Howard, aesthete and poet, never fulfilled his early promise by writing anything substantial.
2. Sir William Rothenstein, portraitist, Principal of the Royal College of Art, father of Sir John Rothenstein and Michael Rothenstein.

to portray the ambitions of Kings. The Renaissance broke away from this, but still set subjects were painted – portraits and classical legends, then the Pre-Raphaelites tried to break away from this again and to paint *what they saw*. But then others, breaking away even more, left entirely to themselves ever since the Renaissance, flew to light and abstract form – just as abstract philosophy never solidifies, so the modern art, brought about by this process, is only to be regarded in the light of an interesting experiment. The gist of his speech was however that all this evil was caused by the public leaving the artist to himself, if they helped him to choose his subjects as they used to he would ripen and develop far more fruitfully. To illustrate this he told us a story of Whistler which is *so* interesting that I must write it down and put it in my scrap book.

In his old age, Whistler in a never-published letter (it would destroy the theories of all biographers) wrote to a friend, saying how he regretted having gone off on his superficial impressionist track and not having started at the beginning and 'understood Ingres when he was a child'. In the same way the new movement, R. said, has petered out: and in Paris they are returning to the old set subjects. He then talked of the necessity for keeping English art English, which pleased me and ended by speaking at great length on the necessity for the employment of our great artists on great public buildings etc. England, richer than Greece or Italy, can't even afford painters for her public buildings. But he owned that vulgar people wanted vulgar art and should have it: he whispered in my ear afterwards alone, that really good art for the masses was no good at all.

Then he answered questions, *brilliant* – softly epigrammatic, a wonderful man – *so* unbelievably unassuming and yet extraordinarily clear, clever and thank heaven unaesthetic, somehow at the same time giving one an impression of saintliness.

All about a person you have probably never heard of before is no doubt uninteresting. I will shew you some things he has done on St Andrew's Day and you will see he is no mean artist. [. . .] His small unassuming portraits are *far better* than those charcoal things by Orpen and Sargent. [. . .] Then after the lecture following Powell and him and talking at the same time, I suddenly found myself in the crowded drawing-room of the Alingtons. *Mrs* half embraced me. This she does to everyone. Lady Lyttleton was there whoever she is – very witty I believe. Then we went back to tea in Howard's room and then to chapel.

After that and tea I couldn't write as I had to play in M'Tutor's jazzband which consists of one piano, two swanee whistles, 1 swanee piccolo, 1 banjo, 1 violin and me – who plays drum cymbal bell hollow box all with two drumsticks. *We really are very good.* Henry comes sometimes plus fiddle. We play innumerable tunes with no music and no conductor – this is genius. [. . .]

Love
Bobs

Robert went up to Merton College on 19 January 1923. He was still a month away from his eighteenth birthday. He always maintained that he chose Merton as being the only college in Oxford with an endowed kitchen, but his father might have added that the fees were less; and less academically rewarding were the tutorials which Robert perfunctorily attended. Cecil Clonmore and Rudolph Messel were already in residence. Robert regarded himself as extremely fortunate to be given the 'second best rooms in college', pannelled and overlooking Christ Church Meadow. He lost no time in gathering up his Eton friends; Harold Acton, whom he described as a 'remarkable sight with his grey bowler on top of black side whiskers and a black stock', Alfred Duggan, large-nosed and hospitable with his scurrilous stories – during a game of sardines his mother, Lady Curzon, 'hid under the bed for half an hour with the Aga Khan to make the party go'. Alfred had a drinking problem so bad that his mother was forced to hire a keeper to accompany him everywhere. Robert's friendship with David Talbot Rice, the future Byzantinist, developed after reading a paper on Turner to the Asiatic Society of which David was President. Robert described him hunting with the Heythrop, soaring over the fences like a heron in flight. Then Gavin Henderson, absurdly rich, to whom Robert became best man and later executor. Bryan Guinness, gentle, shy, romantic, son of Walter Guinness and Lady Evelyn; though a keen huntsman 'Bryan falls off his horse before he gets to the meet'. David Greene, six foot seven, prone to dressing up in débutantes' dresses of scarlet chiffon and one of the earliest fans of West Indian jazz. And Henry Yorke, seldom sober as he admits in *Pack my Bag*.

Robert spent his afternoons hunting through the more obscure streets of Oxford, determined to develop his taste in the experiments of his purchases. These included a picture found as the backing for a washhandstand which he refers to as a Breughel or Van Lint.[1] He took it to the Ashmolean for advice. The Keeper of the Fine Arts allowed that the picture, although not a Breughel, was certainly done in his studio under his eye and was rather good.

In March 1923, Robert went to Italy with Lord Beauchamp as a companion to his son Hugh Lygon, not yet up at Oxford. Robert described Lord Beauchamp as 'one of those indefatigable sightseers who map out every moment of every day weeks ahead'. Seven years later Robert wrote to his mother begging her to go to the Italian Exhibition at Burlington House to 'see all the things that transformed me from an idiot into a person when I went to Italy with Lord Beauchamp'.

January 1923   Merton College, Oxford

My dearest Mother

I am so sorry to have written so little but have been so fearfully busy about nothing all last week and trying to settle in. [. . .] My room is beautiful – one that anyone might envy. I am lucky getting it, as I think it is the nicest room I have seen in Oxford yet. [. . .] I have also spent three pounds on the room, as it is extremely sparsely furnished, and they have done so much and taken so much trouble and are so solicitous after my likes and dislikes, that I daren't ask for any more. [. . .] I still really want two more tables but must wait. The College are providing the curtains, just the colour I don't want, but it can't be helped. I shall get those coral ones one day.

I have not got to know many people inside the college, but a good many out. Miles came and spent an evening in my room the other day and I am going to breakfast with him on Wednesday – why breakfast? The problems of life that confront one here are
  1. How to find time to do any work.
  2. How to get to bed before one (a shilling fine imposed every time you enter the college after eleven – I have been in *once* this term before).

---

1. A Flemish contemporary of Pieter Breughel the Younger.

3. How to get drunk cheaply.
4. How to be rude first.
5. How to sign one's name.

We had a wonderful evening last night. Alfred Duggan[1] the brother of the one at Eton gave a dinner party, followed by a visit to a sort of Los Angelos dancehall in the Cowley Road. After seven glasses of champagne, two of port and the paraphernalia of cocktails and liqueurs attendant on these orgies, I found myself dancing the Boston twostep with feeling and I only then realised what the joy of dancing was. I have a very strong head which is an accomplishment here. Dear Duggan – he is so nice – but so extravagant and generous – and it is so difficult to pay it back. [. . .] He is very witty, and wrote an article about his stepfather Curzon the other day which was so libellous that the printers refused it. He was expelled from Eton – I have always been surprised at what little stigma attaches to this feat. One's day here is something like this.

Roll-call 5 to 8 – bath after or before. Breakfast by fire 8.45. May or may not be lecture from 10 to 12. Lunch at 1.15. Afternoon spent in Darrell's motor or antique shops – I hope to play hockey occasionally. Tea at Fuller's or Ellison and Cavell's as cheap there as in college: may or may not be an hour's tutorial in the evening. Dine in hall at 7.30 – or dine out. Cinema or orgy afterwards. Gates shut at 12 – a life, as you perceive, so fitted to prepare one for the thorny paths of this world. I am making the best of it and have bought some very nice suede shoes for 32/6. Never again, I am quite convinced, shall I have such comfort or such a beautiful room to live in – it is as well then to enjoy it while one can.

I dined in Christ Church Hall the other night with Talbot Rice[2] – such fun – at the guest table – wonderful food and all the Etonians I dislike. I have a regular lunch consisting of cold mutton, mint sauce, salad and bread and butter and Gorgonzola. Quite filling. [. . .]

Best love
Bobs

---

1. Stepson of Lord Curzon and later an historical novelist.
2. David Talbot Rice.

February 1923   Merton College, Oxford

My darling Mama

[. . .] Thank you so much for your letter – I am sorry not to have written much, but in the 'excitement of the new Hell into which he was suddenly plunged, Alastair's soul was deadened even to the ties of home affection, and the beast in him predominated over all the precepts of his mother's knee'. I am thinking of writing a book on these lines – would it sell? As a matter of fact I have found it rather difficult to get any spare time during my first fortnight, having been shoved straight into the middle of a ready-made 'set', so to speak. They are all very nice and witty. There are us at Merton – 'that lot' Cecil [Clonmore], Rudolph [Messel], Geoffrey Taylor and myself. Then at Christ Church there are Talbot Rice (who talks Johnsonian English and Cockney), Harold Acton, the poet, who has lost most of his youthful affectations, and vaguely Dick Darrell, who is an American, Yale's champion wrestler, and has a Ford and a cousin called Mrs Pearce who lives in the outskirts of this disgusting town. At Balliol are 'Alf' [Duggan] who has six hundred a year and offered to mount me out with the drag on a racing mare which he can't hold (I refused politely) – and John Heygate[1] who was in the sixth form at Eton, most charming person. In rooms are Peter Rufer who has been here for years, and Mungo Scone who gives people poisoned chocolates, has a degree, a car and an incredible fund of gossip. Last of all comes Gavin Henderson,[2] who is of course unbelievably wealthy and very hospitable. There are others that I know vaguely, but have forgotten. The great difference between this place and Eton is that you never seem to meet anyone if you go out and so are very apt not to see your friends for days at a time. Alf and John Heygate dined with Rudolph and me in Hall last night and we are going again to dine at Balliol tonight. It is such fun dining in other people's Halls and such a cheap form of entertainment. Balliol has disgusting food and they are all very ill-mannered – as compared with us. Nobody else seems to dine in foreign Halls except us. I do enjoy it. Christ Church is wonderful, because they have a guest table, near a great fire, with a five-course dinner – all the tables are lighted with little candlelamps in the middle, so pretty.

---

1. Writer, later Baronet.
2. Later 2nd Lord Faringdon.

I am sorry about the year's accounts – such a blow, I know the feeling. How delightful it will be now that we can leave the neighbourhood unentertained, with a clear conscience. Such a relief – you know I never want amusing in the holidays. [. . .]

[Last page of letter missing.]

February 1923   Merton College, Oxford

My darling Mibble
[. . .] You don't quite enter into the spirit of my corner cupboards: if I bought them for six guineas and after six months enjoyment, sold them for twenty, I should be doing quite well. If only I could obtain six guineas extraneous to my allowance. I must try and write an article for the *Isis*, or something. I shall start a corner cupboard fund which will prove the capital of my antique business. I am going to keep an antique shop with Talbot Rice.

We had such a lovely bicycle ride yesterday – through Nuneham to Clifton Hamden; the bridge was looking perfectly lovely with the floods up – then along that road by the river – all the water was pouring over the island instead of going decently through the lock – past the gate that won't meet and up into the village. We looked at the church and then to the Plough to tea. The place was looking too lovely, with the evening light maddering everything. Cecil and I walked down to the landing stage and found the boats right up in the roof of the boat house. [. . .] After tea we set off for Abingdon – it was about a quarter to five when we left the village, they told us it was too muddy to go the old way past Sandbank Point – so we went round by Appleford and along the road which the footpath joins. Do you remember that rather wild open bit of country just there on that road – with some haystacks on the left as you go towards Culham (how the wind used to impede our food-laden progress!)? This was looking too gorgeous with a flaming blooded sunset behind the haystacks – great huge black clouds scudding up on top of it – the very fields were red and the haystacks in silhouette edged with glowing ruby – it was perfectly marvellous, we all stopped in amazement to look, we then hurried on as it was getting dark and we had no lamps. We left Sutton Courtenay on the left and shot over that monstrous little bridge at Culham. By this time it was raining in torrents and we none of us had any coats. At last we got into Abingdon, looking perfectly beautiful in the semi-darkness, with the great octagonal brewery and the spire silhouetted and reflected in the river. There a bicycle broke – and hiring another, we struggled on, tearing up and down hill in utter darkness till after being requested by a policeman to walk just before Folly Bridge, we arrived home at seven – wet and happy – the first time I have taken exercise for 3 weeks – must do it again. It was so nice seeing all the old country again, so pretty it looked. Even Rudolph who hates the country and John Heygate, who thought we were mad, enjoyed it intensely.

Goodbye and
best love
Bobs

June 1923   Oxford University Reform Club

My darling Mother

[. . .] I have bought that Van Lint or Wint (Breughel) or whatever its name is: eight shillings: and another to the man who bid and got it cheap, makes nine. Then I shall sell it for ten and make 10 per cent profit. What more could one want?

I did enjoy yesterday [the Fourth of June] – it was perfectly heavenly – there were none of the *hideous* responsibilities of being a boy. Do let me begin at the beginning and bore you to the end. (I can see how bitter you were about the length of my last letter.)

Alfred arrived in car and bowler at midday and found us (Cecil and I) arguing about the play. [. . .] I may tell you to start with that I have got a tie which shortens people's lives when they see it. It is oyster cream silk with just that coffee timbre. [. . .] Anyway in the motor it was hidden under your scarf. There was a lot of traffic: just outside Maidenhead we ran out of petrol, but found that there was an extra tin in the back. Alfred was quite cautious. We arrived at the Burning Bush at 1.30 – there was the usual turmoil. Cecil got out and strutted off to M'Tutor's to lunch with his ward, while Alfred and I went on to the White Hart. There we were ushered past a queue of clamouring misery into a private room (the drawing-room) with a table for *twelve* and a footman – and only Lady Curzon[1] and Marcella and us to eat it as Hubert had been sent up to London with a temperature and a hospital nurse that morning and his friend wouldn't come without him. It was too ridiculous – you know what one generally goes through at the 4th of June with one's food – here in a private room and a footman of their own. Lady Curzon thought it so funny too and explained that she had had to walk up to Windsor and that it had nearly killed her as she never put foot to the ground and that everyone had stared at her so, she couldn't think what was the matter – she's so amusing and sees the point of herself so. Perhaps you saw her photograph in *The Times*. [. . .] She looks horrid in it. [. . .] She had a black and white dress and that coat was a perfect marvel, she was so proud of it too and said that the King had liked it so much, he had had one of his robes made into one for 'Elizabeth'.[2] It was all ermine inside (with no tails – much more effective), outside the very plainest black cloth [. . .] one caught a glimpse of the ermine as she moved. I do like good clothes – one never sees them here at all – it was nice to get back to them, though people are not well dressed this year [. . .] I wish you had been there; you would have looked so much better dressed than most people. Marcella had brought an extra pair of stockings in *case* the others went into holes. I hope you don't think all this very gossipy and snobbish. I do like describing people with personalities, who are really sarcastic and amusing. Then after that ridiculous lunch, huddled at one end of the table, we left in taxis: I got out halfway down the hill and met Cecil who was walking up with his ward, who is small and fair and quite impervious to outward circumstances. Then we went and walked round Upper Club. I saw lots of people I knew, from M'Tutor's – John Spencer looking very handsome and well dressed (3 years of *my* tuition), Henry roaring and gesticulating with a crowd of Aunts and his brother – however we did manage to talk a little. [. . .]

Then we went to the Eton Society of Arts exhibition which was *very good* – extraordinarily high standard covered with portraits of Henry. Then – the accumulation on my chest being intolerable I bought yards

---

1. Grace, Marchioness of Curzon and Kedleston, previously married to Alfred Duggan by whom she had Hubert, Alfred and Marcella Duggan.
2. The Duchess of York, now the Queen Mother.

of thermogine at the chemist and put it on. I could not wear a coat over my coffee cream, the effect of the tie would have been lost. People goggled at it. I was very nearly white – Cecil was all in black – we looked like an advertisement for whisky. I must go now to get that Van Dint, but will continue later. [. . .]

The thermogine was made of cayenne pepper (they told me so) – I found difficulty in not sneezing the whole afternoon. Then we went and took tea in Tulls – so delicious to get back to real *food*. Lobster cutlets, proper salad and iced coffee. How I enjoyed it. After that we returned for absence, where by the grace of God we met Alfred, Lady Curzon having departed to London. Cecil spent some time talking to the Governor-General of Ulster and his cousins: then we struggled down to the procession of boats. It was delightfully gloomy and very cold, but the thermogine saved my life. The river looked very pretty after Oxford!!! The Castle shewed up white against a black sky – it was lovely. It was nice to be back – so different from here. The 4th of June at Eton is concentrated England: after Oxford quadrangles, the schoolyard is so magnificent. Everything is *of the best* and stands for all that one cares for in this world, the institutions of the English Upper Classes. One speaks from this foreign point of view, because except for the dullest most bigoted and most snobbish sets, Oxford produces no vestige of any such thing. Everything here is founded on reason, not instinct, and reason is never right in this country.

However – after the most appalling squash at the Brocas, we got out onto the road and Cecil, his ward, Alfred and myself repaired to the Private room and the footman. Diamonds were sitting in hungry queues on the stairs – pearls and sables clawed the commissionaire. *I* had a private footman. How Cecil and I laughed over it afterwards. Alfred sat bolt upright at the end of the interminable table recommending a quail and deprecating the use of mayonnaise with asparagus. How I admire people who always travel with their own food. After dinner – it was about nine – we motored down, dropped Cecil for the fireworks and got back to Oxford about eleven, after a gorgeous drive in the dark and some more petrol at Henley: so to bath and bed.

I do hope you enter into the joke of the room and the footman. I can't get over it – you know what one generally suffers. ME . . .

My Van Lint is really a very pleasant picture about 27 × 18″ – *Adoration of the Magi*. It includes one cow lying down, 1 elephant and 3 camels. It is extraordinarily bad in parts and very good in others. Are there really badgers in the grounds – it seems *too wonderful* to think that we shall have those grounds for our own to play about in and *make*. My picture dealing mistakes will furnish the nursery – I mean the Lounge. [. . .]

You must HATE this letter by now.

Best Love
from
Bobs

October 1923   Oxford University New Reform Club

My dearest Mrs Brown

Thank you so much for all your letters this week. Yesterday afternoon, after lunching with Harold, Clonmore, myself and a person called Schurhof[1] set off for a walk in the country. Taking a Ford van which we found by the roadside we went to a place called Whiteham where there is a lovely old stone house, tenanted by one Mrs Rose, and lately sold by the Earl of Abingdon to Major Fennell who is unable to obtain possession. In order to spite Mrs Rose he and his wife and daughter live in very large and luxurious tents in a clearing in the woods on the top of Cumnor hill. They have a butler and have built an enormous garage full of fleets of cars. All the woods are guarded by armed men. When we got there Schurhof, who hardly knew them, introduced himself and us to Mrs Fennell, a good-looking woman who treated us like so much dirt and went out to tea somewhere else, leaving the butler, a typical criminal, to give us tea in the drawing-room tent, pitch dark, full of most valuable furniture and tenanted by three dogs, a goat and some ducks, all at home on the turkey carpet. The butler remained with us lest we should steal anything and hinted, if really necessary, he could produce Major Fennell out of a cupboard. Of course they are coiners, and Major Fennell and Mr Rose the same man: there really was an astonishing atmosphere of mystery about it all. They had wonderful black muscatels.

---

1. George Schurhof, of German extraction, friend of Patrick Balfour at Oxford. He later went into the City.

Then we got lost in the woods in the dark and wandered vaguely about, eventually finding a cart horse and man by the roadside, we begged a lift to The Trout. On arriving there we were ushered into their new room, astonishingly pretty and cosy, with a huge fire and great beams, but not rough. Mrs Coleman, the landlady, produced a bottle of milk punch. A Mr Sissons who lives in a barge and whose literary partner has just found it necessary to leave the country, sat in one corner. While in the middle of the room sat the most amazing human being I have ever set eyes on, talking about the latest pictures he had bought in Paris, a perfectly gigantic red-faced man, Lord Effingham,[1] who is accustomed to take tea at The Trout off a decanter of port. I can't tell you what delight the thought of him gives me. He gabbled on in the most pompous way about his pictures and his birds and actors of the seventies and so on. He eventually ended by asking us all over to his house to see his collection next Friday. Meanwhile the decanter of port disappeared and also the milk punch.

Then we walked back to Oxford along the towpath, had dinner and spent an amusing evening at the Hypocrites.[2] I have seldom enjoyed a day more – if only you could see Lord Effingham. Probably no one in England will speak to him. He has wonderful collections of pictures and writes books on the beauties of England: also knows his Debrett by heart.

Rudolph and I are thinking of motoring over to Tewkesbury on Tuesday, to see the celebration of the 800th anniversary. It is such a wonderful building that I would love to see it adorned with the greatest dignitaries of the church and Lord Beauchamp himself.

[. . .] I am longing for you to see my room.

With best love
Bobs

I forgot to tell you how beautiful the river looked by moonlight from the bridge by The Trout; there was something fearfully fascinating, rumbling along in this huge cart, in the dark, sitting among cabbages

---

1. Henry Alexander Gordon Howard, 4th Earl of Effingham.
2. A club frequented by hard-drinking aesthetes, scene of riotous parties until closed by the Proctors after complaints from neighbours as to noise. Robert contributed by roaring out Victorian ballads with piano accompaniment and David Greene indulging in his passion for West Indian jazz.

and smelling that autumn smell of the river. I miss the country terribly and those little episodes are so pleasant – but of course after Savernake seem revoltingly suburban.

––––––––

There is hardly a letter from Robert in 1923 and 1924 which does not contain some reference to the beauty of his rooms. To fit his slender allowance, he decided that collecting Victoriana would be an inexpensive way of furnishing them, besides amusing his friends. Any Victorian production was at the time considered of such execrable taste that the word 'art' could hardly be used; sugary sentimentality and ugliness of this sort aroused horror and derision. Robert enjoyed chasing objects such as wool pictures, Staffordshire figures, and particularly glass domes: domes containing pyramids of artificial flowers with mother-of-pearl petals and Berlin wool leaves or cornucopias of wax fruits. By the beginning of 1924 his collection was so large that he and Harold proposed holding an 1840 Exhibition which was promptly banned as unnecessary by the University Proctors, no doubt in their turn exasperated by the extravagant and unscholastic behaviour of these aesthetes.

The apex of the summer entertainments was the coming of age of Lord Beauchamp's eldest son William, Viscount Elmley, at Madresfield in August. The proceedings were so lavish as to rate the description as 'a phase of civilization either forgotten or derided'.

After a vitriolic exchange of letters with his mother over his plans to go to Russia, which proved abortive, Robert and Clonmore set out for Vienna and Estergom, Trieste and Venice. While in Vienna a visit to the Capuchin Vaults in the Neumarkt to view the Imperial tombs resulted in Robert's first article for *The Times*, for which he was paid £2 10s 0d.

Back at Merton Robert was not sent down after the incident he describes of driving Ponsonby's car, but gated and fined, the reason given by his tutor Mowat being that he had produced one of the best papers they had had at the beginning of term. He endeared himself still less to the Merton authorities by sending out an invitation

Mr Robert Byron
At Home
Eight o'clock to midnight
for the remainder of the Term

Night after night his rooms were besieged by bottle-bearing friends.

In the early part of 1925 Robert made an effort to do some work, spending a fortnight on Lundy Island with Billy Clonmore and his books. But three years of party-going could hardly be retrieved in a few weeks and Robert, to the fury of his mother, got only a third in History and never came back to take his degree. In the summer of 1925 he became editor of the *Cherwell* and spent much time on the telephone wrestling with the printers in Birmingham. It was a prelude to his journalistic career, which he lost no opportunity in fostering.

February 1924   Merton College, Oxford

Darling Mibble

I am sorry you were so agitated. Having once read you the letter[1] – which you found too dull to listen to – I thought there would be no more cause for complaint. The Press have taken it up splendidly. Inaccurate tirades have appeared in the *Morning Post* and the *Daily Herald*. On Friday morning an alarming young man advanced on me shivering in a dressing-gown saying 'I am the *Oxford Times* – I want to know why . . .'
Consequently an 'interview' appeared in the *Evening Standard* with Mr Byron who said he thought the exhibition would be both attractive and amusing, ending with an incredibly snobbish reference to Lord Effingham. The final pitch of absurdity was reached on Saturday morning, when this appeared saying he was the *Graphic* and the *Weekly Graphic*, papers which he hoped I did not class on a level with any others. I replied not. We talked for hours – at last he took a photograph of all my domes in a row, to illustrate the harmlessness of the proposed exhibits – and then, utter degradation, of me holding a basket of wax fruits. He suggested

---

1. Robert and Harold Acton had published a letter in the *Daily Mail* protesting against the decision of the university authorities to prohibit their 1840 Exhibition.

that we should get the American Club in London to lend us its rooms in the summer. We will try: anyhow it is by now splendidly advertised – and ourselves as well. Please believe that that was the *only* reason that induced me to pose – when one has to squeeze a living out of journalism, such opportunities are not to be missed. But it is all very revolting and I can't say I feel very pleased about it. I told him my sympathies were all with the Proctors. Philip Guedalla[1] sent a telegram: 'Why not include Proctors in exhibition' – amusing I think. But think of my domes in a row!!

The *Nation and Athenaeum* sent me a book to review yesterday. It is called *Daphnis and Chloe*, a reprint (very art) of a 17th century translation from the Greek: and is very like a modern novel, in English much too good for it. I have spent today diving into encyclopaedias – late Greek literature was never my forte and as they want 750 words, I suppose it calls for notes on the various editions that have appeared. Very boring, but I suppose worthwhile, as the paper is so cultured and I am told that they always send one a difficult book first as a test. It is worth 18/6, as I have already scored it thickly in blue pencil I trust they will not want it back. There is no news from the *Tatler*,[2] but I am told that some papers do not pay until a month after publication.

Elmley[3] drove me to Sandhurst yesterday. It is really incredible, the discomfort and horror of it: nauseating green and brown tiles *every-where* and everything numbered. One room each, about a sixth of the size of one's Eton one, with a splintery floor and a smell of corps clothes – awful. It is not the discomfort of it, so much as the drab gloom, that must be so ghastly: and the people – they are horrible. As Erskine (the boy in the electioneering cab photograph) says, Tom Soames[4] is an oasis. We met him: myself clasping a large woolwork picture which I had just purchased at Wokingham, for 15/-. He hurried on, afraid. It is a wonderful picture, really very very pretty, a love scene, foliage, dog at troubadour's feet, lake, mountains and sky – and filling up the whole of one side a marvellous Gothic shrine, built of chocolate bricks (so

---

1. Prolific author of *The Second Empire*, *Palmerston*, etc.
2. In March 1924 the *Tatler* printed an article of Robert's entitled 'The Victorian Revival in Oxford'.
3. William, Viscount Elmley, became 8th Earl Beauchamp.
4. Son of a neighbour in Wiltshire.

domestic) and carefully broken pinnacles and tracery. I am dying for you to see it: it was very cheap and has a lovely frame.

Lord Birkenhead[1] has been prowling about Merton today. He peered in at my window, so I leapt across the room and drew the curtains with a clatter. He must have been surprised. Judas.

Incidentally, *do* you think it would matter very much if I was sent down? I can't say from the most expeditious point of view that I think it would matter very much and I feel more and more that I *must* go abroad for a year before settling down to anything – I must get some experience before I can write and I should like to go to America. But I don't know how it can be managed. [. . .]

With best love
from
Bobs

5 May 1924   Merton College, Oxford

Darling Mibble

[. . .] Lord Beauchamp came here on Saturday for an hour or two. He has grown fatter. We had lunch in the Magdalen guest room and a bottle of Tokay, that the steward had bought from the cellars of the late Emperor Karl of Austria. It has the most wonderful taste – so extraordinary as to be like seeing a new primary colour. Elmley's coming of age celebrations are to begin on August 5th. There is to be an agricultural show in the grounds and a house party of thirty. Lord Beauchamp was full of it. Elmley has to make seven speeches. The term ends on the 20th so I think the best thing is for me to come home for a fortnight, go off on the 7th of July, pick up Cecil at Brussels and David [Talbot Rice] at Vienna – they want to go on before going to Russia –

---

1. Lord Chancellor, 1919–22.

and then go up through Warsaw and Cracow to Vilna, the frontier station. The American Express company say they can book one here second class for eleven pounds. Thence everything is uncertain, but from all accounts there will not be much difficulty once a visa is obtained. I will come back by Aug. 5th and go straight to Madresfield and after that be able to spend an unbroken two months at home. Do you not think this the best arrangement? Will you ask Father about selling the gun to a member of the family? I must have more money than forty pounds – about sixty or seventy and am selling everything in my rooms – or trying to. I am determined to carry the thing through. You see most people go abroad and lead exactly the same Oxford lives in foreign capitals, drinking perhaps something new, but flitting from café to café etc. I don't want to do this: I want to go somewhere where there is not an Oxford life to be led, where a little energy is required and if such a thing is possible something *new* – different conditions of life. It is not a mere extravagant whim to be the first undergraduate to Russia or anything of that sort. I am sure you can understand. Why, I haven't made an effort since I went to Eton! So will you ask Father about the gun, I will write to anyone about it, if he will tell me whom he thinks best.

My newspaper syndicate[1] wrote and asked me for a description of myself and my 'furious publications'!!! Pray heaven something will come of it all. Meantime I am slaving at a love story called 'Reading and Sandhurst'. Such a marvellous setting, if you only knew it, all hanging round the incident of the young lady who turned to Elmley and said '*Are you a viscount?*' Yes Reading beats everything – there is a certain picturesqueness about Chesterfield, a certain unique squalor about Bridholme, but the Reading *palais de danse* in the Chinese style just tops the summit of middle-class repellency.

We went over to Thame yesterday in David's motor and saw Fothergill:[2] he was most amusing in buckled shoes, he gave us Greek wine for tea. I hear he has spent most of his life in prison or exile. Oliver Baldwin[3] is writing a book about the Armenian army; I think it will be

---

1. The *Express* Group.
2. John Fothergill, innkeeper and author of *An Innkeeper's Diary*.
3. Son of Stanley Baldwin, whom he succeeded as the 2nd Earl Baldwin of Bewdley. Imprisoned by the Bolsheviks while serving with the Armenians. Author of *Konyetz*, *Six Prisons* and *Two Revolutions*, etc.

interesting. Thame is pretty – but how horrible the country is round Oxford – such terribly squalid villages and *filthy* children. Lady Beauchamp sent me a lovely box covered with shells. It fits my period perfectly. [. . .]

With Best Love
from
Bobs

May 1924   Oxford University New Reform Club

Darling Mibble

[. . .] I have just received a letter from America – some magazine I wrote to – saying that my proposed articles sound very interesting: would I send them! – unfortunately I can't remember what they are to be on, but I think it was class grades. I shall get in the story of Mrs Asquith and the brandy bottle, I think – do you know it?

Oxford really surpasses itself in eights week – oh it is *awful*. I am having tea, or rather giving it, on the College Barge with Mrs Gibson and Phoebe[1] and Drury Lowe and Mrs Drury Lowe who always wears Paquin and very large diamonds in the daytime. She used to be the joy of my life at Eton. I don't know her.

Have you read *Konyetz* yet? Oliver Baldwin came to lunch with me on Friday – he was so amusing – the most bitterly sarcastic man I have ever met. He went through 2 years in France, then a year and a half in a Bolshevist prison amidst unspeakable horrors, escaped 2 days before his arranged execution and spent some time more in the Armenian army murdering Bolsheviks in cold blood and now he is 25.

Six of us went over to Sandhurst[2] on Saturday and of course got mixed up in a scuffle among the gentlemen cadets, which ended in my being thrown into the lake, and our friends arrested! Picture the ignominy of it – being swung out over a vast moon-swept stretch of

---

1. Grandmother and sister of Rudolph Messel.
2. This incident is said to have passed into Sandhurst legend: see *The Memoirs of Anthony Powell*, Vol. I, *Infants of Spring*.

water just like a Macwhirter picture – and then the taste of old roach and droppage of a penny and two sixpences! How I laughed – especially when Hubert Duggan motored over the tennis courts to my rescue. But the forty-four miles in the middle of the night would have given anyone but me pneumonia, I am sure. [. . .] the colours in my Roman tie did not run – wasn't it lucky? Otherwise my clothes were old. We were supposed to go over yesterday to give evidence at the Court Martial – such a pity the wire arrived too late! I should have gone in a frock coat.

I had lunch with Cecil and Lord Frederick Hamilton[1] on Sunday. He was very interesting but had a tiresome habit of using the rhetorical question. Hugh[2] and I spend our days visiting Cinemas in search of Lord Beauchamp meeting foreign royalties on Dover pier. [. . .]

With best love
from Bobs

June 1924   Merton College, Oxford

Darling Mibble

I have just been to breakfast with Harold who shewed me the enclosed – isn't it delicious – I mean the Osbert Sitwell article.[3] I do think it is the most perfect sarcasm don't you? Really the Sitwells might have been great if they hadn't got the reputation for serious poetry. [. . .]

Cecil and I are giving Elmley a gigantic scrapbook for a present, bound in white suede with gold ciphers, which I spend *hours* designing.

Rudolph proposes to produce a film here next term. I spend my days writing to plausible film companies. I must own I am very interested in the cinema.

Oliver Baldwin came to lunch with Harold on Friday. The latter left early and O. and I spent the afternoon together. He *was* interesting –

---

1. Diplomat and author of *The Days before Yesterday*, *Here, There, and Everywhere*, etc.
2. The Hon. Hugh Lygon, second son of the 7th Earl Beauchamp and brother of Lady Lettice, Lady Sibell and Lady Mary Lygon.
3. The enclosure is missing.

the only person I know of course who is really Conservative. It is the most extraordinary thing up here, and among everyone one meets who is in any way ambitious, the way in which foreign politics are completely ignored in these days. People will rave and rant over Bengalese birth statistics, Australian rabbit problems, beer for the miners etc., etc. When they see a speech of Trotsky that Russia is going to fight for Constantinople it conveys nothing to them. If we can't manage Russia I shall certainly go to Bessarabia: that is northern Roumania, once Russian. There the fighting will start – and if one knew the country or happened to be there it might be a tremendous chance to get on the staff of a paper. It is certain to come and I suppose we are certain to back the Turk – or throw away the policy of over a century.

Also the Grand Duke Nicholas is in Paris working hard for the restoration of the monarchy. Cyril has been crowned in Paris. Apparently they have a large organisation over the whole of Russia and it is believed that the Soviet will not last. Think of having a finger in that pie. I am really going to try and learn Russian. Oliver Baldwin said his Father signed the trade agreement with Krassin,[1] *knowing* that his son was in a Russian jail. He had an *appalling* time – went out on invitation to train Armenian troops and got captured. He says he has nightmares once a month, when he thinks he's back there – the awful feeling of despair.

He is standing for Parliament next election – in Worcestershire at the very next constituency to his Father – as Labour. He would have stood for the same one, if it hadn't been entirely agricultural and conservative. His views are diametrically opposed to Labour in every conceivable way. To begin with he is a rabid militarist. [. . .]

I was on the point of selling everything in my room the other day, when Cecil arrived with the most exquisite 1827 woman made of shells entirely – under a dome. So of course I couldn't. How you will love it.

I must go – to lunch with Hubert Duggan. He gives us caviare. [. . .]

Best Love from Bobs

---

1. Soviet Commissar of Transport and Foreign Trade, signatory of Anglo-Soviet trade agreement of 1921.

11 August 1924   115 Park Street, W1

Darling Mibble
   [. . .] We start at Victoria at 11 o'clock today, reach Paris at six,
where we stay the night and then go straight through to Vienna and
from there down the Danube. How depressing it all will be. I wish I was
at home. [. . .]
   Really Madresfield was tiring. What a horrible existence it must be
flitting from one house party to another, making meaningless conversation to vapid girls, who for all you know expect to be made love to,
wandering aimlessly about, worried to death lest you have not got an
invitation to the next [. . .] cultivating a tolerance which you do not
possess or wish to [. . .] putting up with indulging in the kind of
humour that wakes up elderly invalids in the middle of the night, breaks
the china and ruins the furniture, ugh!
   The whole effect was most odd. Lord Beauchamp at last reached
such a pitch of exasperation, he took to ordering the girls about as if they
were servants. The organisation was marvellous – all of us given
typewritten slips with whom we were to take into dinner on them [. . .]
There were one or two quite charming girls there: Lady Anne Lindsay,
the daughter of that peculiar man, Lord Crawford. She lives in Wigan
and gets her hats at Woollands. She was charming. Lady Winifred Cecil
was there – she said Lord Brownlow had gambled away all his money in
early youth and that his relict was a great drain on their resources. [. . .]
   Lord Beauchamp wore his garter to the servants ball – but I can't
really describe it to you, except that all the frequenters of such functions
who were there say that there never has been a party on such a scale
before. Elmley remained quite oblivious of everything. I haven't the
smallest idea *when* the *Daily Sketch* got hold of me, damn them – I
remember running away from one or two – but I imagine the *Tatler* will
be full of it all – do keep the *Daily Sketch* – I want to see when it was.
   I went for a long drive on Friday to Symonds Yat. How hideous all
that Beauty spot is! Unfortunately we could not get to Tintern.
   I must get up, as I have only an hour to dress and pack – Goodbye.
We have decided to pick a quarrel with an American every day.
                                          With love to Anne and Lucy and Papa
                                                                    from Bobs

November 1924   Merton College, Oxford

Darling Mibble

[. . .] It was nice having that cheque from *The Times* as I had the most expensive weekend.

Cecil, Hugh and I hired a taxi for the day to go to Eton as it was only 3/- more expensive than the train and the trains back were impossible – off we drove and broke down in Henley at *exactly the same spot* where Darrell's Ford collapsed a year ago on the way to the Derby. Then we went on, and arrived rather early had to talk to M'Tutor, who was if anything less difficult than usual, though my suit gave him a shock. How curiously horrible everyone seemed that I had not seen since they left – all the boys who had gone into the army etc. just exactly the same – still hanging on the witticisms of those to whom they used to toady – still giving vent to the same snobbish categories of promotion though in the regiment now instead of the house eleven – mouthing the newest humour with perhaps a little more assurance. It was just so awful that after lunch and the purgatory of being photographed in their company – (jokes cracked by the wits) I took a bus with Oliver Messel to Windsor to look for domes. What a success! I have got the most lovely one of shells – calceolarias made of inverted small shells – it really is quite beautiful and *when* are you coming to see it? You will come and see my room once more won't you. It is so depressing having to leave it and fearfully hard to get rooms, as they are *all* taken – I shall have to go into some much too expensive ones I am afraid – there are simply none to be had. The ones I have fixed on were burnt last night – but no damage seems to have been done. [. . .]

On Sunday I travelled to London by the one o'clock train with Oliver Messel and we lunched off a bag of ham – reached Paddington 20 minutes late and only plumped into my seat at the Albert Hall as Clara Butt began the first notes of 'The Wanderer' (I could have given her a hint or two). She sang also 'Three Fishers' which I thought quite lovely and 'Abide with Me'. But the crowning moment was when after the encore to the second series of songs a small bunch of Chrysanthemums was carried up and she announced 'I have been asked to sing Hatton's "Enchantress".'[1] And she sang it – it really was too wonderful for words

---

1. A favourite from Robert's repertoire of Victorian songs.

to describe: we got up on our seats and waved and shrieked. For Mark Ogilvie-Grant[1] had previously written to warn her of the advent of two undergraduates interested in Hatton and would she etc. etc. – and then that morning which he had spent in London he had bought (with Guinness money) the bouquet and affixed a note saying that it was from an admirer who hoped to hear 'The Enchantress'.

I can't describe to you what a moment of delirious triumph it was when she said she was going to sing it.

Then we went and had tea with the Guinnesses[2] – a vast palace in Grosvenor Square with great trees and plants of flowers made of jewels lying about – a whole conservatory of them in the drawing-room too exquisite for words – I have never seen such riches. We then went to the cinema with Oonagh Guinness and saw *Nellie the Cloak Model* who was just being burnt when we left for dinner. Mrs Guinness wore the large pearls in vogue only *real* and after dinner took us upstairs to a jumble sale she is organizing and dressed up as a Belcher woman – Frank Reynolds with beads on the toes – and 1916 coats. I've never laughed so much in my life, she just buys everything that is sent her to sell, as she can't part with them. There were some Victorian plush and lace caps with yellow feather butterflies in them – I purchased a Cleopatra headdress and a pair of elastic sided boots for one and four. Then we had to go and arrived back very late and tired. [. . .] Next morning I got up at 6.30 to do an essay – today I have attended the service at the War memorial.

With best love
from
Bobs

---

1. Mark Ogilvie-Grant, first cousin of Nina, Countess of Seafield. At Oxford with Robert where they sang together. Honorary attaché in Cairo, 1929. Lived in Athens after the Second World War.
2. The Hon. (Arthur) Ernest and Mrs Guinness, parents of Aileen who married the Hon. Brinsley Plunket, Maureen who married the 4th Marquess of Dufferin and Ava, and Oonagh who married the Hon. Philip Kindersley.

November 1924   Oxford University New Reform Club

Darling Mibble

Thank you so much for your letter. It ends with such a sweet wish that I lived at home. I am afraid this is only too likely to be realised as the most awful affair took place last night. After a terribly tiring day with Oliver Baldwin, we dined midst a huge party including a woman called Julia Strachey[1] – all went on to Richard Greene's[2] rooms – and suddenly realised it was past midnight. A lot of people from Balliol had to be helped in by the fire-ladder. Taking the Foreign Secretary's motor bought with his ministerial salary, a poor Ford – we drove them to the window, but were suddenly surrounded by police. I had a licence: and in order to save all these wretched people and a case in court, produced it. Then drove off, the Foreign Secretary's son[3] by my side, before the other names were taken. Meanwhile the police have got the number – how surprised the Foreign Secretary will be when he hears of his pathetic little car's adventures.

I am afraid that as mine is the only name taken they will be very upset, as I suddenly discover this morning that there is a new rule forbidding one to drive other people's cars – and then being out late. So if I arrive with some books and domes, I hope you will be able to bear it. Anyhow it will only be for the rest of this term and I shall get much more work done and save much more money. But of course there is always a hope that they will not mind. Only it is all so difficult as one of them gave a false name – I suppose I shall have to pretend it was all my fault! How like a Kipling melodrama this must read.

I am very sorry that it should have happened especially over losing my room – but disaster may be averted. In any case it will make no difference, except that I may get a second instead of a third if I come home and work!

---

1. Novelist. Niece of Lytton Strachey.
2. Eldest son of Harry Plunket Greene (baritone) and Gwendolen, daughter of Sir Hubert Parry, and brother of David and Olivia.
3. Matthew Ponsonby, son of Arthur Ponsonby, Under-Secretary of State for Foreign Affairs.

I am just going to tea with Harold to meet a publisher's reader – novelette in hand.

Think of the Foreign Secretary!

Goodbye and best love and hoping to see you soon

Bobs

November 1924   Merton College, Oxford

Darling Mibble

Thank you so much for your letter – I am glad you liked my At Home card – people I don't know keep coming up and asking for one to put on their mantelpieces. [. . .] I am glad you agreed with me about Raymond Savage's[1] criticism. But I think his letter is more than satisfactory, considering that in the first place he is supposed to be the best and most enterprising agent in London: and also that he is so totally out of sympathy with my style of writing. His is the typical modern rather journalese mind, which I intend to shatter one of these days! It is nice to feel so sure of success isn't it – how awful it will be if it doesn't come! I am seriously wondering which paper to try and get on to now, as I think I could manage an introduction to most of their editors or owners. Which would you suggest? *I* think the *Daily Mail*. My object is not to make a success as a writer for the next five years – or try to – but to adopt that form of journalism which will give me most experience and make me travel. I must travel a little more as all I want to write about is England and the English, and a knowledge of abroad throws them into such high relief – especially seeing English people abroad. [. . .]

This term has been one continual round of expensive parties – quite quite extraordinary. I owe more meals than I can count, yet feverishly ask people to lunch every week. I shall have to work hard when I get home, harder than I did, as I do very little up here. So may I have that room again – it really was ideal and quite undisturbed. Hugh has asked me to a party at Madresfield on January 2nd, if it is going to be anything like the last I don't think I shall face it. I cannot stand the smart guards officer with his loud voice and *savoir-faire*. [. . .]

---

1. Robert had sent Raymond Savage part of his novel for criticism.

Will you ask Father to sign the enclosed horror – how depressing it is, the whole idea of living in such a place. I could have gone to Mrs Dickinson's, but she is always drunk and there is generally a gramophone. [. . .]

Best love
Bobs

February 1925   40 Beaumont Street, Oxford

Darling Mibble

[. . .] Elmley was here for the weekend – he has sent my 'credential' to Barbara Cartland, who has sent it to Beaverbrook, who has sent it to his editor (Beverly Baxter, what a name!) who is returning to England at the beginning of this month, when I shall have to write some specimen articles. I do not know whether it is unfortunate synchronising thus with the pearls – but the *Daily Express* pays *very* well I know. You see, what I feel is that despite all its disadvantages, Journalism would give me a few years' experience of various places and sides of life which business would *not*. Nothing in the world would be more delightful than to settle down *in* London where one's friends are or come and go to a business which one likes – but I can't help thinking it might be a mistake – though I suppose one could write at the same time. However we can talk about it when you come.

I went to see Richard Greene at the private public school[1] on Sunday. A queer Greek revival house low down among preposterous specimen trees – all the boys in top hats like Eton and three masters who all teach everything. It was like a book. Richard has just become engaged to a girl called Elizabeth Russell and her people are furious and refuse to give or leave her a penny unless he has £500 a year settled on him – they are very well off – her father a grandson of some Duke of Bedford – and do nothing to get him a job. He thinks he can earn £2,000 a year teaching music in Canada. I went over with Anthony Russell, prospective brother-in-law and Matthew Ponsonby – it was all exactly like a book

---

1. Aston Clinton.

Youth and Hope with capital letters – I said so and everybody laughed! Richard seemed quite happy really. [. . .]

I went to lunch with Mrs Yorke yesterday – a breath of heaven to hear her talk. She had asked Anne and Lucy to go shooting just after they went away – till Friday.

Best love
from
Bobs

February 1925   40 Beaumont Street, Oxford

Darling Mibble

It was so nice to find your letter waiting when I got back last night. [. . .] I had a lovely time in London [. . .] went to the cinema with Olivia[1] who has Elizabeth Russell staying with her and Mrs Greene has gone away for a rest cure. A new servant of uncertain sanity arrived while we were having tea. In the evening I dined with Bryan[2] and a youth of still more uncertain sanity called Martin Wilson[3] – saw Elmley and *his* young woman who is *very* pretty and very nice and told me all about how to write to the *Daily Express* etc. – (I *shall* at once if I don't hear from the pearls) – and then went to the party which was most amusing – all the people that one has ever seen in *Punch* come to life – Winston Churchill hopping about like a little round ball etc. Baldwin received at the top of the stairs with Mrs B and Lady Evelyn Guinness, who looks literally about eighteen in a débutante's dress of chiffon, and long golden red hair. It was a terrific crowd even in this vast palace – and we and the more adventurous politicians danced in the middle of it. Lettice[4] was there; Betty Baldwin and I asked her why. I felt distinguished dancing with the Prime Minister's daughter, she is too

---

1. Olivia Greene.
2. Son of the Rt. Hon. Walter Guinness (later Lord Moyne), Minister of Agriculture and Fisheries, and of Lady Evelyn Guinness.
3. Friend of Brian Howard and later Baronet.
4. Lady Lettice Lygon.

charming and rather ugly and asked me to tea at Downing Street – I shall go one day to see what it is like.

At length we went on about 12.30 to a new and exclusive and law-abiding night-club started by some Tennant where there was nobody and thence to the 50–50, another frequented by the stage, where there was also a pleasant atmosphere of tea drinking. However it is considered a little *risqué* – imagine our surprise and that of her nieces, when suddenly Lady Evelyn appeared with her son having got rid of her thousand people by half past one and determined not to be left out of anything, it was too funny. So we sat there till three (the band went at two) and then Bryan and I, David and Michael Rosse[1] whom you don't know, went and saw Tom Douglas[2] who never goes to bed till dawn and then Michael and I went home and I had great difficulty in getting in. Up at nine! Went to the National Gallery in the morning, where the pictures made me quite homesick for Italy and in the afternoon to the hospital at Wormwood Scrubs, where we talked to the ex-servicemen who are incurables and matched their bags of beads etc. There was a very happy atmosphere about the place – they seemed so contented – but it is a depressing place to go to – however I went away quite cheered and full of material for an article and went to the cinema feeling I could not face tea with Tom Douglas who is an American and I cannot understand what he says. Home by nine and talked to Harold. I am rather sleepy

---

1. 6th Earl of Rosse.
2. American actor.

today and am just going to the cinema with a free pass and then dining with some Cambridge people who have come over to see the O.U.D.S. performance of *Peer Gynt*, which I am going to slang in next week's *Cherwell*. [. . .]

Best love
Bobs

February 1925   40 Beaumont Street, Oxford

Darling Mibble

[. . .] Thank you so much for your letter and letter card. No, it is curious, but that article in the *Cherwell*[1] was one of the few things that I have written straight off – a whole day with half an hour for lunch. Of course you cannot be expected to understand a great deal of it – Garsington's owl of wisdom for instance – Garsington is a sort of salon held by Lady Ottoline Morrell, where all the bores of Europe and Oxford congregate – and of course you want to have seen *Peer Gynt* and know the play. I find it hard to discover what has been said by the O.U.D.S. as no one I know here knows any of them. They were of course perfectly furious – each person became, quite literally, speechless as he read it. Apparently, which is very disappointing they are not going to write anything back as they are afraid of my tongue. However there will probably be a good many answering protestations from other sources (the Banbury Road) and if there are I will send them to you. [. . .]

I had an amusing day yesterday. It started at the beginning of the week by my seeing an advert in the Agony column – the Marble Arch Pavilion wanted a poster for a film entitled *So this is Hollywood*. (Hollywood in case you don't know is where they make films.) So I wrote for particulars, received them on Friday and had to get it done by yesterday, Monday. I slaved and did I think quite a good thing in black and white, with great arc lights crossing and a group of producers and people in the foreground. I really went in for it to see the type of person

---

1. In the *Cherwell* of 21 February 1925 Robert had written a scathing attack on the OUDS' performance of *Peer Gynt*.

that did also. After the most exhausting day – on Sunday William Acton[1] gave a lunch party to twenty-three, Elizabeth Ponsonby a tea party, and Hugh [Lygon] a wine party – I sat up till three doing the letters – then got up at six by an alarm clock, emerged from Paddington breakfastless and reached the Marble Arch Pavilion by 9.30. Literally, like the tea party, those people will haunt me for ever. They were like the Bohemia of Punch, only hungry and tragic – weird old men with great capes of white hair down to their shoulder-blades. Curious peaky youths in roll collar jumpers and boots, odd women in starched frills and high collars – all in the wet outside the building, each one carrying a portfolio. I was ashamed of my neatness, unrolled my umbrella and pulled my hair over my eyes. Suddenly an American came along saying 'D'you mind getting out onto the pavement to be photographed' – and a bevy of press photographers appeared. Naturally I hid behind a pillar though tempted to place my bowler among the roll collars, when suddenly I found a man creeping round the corner with his camera raised. I darted off: but have seen no papers yet this morning. Inside we were shewn two reels of the film and made to do a lightning sketch to prove authenticity. Then I went away – came back at six – and naturally did not get a prize – but my poster *may* be one of the ones exhibited in the vestibule. It was all rather stupid, but well worthwhile just to see those people. [. . .]

Then I got shaved and went to lunch with the Yorkes – Henry being in London. Miss Yorke and Mrs Yorke, I never stopped laughing and after that to the cinema – a new film I wanted to see which was very bad. There I met Michael Rosse and his mother and Bryan Guinness and we went on to the Café de Paris for tea, where I was made to dance, Mark's cousins Aileen Guinness and Bettine Russell appearing. It was rather fun – and back to the Pavilion – and to dinner with Bryan Guinness before going back to Oxford on the 7.40.

We had a tremendously amusing evening at the Reading *palais de danse* the other night – Mark and I announced we would give a birthday party there later this term. [. . .] and Lady Evelyn Guinness has got to hear of this and invited herself in a white wig, which she wore at the Embassy[2] the other night and everyone made hunting calls – a very odd

---

1. Brother of Harold Acton.
2. Night-club.

woman. A *vast* house in the middle of London – quite quite lovely – with very old pre-Tudor rooms in it, which she has made really beautiful – from the description horrible – and peat – so that the rooms are filled with a real smell of the country. It shews what Libertyism can be when you know how to do it.

Goodbye – I hope this letter is not too long and boring.

Best love
Bobs

On 31 July 1925 Robert left for Athens with Gavin Henderson and Alfred Duggan in Gavin's car, a touring Sunbeam whose beautiful body was far too low-slung for the increasingly bad roads they were to encounter beyond Naples. Gavin appeared to have endless acquaintances dotted round Europe and could make 'inexhaustible conversation to any living creature that understands a single word of French, German or English'. Alfred was 'upright and neat. He affects a pearl pin and stiff collar. Whenever possible he likes to dress for dinner.' He resolutely avoided any sightseeing and invariably made for the lowest bar he could find. The fact that he was 'armed with letters to all the Legations' from Lady Curzon hardly compensated for the fact he was unable to change a tyre. In Italy the average was between one to three punctures a day.

Robert's light-hearted account of this journey in *Europe in a Looking Glass* only indicates the beginnings of his love affair with Greece and his passionate protagonism of its post-classical culture, first revealed by the mosaics in Ravenna. Surprised at the excitement his name aroused everywhere he went in Athens, he was inveigled into a meeting with Dr Skevos Zervos OBE, ebullient leader of the Dodecanese Islands and their representative at the Paris Peace Conference, but now exiled. A friendship began with much exasperation on Robert's part and, on that of Zervos, a flood of Dodecanese propaganda and presents of gigantic sponges.

The islands, with their capital Rhodes, had been occupied by the Turks for nearly four hundred years until captured by the Italian forces in 1912. The Italians managed to retain the islands through the First World War and the ensuing settlements in spite of promises to the islanders of their return to Greece. As Zervos was never tired of pointing out, their grievances under the Italians were the suppression of the sponge industry, compulsory teaching of Italian in the schools, Catholicism being thrust upon them, and the loss of most of the intelligent Greeks who had either fled, or been banished like himself, to the mainland.

Owing, however, to the belligerent policy of the Greeks in attacking the Turks in Asia Minor and the return of a government under unpopular King Constantine, sympathy in England for the Greek claim to the islands had been much diminished, as Lord Beauchamp rather wearily pointed out to Robert when appealed to for help. Robert managed to get an article published in the *New Statesman* and also in the American *Nation* pointing out the miserable conditions of the islanders and the threat of Italian fortifications increasing Fascist domination in that part of the Mediterranean. The article, though enchanting Zervos, did not please our Legation in Athens.

On returning to Merton Robert wrote 'People tell me to my face that what with the Dodecanese and the *Cherwell* I have become the greatest bore in Oxford.'

August 1925   Salzburg

Darling Mibble

We have arrived here to find no Mozart until Wednesday. So we leave tomorrow in a temper for Italy. What the heat will be like I can't think. We go over the Brenner which is not very high – only 4,000.

We had a lovely drive here all through Bavaria – most beautiful. Yet in a way it is a relief to be out of Germany. The frontier took hours in the dark last night but luckily the local Austrian custom official was attending a village dance and so could not be bothered to examine our trunks.

We are very imposing and cause great amazement. We had two punctures yesterday – so now have no spare wheels ready. There are however 2 dozen inner tubes and 2 outer covers besides 4 new springs in the back. Also petrol and oil. Yesterday mending a puncture in Wasserburg on the Inn, the crowd became so great that it was almost impossible to move. [. . .]

I now eat very little and find that I am feeling ever so much better than when I left. I was really rather unwell, tho' you did not realise it, and had perpetual trouble with my eyes. Now that is all gone. Also I am beginning to feel mentally revived – it is a relief to be away from everyone and in strange surroundings yet, having been abroad before, not too strange to be worrying. Alfred is most charming and very amusing. I sit in the middle – the back of the car is entirely occupied with luggage. When people motor in Germany they literally have only their noses shewing. We caused amazement in only shirt sleeves and flannel trousers.

The roads in Bavaria were quite good and we could go sixty for long stretches at a time. The result was that whenever we passed a hay cart we took a large quantity of the crop away with us.

When it gets cooler Alfred and I are going for a walk in the mountains – he has got up in plus fours for the purpose. Isn't it annoying – I have lost my paint box.

Love
Bobs

August 1925   Bologna

Darling Mibble

I am sorry not to have written for so long. We should have been at Florence today, only the car has broken down.

We have had an adventurous time. Leaving Salzburg on Monday, we crossed and recrossed the German frontier and slept at Innsbruck, a squalid town amidst enormous mountains. Then to the Brenner Pass, where the Italian officials refused to admit the car, owing to a defective form. We stormed and raged, got the Austrian officials to forge documents for us, but all to no effect. Then we telephoned the Embassy at Rome which was shut and inaudible. Meanwhile I was left with the car. They wanted me to move it back. A horde of gesticulating douaniers stood screaming round and a harelipped porter interjected words of English. I turned my back and settled down to complete a sketch. They tried to take the sketch from my hand. The porter told me to fetch my friends, so I stood up and roared abuse at the top of my voice, with the result that they fell back aghast. The afternoon we spent telegraphing to Rome and drinking red wine in the post office. To crown the horror and despair of it all the most loathsome of all loathsome human beings in this world arrived in a car on his honey-moon – a man named Bobby Jenkinson whom I had met at Madresfield.

About six it began to rain – 4,000 feet up. Gavin then started an argument in 3 languages, won over one official, then another and finally by telling him on no account to let us in, as it would get him into trouble, got him to let us in. We arrived at two in the morning at Verona, after a hair-raising drive round and round mountain roads.

At Verona we saw a performance of the opera *Mosé* which beggared description. I am writing an article for *The Times* about it though they won't take it.[1] It was in the *vast* Roman amphitheatre at Verona. The whole of the 12 tribes of Israel (about 700 people and Pharaoh's army) was on the stage at once. Moses, a striking figure with the traditional horns roared operatics. God was a baritone behind the scenes – the tables looked very new. The lightning effects were heightened by the summer lightning that flashed across the sky every other minute. The orchestra was vast – there must have been about 10,000 spectators. In the intervals we drank beer where formerly the lions had been starved to give them appetite for the Christians.

The last scene was indescribable: the back of the enormous stage was occupied by the Red Sea, rolling and heaving in the most realistic manner. The tribes of Israel led by Moses and Aaron sang a farewell song. The love interest was also wound up. Then they spied Pharaoh – with operatic shrieks they rushed into the sea which parted to receive them. Pharaoh appeared on a rock *recitativo*, then led his army into the sea. It closed up, but for a few moments was punctuated by many arms and spears. Meanwhile the orchestra grew louder, real thunder and vivid flashes of lightning added to the effect, at length a red sun rose over the sea – the orchestra quietened down and that was all.

Moses took his encores in the midst of a gargantuan wreath supported by the Fascists, who abrogated to themselves his applause.

Yesterday we arrived here for lunch. Then set out to Florence, got lost in the Appenines, went down literal precipices on the lowest of four gears, forded a river bed and then stopped dead on the main road. We could do nothing, though we tried for 3 hours. Then two fat men arrived in a lorry. Three times they set the engine on fire howling with laughter as the whole car burst into sheets of flame – then produced

---

1. This article, 'Rossini's *Moses*', was printed in *The Times* of 29 August 1925.

some mangled bits of string and towed us back to Bologna. I sat in front of the lorry. It was delivering Bolzano beer and we stopped at each public house. The occupants – all sitting barefoot in six inches of dust in the road – all cackled with laughter. The man explained he had a son who spoke German and English. At length we telephoned to a garage for a chauffeur – I had to do it – it was awful. We arrived back here in the dark, in a state of impenetrable filth. You cannot conceive the dust – it penetrates every pore – and makes one's hair feel like a cat's tongue.

After dinner, we went to a Café and an immense woman made love to us from over the counter. There was also a young Fascist who spoke four words of French. He promised to have us enrolled as Fascists. We met him this morning, and he took us to the 'lodge' but unfortunately we had to be resident in Bologna. So it was no good. He had been up at six, as his father, a policeman, was ill so he did duty instead. I have just left him talking to Gavin in a Café.

The heat is strong but not unbearable. Lady Curzon has wired to say that she has got a Turkish *Laissez-passer* for the car so we are now going to attempt to drive to Constantinople, via Salonika. I doubt if it will be possible. Do not forward any more letters after you get this, until I let you know where. I think the British Legation Athens will be the next. [. . .] I am enjoying a day's peace – we have had rather a strenuous time lately. Alfred is a model of good behaviour, and being so very well read, is most interesting to travel with. He is standing for Parliament at the next election. [. . .]

Of course we have mistaken the date of the Palio at Siena – so we shall probably go more or less straight to Rome, after Florence. Thenceforth the heat will be fabulous I suppose.

Goodbye –
Best love
Bobs

August 1925   Naples

Darling Mibble
    We left Rome at one yesterday morning – having intended to get off at nine.

What a drive! Roads are awful south of Rome – we had two punctures in the first fifty miles – the third would have meant changing an inner tube – but we averted it by picking up two *Jungen Bewegen* (that is by charity) at a level crossing, German walking tourists, poor brutes in this heat. They perched on top of the luggage and we drove along looking like a Victorian war memorial. The South of Italy is wonderful – covered with Roman remains in the fields – the women all in peasant costumes that our grandmothers delighted to sketch – the men on donkeys with huge panniers – everywhere Vesuvius and an umbrella pine on the horizon. A particularly lurid sunset completed the effect – we might have been moving in a world of Victorian watercolours.

The dust was terrific – each cart made a cloud, the bumps were awful – great holes. We passed Caserta, a vast palace so beloved by the Sitwells. It has a magnificent avenue up to it in the *middle* of which they have put not only a level crossing, but the station. It is tragic and all very squalid. As it was practically dark we could not stop to look at the water garden – the biggest in Europe.

Then we came on a town decorated up to the eyes with electric fairy lamps and religious processions, horribly pagan. It was past eight and had been dark an hour when we arrived – in a state of filth quite indescribable while the *Jungen Bewegen*, having had no windscreen to protect them, looked as though they had fallen into flour barrels. They offered to wash the car out of gratitude.

Tomorrow will be the worst drive – it is nearly 200 miles to Brindisi over those awful roads and we shall have to start very early. It is terrifically hot, but I don't mind it when I am doing things.

The Capri boat has just gone out. The excitement of actually arriving in Greece will be too terrific – but I can't believe we ever shall. Is Greece likely to possess a crane strong enough to lift a car?

Still we have a letter to the minister and from the Greek minister – and we know Leonard[1] – and I am me – I hope it will be all right.

Love
Bobs

---

1. Leonard Bower, attaché at the British Legation in Athens.

31 August 1925   Athens

Darling Mibble

We arrived last night an hour after dark and I am now writing before
dressing – so cannot as yet tell you of the beauties of the Acropolis. Our
travelling lately has been rather tiring. We left Brindisi Thursday night,
after the most appalling scene getting the car on board. Next morning
from Albania a large herd of cows arrived in a lighter and were settled on
the first class deck. Then we passed Corfu and arrived at Patras (at the
entrance of the Gulf of Corinth) at four next morning. There was no
quay and the car had to be craned into a lighter. It was quite awful to
watch it – we all struggled and pulled – it fell through the hold and was
then picked up by the nose, but eventually landed. Then we discovered
there was not even a path from Athens to Patras, so we spent the night
there – next morning we rose at five again and caught the train to
Corinth, the car having gone before. But we passed it on the way and
had to wait from 12 until 6 for it in the filthiest waiting room. I went
and paddled in Corinth's Gulf. Then we had to lift it bodily off the
wagon. Finally we started. The bridges of the road which wound along
the face of a cliff descending 300 feet into the Aegean were either gone or
merely planks of wood – it was all very hair-raising. We arrived about
9.00 – it gets dark at 7 – and found Leonard Bower expecting us. The
rumour is already round the town that Lord Byron is here.

Greece is fascinating – the Gulf of Corinth quite lovely stretching for
eighty miles between high mountains – a brilliant deep blue and only
about a mile wide in places. We had a delicious bathe. Ancient Greece
so far we have been spared. [. . .] Nothing suits my health better than
this sort of thing. I love having something to *do* – I burst into art at
Brindisi – horrible 'modern' pictures – unfortunately of the French
water colours I bought at Siena, the chrome yellow has turned out the
colour of a crocus and so everything is much too hot.

We have made no plans, so I cannot give you another address yet. I
am getting rather worried about money, as I only have ten pounds left –
having had my small wallet stolen in a tram in Naples. Luckily I had left
my letter of credit in the hotel. It was very tiresome and I felt such a
fool.

It is almost too hot to go out – however Leonard is taking us to bathe
this afternoon – I find that abroad I don't mind the heat at all, and am
much more active than anyone. It is amusing to see people in fustanellas

but the heat of them must be quite awful. From Patras we could almost see Missolonghi across the Gulf – I felt a pilgrimage was expected. I must now write my diary and then to art. I have a plan for formalising the Gulf of Corinth.

Goodbye – best love
Bobs

September 1925   Athens

Darling Mibble

I am so sorry not to have written for so long, but our plans have been in a state of flux and I have been waiting from day to day to know what we shall do.

The big-end of the car is broken. Prince Andrew's late chauffeur says he can mend it by the end of the week. Tomorrow we go to Namplia (?) by boat to see Mycenae and if possible Sparta and the entirely deserted Byzantine town adjoining it. Then I shall probably come home with Alfred unless Gavin shows definite signs to driving more or less straight: which he probably won't. [. . .]

Greece is more wonderful than you can imagine. It is entirely unspoilt. One still sees cartloads of inflated pigs containing wine – etc. The other day we took a car to a place called Porto Rafti – thence a sailing boat and went out across the bay to an island, which we had to land on by swimming. [. . .] On top of the island, cone-shaped, is an old Greek marble figure of a woman looking out to sea. She lived on this island all the time her husband was at the wars: and when he came back she was dead. He put up this statue, which still looks out to sea, waiting for him. The island was covered with potsherds and remains of Greek vases etc.

I have been doing political interviewing. Have you seen two articles in *The Times* on the Dodecanese? Yesterday Leonard took me to visit the patriot leader of these islands.[1] His room was decorated with sponges and modern oil paintings of the islands. He discovered my

---

1. Dr Skevos Zervos.

name, took me by the hand and we swayed up and down sweating and shouting about Liberty and the new Byron in French. It was very gratifying. Then we went to see the man[1] who made the last revolution. He is a director of air services and educated in Glasgow. I explained that I had my living to make and should he want a King . . . he said he would keep it in mind. There is a revolution every October and the present dictator has now reached the end of his tether, something is bound to happen. Leonard says that he wants the throne for an heir descended from Henry VII. He is known as Boover: I and my namesake as Vironos. The small boys have Lordos Vironos (ΛΟΡΔΟς ΒΙΡΟΝΟς) embroidered on their sailor hats. How will you enjoy being the new Napoleon's mother!

After lunch
I have just finished my article. It is not bad, very suave and moderate. I do hope they publish it. I think, even if they don't they will give me some credit for having gone and interviewed the man whom the British Legation only just prevented from kidnapping the Crown Prince of Italy in Rhodes. Though of course nobody knows this. It is called 'The Dodecanese. The Greek point of view.' It is extraordinary how in half an hour one becomes an authority on the near east. A man named Kartali[2] dined with us last night who had driven through the streets of Smyrna over thousands of massacred bodies, with his father and mother in the back green and chattering, with their eyes starting out of their heads. They got away on a Japanese boat.[3]

I am just going to bathe – Goodbye
Bobs

---

1. Mr Kokkinopolous, Director of Greek Air Services.
2. Sotiri Cartaliss.
3. In August 1920, under the abortive Peace Treaty of Sèvres between the Allied Powers and Turkey, the district of Smyrna had been placed under provisional Greek administration, in effect under Greek military occupation. Hostilities ensued against Turkish nationalist forces under Mustafa Kemal, who reconquered Smyrna in September 1922. There was much bloodshed and many Greeks escaped by sea. After the Turkish entry a conflagration destroyed the larger part of the city.

6 November 1925   40 Beaumont Street, Oxford

Darling Mibble

I have ordered the *Cherwell* for you regularly – and Anne – how it will brighten your Monday mornings.

The article comes out rather well, and evoked torrents of praise from the compositor in Birmingham over the telephone.

Oxford is too depressing, I shall be thankful to go down – too many have gone already.

A party of queer men from London arrived to see Hugh yesterday, as he is at Madresfield celebrating his majority with becoming pomp, I looked after them, Ché, named Murdoch, is a magnificent example of the successful journalist. He has money to throw away and lives at the Carlton. He does it all by writing for American papers – though frequently employed by English, such as *The Times*. He says I ought to go to America. I am going to cultivate him assiduously this morning and cover him with *Cherwells*. I have written to Lord Beauchamp over the Dodecanese – and am getting a Don at Christ Church to write to all the Liberal MPs. I suppose it will be no use. Oh! these lost causes – I feel like one myself.

[. . .] I dined with Henry last night. His book[1] has been accepted by Dent's – isn't it a triumph – I am so glad and he is so pleased – it is, I think and he agrees, little more than the mental processes of a blind youth. There is a lot about me and Brian at Eton in it, in diary form, which I am told is quite irrelevant.

Last night was Guy Fawkes night – tremendously celebrated. Henry and I suddenly found ourselves addressing a mob of 3,000 people in the Cornmarket from the windows of the Liberal Club – at least we booed at them and called them 'girlmen' and they screamed for a speech and threw rockets in at the windows till the whole club was flaming and the steward in tears. Luckily the entrance is about four doors off, so that no one could find it. The awful thing is that in the turmoil I lost my hat, just as it is beginning to get the right shape – but I think I shall find it again all right. [. . .]

On Saturday I go to London to see the Private View of the International Exhibition (run by Francis Howard[2] and opened by Birken-

---

1. *Blindness* by Henry Green.
2. Hon. Secretary of the National Portrait Society; father of Brian Howard.

head) – lunch with Harold's sinister friend Condamine – and then I hope see Cecil. It will be interesting to compare this exhibition with that in Venice last year and see if any pictures are the same – Harold's Father is represented – and as Harold has never seen his pictures, he is naturally amused to go.

Goodbye   Best Love

Bobs

9 November 1925

Darling Mibble

I really have no time to write and tell you all that I want to. I am going to London tomorrow to see the Foreign Editor of the *Daily Mail* and then dine with Mrs Locker Lampson[1] at the Carlton, go to the first night of the new ballet,[2] with Oliver's[3] masks in it, and then to the Armistice Ball: then lunch and motor back with Bryan Guinness the next day. Won't it be fun – I arranged it all in an hour on the strength of the 'Foreign Editor'. Murdoch has provided the introduction. I *shall* go to America directly I get the chance – don't you see that then there will never be any need to go again – like having an eye tooth out.

The college is now upset over the Guy Fawkes night business and says that I am wasting my time up here. I replied that I could have told them that and the end of it was that I have arranged to come down – or rather they arranged it on Nov 29th after keeping the official term. This will enable me to get ahead with my diary – as I cannot do a *word* here – and Murdoch says that if I get a job they will probably want me to start at once – that is about December 5th, but probably nothing will come of it.

[. . .] Gavin's [Henderson] back with Cartaliss – I shewed him round Oxford in a grey November foggy twilight – he was astonished that anywhere could be so Gothic – it was astonishing to think that here was a Greek from the temples and the Aegean among this decaying stone.

---

1. Bianca, wife of Commander Oliver Locker-Lampson.
2. *Zéphyre et Flore.*
3. Oliver Messel.

I am going to have a leaving dinner on November 15th – that is next Sunday – do you think you could send a great wodge of green stuff, with which to decorate the room and the table – it doesn't really matter if it is a bother – but would help a great deal, as everything is usually so bare and I have no money to spend on decoration. [. . .]

Love from
Bobs

November 1925   40 Beaumont Street, Oxford

Darling Mibble

[. . .] I had a most enjoyable time in London – went up midday on a lunch train, and sat opposite a fat Scotch business man, who had been to see a polo pony breeder (A I socially) in prison for manslaughter and drunken driving – he said he saw no art in jazz and that he knew humanity through and through and could see also that I was one who would broaden my views. I said that my life was devoted to narrowing them – he then spoke of the gospel in the United States.

After that we arrived at Paddington, and I bought a top hat at Lock's and also a new pair of black shoes so that is two stages towards Betty's wedding.[1] Richard [Greene] and Elizabeth [Russell] are also being married on the 21st – their relations have come forward in thousands and they now have nearly eleven hundred a year.

Poor Mrs Greene has to have a very dangerous operation after it all – isn't it dreadful – I am so sorry. Do go and see her when you are in London. If I am up next week I will let you know.

We dined at the Carlton – Bee Locker Lampson, Gavin, Cartaliss, Peter Rodd,[2] and Rosemary Wilbraham – then went to the new ballet where Gavin had of course managed to get the royal box. The scenery vile and dresses, but Lifar is very good. [. . .] Then we went to the Ball, where were Michael and Bridget (Parsons)[3] and a party and Bryan

---

1. Wedding of Betty Byron, a cousin.
2. Second son of Sir James Rennell Rodd, subsequently Baron Rennell of Rodd. Future husband of Nancy Mitford.
3. Sister of Michael Rosse.

Guinness and Lady Evelyn in a most wonderful really old crinoline of tartan taffeta, trimmed with muslin frills and a suite of topazes. It was not easy piloting her round the room to a very bad band. There were one or two quite good dresses – not many. The judging was very badly done – Gladys Cooper is as fat as a German sausage – the band was abominable – but I enjoyed it all very much – to bed about three.

Next morning I traipsed off very cold in my tight new shoes to the *Daily Mail*. Crawford, the Foreign Editor, was most kind. I have told Father what he said. I think really that he did not like to commit himself for certain until he had seen the things that I have written. He shall have them with a vengeance.

Then I went and saw the Greenes – Olivia *just* off to Oxford for her music (?) lesson expecting to see me. Then to lunch with the Guinnesses. Bridget who was there, and I pumped Walter Guinness about the foot and mouth – he said he was that evening issuing a fortnight's restriction over the whole Midlands at which Bryan said he was hunting that week – whereupon his Father rushed to the telephone and discovered that it wouldn't be necessary after all. This is history made. He is in the middle of a bye-election at Bury St Edmunds – is it anywhere near Aldeburgh and is Granny there now – we might go over and drive a car on polling day. I love elections. I must go and buy some tinsel for my party. It will be very depressing. We went to *The Silver Fox* in the afternoon – very risqué – quite French in fact. [. . .]

Love
Bobs

2

Greece
1926–1927

ROBERT FINALLY came down from Oxford at the end of November 1925. His leaving was a relief both to the university authorities, convinced that he was only wasting their time, and to Robert, eager to pursue his journalistic career. He had, however, fulfilled his statutory three years, enabling him to take his third-class degree. This he never bothered to collect.

In January 1926 Robert, moving to London, took rooms in 'a dear little Georgian house' in Upper Montagu Street off Manchester Square and on 18th he arrived 'like a shy maiden' at Carmelite House to start as cub reporter on the *Daily Mail*. He trekked round London, interviewing such people as 'old lady who throws burglar downstairs' or 'ventriloquist vicar inhabiting public house in Peckham'. But his was hardly the human approach required. The combative style he had practised for the *Cherwell* could not be moderated to suit the news editor, who complained that his stories were not bright enough, and by the end of February he was out of a job, sacked on his twenty-first birthday. This rather humiliating experience gave him time to finish his first travel book, *Europe in the Looking Glass*, and to rough out a synopsis of the grand design of his next project, the first part of which was to be a history of Byzantium and the second taking the reader up to the Greece of 1923.

His visit to Greece in 1925 had inspired Robert to pursue his studies of Byzantine art, especially in the location of almost unknown frescos including those of Mount Athos; and these discoveries which he was proposing to present to the world must be backed up by a comprehensive survey of the civilization which had nurtured them.

On 1 April 1926 he signed a contract with Messrs Routledge for *Europe in the Looking Glass* and on 15 April they concluded another for the first volume of Byzantine history, giving him an advance of £69: brave men to take on an unknown author with a mere third in history at Oxford, writing on a subject of which relatively few people, reared on and blinkered by classicism, had ever heard. However, the discernment of Mr Stallybrass, senior partner, was confirmed sixty years later when his firm reprinted this history, *The Byzantine Achievement*.

With Routledge's advance and the money paid for two articles in *Vogue* – enough, Robert hoped, to take him to Mount Athos – he set out on 19 April for Athens. He was determined that a visit of nearly six months would enable him to complete the formidable amount of research which he had planned during the winter. He was invited to stay with Leonard Bower, attached to the Legation, until he could find rooms of his own.

April 1926   [Paris]

Darling Mibble

We[1] arrived with the utmost safety yesterday afternoon – having caught the early train by hours, with Aunt Gladys and Aunt Phyllis to see us off and Mrs Acton[2] wearing all her pearls in the neighbouring Pullman. The crossing was rough, but Anne lay down at once and survived it intact.

I am staying at a *very* comfortable little hotel in the Boulevard St Germain the other side of the river – for 35 francs a day – the Bonne Hostesse it is called. Hugh Lygon has just telephoned from across the road that he has overslept and failed to arrive at the bank – will I go round.

I cannot tell you how harassing the last two days in London were. I arrived to find that my boat had been cancelled – after all these arrangements, so now I have to travel 2nd class *right* down to Brindisi and get a cattle-barge – the whole cost of which is even cheaper than the other way – the unfortunate thing being however that I know, if the Adriatic is rough, I shall be tempted to board a Lloyd Trestino – especially after two hideous nights in the train, but they run 2nd class sleepers from Milan.

---

1. On his way to Greece, Robert had travelled as far as Paris with his sister Anne after entertaining her in London with his friends.
2. Mother of Harold and William Acton.

Then the bank made no attempt to get the letters of Credit that I had ordered – that was on Monday. Late Tuesday evening a draft arrived on the Bank of Athens – leaving me forced to start with no possibility of obtaining one single penny between London and Athens and Athens and Constantinople. The manager had no idea that fortunately I had a friend in a bank in Paris who could cash me any cheques I wanted. I had pleasure in writing to tell him that my surprise at his incompetence had changed to annoyance and that I was complaining to Head Office. Which I did at some length, demanding that a letter of Credit should be sent to Athens immediately – this means they will probably communicate with Father. Will you tell him there is really no immediate hurry and that I am writing to him on the subject.

I think Anne enjoyed her day – we lunched with Bee[1] at the Berkeley – Peter Rodd, Betty Baldwin and David [Greene] – then to a little bit of a film – to tea with Atchley[2] 'the mainspring of Anglo-Greek relationships' – in a Lyons in South Kensington – dined with Babe.[3] [. . .]

When we went to Margaret Marks,[4] Julia Strachey who works there said that she had a job for me on the *New Statesman* helping run the Literary side and writing what the literary Editor, Desmond McCarthy, was too lazy to do! which would have been an *ideal* job – though only £200 a year. I wish I could have taken it, but with contract[5] in pocket so to speak I felt impossible to upset all arrangements.

I have come out loaded with cards of introduction – I saw John Stuart Hay[6] for a moment – Douglas and Thyatyra[7] and I really go to Athos on June 28th. Atchley said that while paying an official visit to the Italian Legation in Athens he noticed the *New Statesman* lying on the table. He says that Zervos will be off his head with glee at the new article. Peter Rodd says that he has an ancestor's escutcheon on one of the towers of Rhodes and intends to visit the island in his father's yacht this summer – in that case I shall be *fully* qualified to go to America and lecture on their oppression.

---

1. Beatrice Dawson.
2. Shirley Clifford Atchley, translator at the British Legation, Athens.
3. Babe Plunket Greene, wife of David.
4. A dress shop.
5. With Routledge for *The Byzantine Achievement*.
6. Art critic.
7. Archbishop Germanos, Metropolitan of Thyateira.

I have got the address of a man to whom it would be of some use sending the Dodecanesian pamphlets for distribution – but am too lazy to find it at the moment [. . .] I leave here on Saturday night, perhaps earlier, carrying all my books so as to avoid registration of such weight.

Goodbye and best love from
Bobs

2 May 1926   British Club, Athens

Darling Mibble

[. . .] We have just had the Easter celebrations – the whole place thick with sheep – every family has its own, which it makes a pet of, then kills. We had two bleating in our own courtyard as we bought one ourselves – which we ate last night down at Gladys Stuart Richardson's. This is the most extraordinary and rather disturbing ménage Leonard's, as there are only 2 rooms – no kitchen cupboards or anything – a large family above – and an old woman who lives in a kind of hovel in a corner. I have bought a deck-chair, in which I sit, down in a sort of stone area, shaded by vines and very strong smelling honeysuckle – and read. My subject increases in difficulty each moment – it is so very large – but I shall be able to carry it off, I think.

I rushed to see Zervos – he has a family of cats in that room now – also a lot of money come from a book written at government order. We dine with him tomorrow night. He was entranced by the article in the American *Nation*, which he had not seen. It is appearing in an Athenian newspaper, *without* my name.

'*Vous êtes bien nominé l'autre Byron*' said he as we parted last. He is going to give me Greek lessons. But I don't really think I shall have time for them, or French. I cannot even keep my usual diary. I *must* get on with the cause.

I am looking for two rooms but they are not easy to find here. However I daresay some will turn up.

We go to Mistra in Sparta at the end of this week – one goes on mules from Sparta. It is Byzantine renaissance – a monastery and a collection of churches.

There seem to be no flowers and almost as much dust. My Fortnum and Mason trousers are a great success. The ikon which I described in the book is now in the hands of a M. Franco. We went by train to the suburbs yesterday to have another look at it. I am trying hard to get hold of it as it is dated 1741 and would therefore be a good example of how the Byzantine tradition survived – it is magnificent. I could use it as an illustration to the book [. . .]

How *dreadful* this is about the coal strike – disastrous. Leonard says that in his family mines, which have been run for years on a friendly profit-sharing basis, the capital has always paid a comfortable 10%. [. . .]

Goodbye
Best love from
Bobs

My health is unimpaired.

19 May 1926   British Club, Athens

Darling Mibble
[. . .] We had the most wonderful time in the Peloponnese. Leaving at 6 in the morning we reached Tripolitza at 4 in the afternoon and thence motored to Sparta – with 10 others in a very moderate sized motor going up the most terrific mountains. The country of Greece is too beautiful for words – with none of the hardness of Italian colour – shepherds in fustanellas playing pipes among the olive groves, groups of peasants doing slow circular dances to their own chants upon the skyline – frogs croaking as they did in the plays of Aristophanes 'Brekekekex Coax Coax' from the ditches – birds with voices like bells, and the rippling bells of goats and sheep on the mountains – soft and low like a sort of musical ocean, unlike the clear-cut tinkles of the Alps.

We visited the excavation, I having a card to the man in charge, and the wife of his subordinate being fetched out of her bedroom in the hotel in her petticoat in order to translate my desire for hot water.

The hotel had only rooms with windows on the passage and as such sanitary arrangements as existed were only five yards off, we decided in future to seek hotels without sanitary arrangements.

Mistra, the only Byzantine town in existence, is about $1\frac{1}{2}$ miles from Sparta – the weirdest place – perched on a precipitous hill – all the houses and a huge palace still $\frac{3}{4}$ standing and nearly uninhabited.

Wonderful frescoes open to wind and rain – cisterns, fireplaces, ovens – all the domestic life is apparent. We spent the most entrancing and tiring 2 days there, our shoes being cut to ribbons on the rock.

In one little vaulted hole, seeing a piece of window moulding I took off my coat and crawling in on my stomach unearthed four whole skulls and three skeletons – how prosaic skulls are.

Leaving Sparta by car we drove to Gytheuri right in the south – this time with eleven people and Alastair[1] sitting on the brake. Huge oak trees rose from the red earth among the rocks of the mountain slopes – Reaching the port we could communicate with no one – but knowing the name Monemvasia – the Greek for Malmsey – where the wine came from – we uttered it, to discover there was a boat leaving in a quarter of an hour.

We arrived about 6 and put our luggage in a room in a sort of public house, general store – reached by an outside staircase which was shared by three families of children, their grandmothers, mothers and fathers, a cat and its family that all had lupus, a sheep which befouled the well and several dogs which were so indistinguishable from the compound of dung, dust and refuse which covered the courtyard that it was impossible to count them. Alastair picked many fleas off my bed and a number of bugs – but as they never come near me I slept in peace. He did not and now has a body like a leopard.

Malmsey is lovely – perched on a rock right out at sea, connected by a causeway to the land – most inaccessible.

We climbed up to the castle the first night to find it locked – the second morning was the same – locked though, with the original iron clamped door in its Frankish fortifications. We determined to break in and were hurling great boulders at the fastenings when a man appeared with the key, which of course refused to work after the damage we had done. However eventually it did and we got in after an embarrassing moment.

There was no food except cold hake kept in a drawer. Then a storm got up and we were almost all drowned – I mean the other occupants of

---

1. Alastair Graham, sometime honorary attaché in Athens and Cairo. A close friend of Evelyn Waugh.

the boat – trying to reach the steamer, which was very comfortable and we arrived in Piraeus early next morning having been away for five nights.

On Friday we go to Mitylene, Smyrna and Constantinople, so that I shall probably write next from there. I am too excited at the prospect, having been doing nothing but read about it since I saw you last.

I am told that the Italians 'know all about me' here so that very soon I am going round to apply for permission to go to the Dodecanese, and when they ask why, to say 'In order to examine the fortifications' – this will probably give them such a shock, that it will be amusing.

Mussolini appeared at a women's conference in Rome the other day on the arm of his mistress. In view of the fact that he has closed the dance-halls in Trieste and has a wife, 3 sons, and a daughter living in obscurity near Milan, I feel that this will give point to some attack very soon.

So glad the strike is over – it must have been maddening being so cut off. I get wild letters from Oxford describing how everyone has gone down in order to handle fish.

I must go and buy a refrigerator. Goodbye and best love, how I long to be home – or rather wish that you were out here.

from Bobs

26 May 1926   Constantinople

Darling Mibble

Here we are lying in the Golden Horn, waiting for the Embassy launch to fetch 'the bag', a kind of perforated mackintosh sack, which Leonard is conveying – thus getting a 50% reduction on the fare, while we get 15% also – as being 'press reporters' for some obscure reason.

Yesterday we lunched in Smyrna – the entire town in ruins – forced open safes still lying beneath heaps of debris – the British Club where we lunched, very grand with band – full of British Levantines all talking broken English to one another – most odd. Leonard purchased a Greek head out of an *altis* that had been looted from the burnt museum.

We identified Cartaliss' house on the quay, gutted but standing – the only one. There were also delicious horse trams.

The approach to this city is more beautiful than you can imagine. There are *no* mountains or hills behind – just a sort of undulating mass of houses and trees running down to the walls on the water's edge – the whole stretching for *miles* into an infinity almost and everywhere punctuated by the flat white domes and white minarets, that look literally like fairyland – above, a huge expanse of sky with great white fat clouds hovering over the town and throwing shadows on the pinky-grey chequers of the houses – below the sea, a dark untheatrical blue, with a number of jellyfish and a good deal of refuse, which is borne out by the very strong current. Across the other side Scutari rather modern, though too distant to be offensive, and a few Asiatic mountains, a dark dull blue. I had read so much of its history lately, that I could identify many of the places as we sailed in, which we did very fast.

Gallipoli we passed before it was light – but I saw dawn at Chanak, the North of the Dardanelles – perfectly lovely – the eastern range of hills black as an essence of damsons against a very soft rosy orange sky, with the water beneath them gleaming absolutely calm, in long silver streaks. [. . .]

Here, I think, comes the Embassy servant. I will go on with this in the hotel.

It was the Embassy servant – we landed and are now staying at the hotel [. . .] for a pound a night for the three – which is not too expensive – only the food and drink cost something fabulous, as the government in its new-found nationalism imposes a 30% tax on everything – Leonard finds it all rather depressing, having spent the Oxford of his youth here in the army of Occupation. It is far more like a capital than Athens, with far better shops, etc. We spent between tea and dinner in antique shops, they are most of them selling up and leaving, as there is no custom. Lots are still just filled with Russian personal effects – dressing cases, each bottle and brush of which are quite obscured beneath *enormous* coronated monograms laid on in three precious metals.

It is impossible to distinguish Turk from anyone else – except they seem rather whiter and cleaner than the Greeks, some have very cruel faces.

This morning we are going to St Sophia – a great moment – I can hardly wait – and must now stop, so as to write up my book about Smyrna and our entry and not forget it all. [. . .]

I do so wish you were here *all* the time seeing everything too. Please write *every* day.

With best love from Bobs

29 May 1926   Club de Constantinople, Pera

Darling Mibble

I am still here – quite exhausted with the interest of the place – nervy in fact with a kind of intellectual satiety – that I have not felt since being in Italy with Lord Beauchamp.

The others left early Wednesday – and I have enjoyed myself enormously being here alone, as we live at such close quarters in Athens, that it is a relief. Borough the Chaplain has been most kind in helping me in every way possible, collecting material – if only it wasn't so expensive, I should stay another week or fortnight – as there is so much to find out and I am as anxious to further the Turkish point of view as the Greek. Philhellenes are so fanatical, that it is almost impossible to get any truths out of them.

This morning I spent at the Patriarchate talking to the Metropolitan of Sardis and the chief Dragoman Constantinides – the whole establishment lives in terror of its life. I had hoped, incidentally, to publish in an article, an interview with the Patriarch himself – but as they said it would be most dangerous for them if such a thing were to occur, I did not bother to see him.

Borough, the Chaplain, has devoted 16 years of his life to the reunion of the Greek and Anglican churches. He is very interesting on the subject, and hopes to see it accomplished.

This town itself is so wonderfully attractive – everywhere are huge big shady light green trees, with masses of cherries, strawberries, drinking fountains and roses.

I attended a Moslem service in S. Sophia, if such it would be called on Friday, their Sunday – it was interesting only for the smell of feet, which in places became positively a reeking stench – not more than 150 people in the whole huge building.

I hope anyhow to write the article for *The Times* – at present Constantinople is no part of my book – and I can afford to.

I am becoming so mentally exhausted, that I really don't know what to do – the subject is ever with me – there is no getting rid of it.

I have taken a lot of photographs and only hope that they will come out – the ones of Smyrna are of interest – I am trying also to get hold of some photographs of the atrocities – but do not know whether this will be possible, as since the army of occupation left, the Turks have been suppressing them.

My Turkish is extensive. *Yok* means no, *su* water – the latter saved my life the other day. I had walked six miles along the outside walls and back revisualising all the main events of the last siege in 1453 – the stone cannons are still lying about – and should have died of thirst, if I had not known it.

I am now going to drink beer at an establishment called the 'Deutsche Teddy Bar' where Germans play and sing – I think I return on Tuesday by a very fast Roumanian boat that gets me back in time for a party at the Legation on Wednesday, though I assure you that is not the reason.

Goodbye and *best* love from
Bobs

4 June 1926   British Club, Athens
Floreat Etona!!!

Darling Mibble

[. . .] I am frightfully busy, as the *Morning Post* Correspondent wants me to go off tomorrow to Megaspelion, a mediaeval monastery in a cave, and from there to the Styx. As I am most anxious to talk to him alone, this would be a wonderful opportunity – and I think I must take it. So have an awful lot to do. Zervos is palpitating with excitement, as an invitation for a conference on the Dodecanese has come from Mussolini – he, Zervos, is being financed from Alexandria – and does not know what to do. Atchley the chief protagonist is away – so that the fate of a nation falls heavily on the shoulders of Leonard and yrs truly. I am *busy* drawing up terms which they shall negotiate for and there is some idea that I shall accompany them to Rome – this might be very convenient, as the conference, if it happens, would do so about August and it would be on my way home.

However it is all such a joke, that I hardly take it as seriously as Leonard likes, and caused the most awful complications discussing the question in front of an Italian attaché last night.

We hope also to return to Smyrna in search of antiquities from the burnt museum – and also to visit Ephesus with an armed guard. This would give me a view of the hinterland of Asia Minor, which I need, as the book deals largely with it. I have also squeezed an introduction to Aladdin Bey, chief of the Smyrna police, out of a Mrs Piet de Jong, who is Scotch, and her husband Dutch, having spent his boyhood in Leeds. I first met her in her petticoat in Sparta, in which she was fetched from her bedroom to translate my desire for hot water.

Yesterday I visited His All Holiness the former Oecumenical Patriarch of Constantinople, which is New Rome, Meletios IV, now His Beatitude Patriach-elect of Alexandria. He had some very fiery liquor which made me cough. Today we lunch with a Greek professor, who has a good cook. [. . .]

Goodbye and forgive haste
Best love
from Bobs

June 1926   British Legation, Athens

Darling Mibble

I write under indescribable conditions at the monastery of Osios Leukas – left Delphi at 7 this morning on a very fast mule – and rode for 8½ hours with one interval of half an hour. The grandeur of the scenery is indescribable, with the most lovely colours, nothing hard like Italy or Switzerland – and where there are springs, huge plane trees and asperns, with shepherds in kilts and alpenstocks shepherding their herds.

This monastery is perfectly wonderful – for the first Byzantine church in Greece with superb mosaics – and all marble panelled, just as we use wood – with even the veins of the marble transposed so as to make a pattern like our dining-room table. We arrived at 4.30, I so dead that I could hardly move, saw the church while light – and then I went to bed – even in daylight it was covered in fleas.

At eight we had dinner with the abbot – there is thank heaven another man staying here – but even he speaks nothing but Greek (I forgot to tell you that I was alone – Alastair was ill when I left). The dinner consisted of a vast plate of rice interspersed with suspicious? very large bits of meat – it was really very good. The abbot, filthier than words can describe, said an inexhaustible grace full of *Kyrie Eleisons*, while the other man crossed himself in the Greek way, which I can't do – then we set to, the abbot like a maniac, only pausing to wipe great glyceriny layers of sweat from his brow – while I fingered nervously with what might have been eyes and kidneys in the growing gloom – then the lamp was lit by the attendant monk. The abbot would keep asking if I thought it good, while 2 emaciated cats literally tore my trousers from my legs under the table. Then, as I did not eat all mine, or any cheese, they cooked two eggs for me – a faggot of bramble was brought up from below and the whole bonfire relit in the neighbouring room – For an awful moment I thought that my guide, whom it had not occurred to me to distinguish as human, was going to share my bedroom – but luckily he has this moment removed his things – and my tomorrow's coffee and gone. The other man is leaving at 4 a.m. – so I shall go too and get out of this hell of fleas. I have almost smeared half a bottle of insect powder on the bed, but I believe they eat it.

If only I wasn't so desperately tired, what a lot I should have to say, the description of this country would fill pages. Parnassus had snow on it – a huge soft silvery pile dotted with dark trees with white patches along the top – we climbed up very high, then went along a wide fertile valley, very cool, with the mountain on one side and another on the other – then a descent into sweltering heat (fortunately it was a cloudy day) with lizards (huge ones), snakes, hornets, tortoises were all frisking about. As we approached the monastery, the path suddenly disclosed one of the most wonderful views I have ever seen – sheer below to one side stretched great sort of flying buttresses of bluey grey earth, about 200 feet down, where they were met by smaller and more luminous ones, a purply pink – and on them very *bright pink* clumps of oleanders. Beyond a vast panorama of infinitesimal cultivated patches, olive trees and huge mountains rising again. Around one, yellow clumps of broom and hundreds of strange thistles, whose leaves looked as if they had been dipped in Reckitts blue – while huge iridescent beetles buzzed from bloom to bloom – and swallowtails, marbled whites, white admirals and all the blues flying everywhere.

Meanwhile I have said nothing about Delphi – I had the most appalling night I have ever spent getting there as I ate something that disagreed with me on the boat, and was sick all night – I was sharing a cabin with 7 other men – really I suffered – such pains in the stomach, then a very ancient cab up – 3 hours – and went straight to bed for the day.

That evening some Greeks arrived whom I knew, mother and daughter, and two deliciously common English people, the man setting up Shell (oil) plants all over Greece (just the person I wanted as the Treaty of Lausanne hinged entirely on oil and he told me the details). We all went down to the sacred fountain and drank and wished – the woman was delicious – (they were very rich and extraordinarily nice) – her cockney accent would keep breaking through her refinement – 'Oh thoese wonky stoenes' was one of her expressions.

Then my nose began to bleed and they all bound it by moonlight and an American *pro*-fessor said that he and Mrs Bragg were going on to so and so by what in his judgement constituted one of the best *aut*-omobile roads that he had *en*-countered in Greece, as good, sir, as any to be found in England or the *U*-nited States – and a Miss Chapman, very old and homeless, would insist on the superiority of the Quorn over what she termed the Pitchly. To complete it Madame Skeleri (the Greek) would do nothing but hum alternating 'What'll I do' and the tune of that quite unrepeatable song 'She was poor but she was honest'. All this at perhaps the most historic shrine in the world – though the water, which I climbed in and got them, was full of tadpoles, as I had been there in daylight. I would not have missed that evening for a lot, especially as the Littler-Powells (she used to breed bloodhounds) had their own supply of whisky *and* soda, which they had brought. I am going to see them if I go to Salonika; it was all burnt in 1917 – and according to them the modern town is perfectly magnificent, every street 30 metres wide – and every crossroads a circus.

I am dreading the 8½ hours back tomorrow.

Goodbye and best love
Bobs

27 June 1926   c/o British Legation, Athens

Darling Mibble

[. . .] The heat grows more and more – I had a fabulous journey home after the letter I wrote you – left the monastery at *four* a.m., and dragged my guide 25 miles in *pouring* rain by lunchtime – people here loathe rain – he nearly died of it. As a result I have been rather overtired since. [. . .]

Zervos dined last night – the Dodecanese rests heavier and heavier on my shoulders. He also produced 10 copies of *The Dodecanese*, a paper published in Alexandria, with my article again reprinted – I must send you some. He also has a female emissary taking photographs of the Italian naval base at Leros, which she sends home in bits of bread – so that I hope to return home with some good material for articles on East Mediterranean Politics. Meanwhile he hopes to go to Rome – regarding the approbation of Leonard and myself as that of the British Government – and if he is not allowed, there will be even more material for articles.

Cheetham,[1] our minister here, was *most* upset by my article in the EMMOΣ – they traced it (the Italians) to someone who was staying with Leonard, and are furious – I am delighted as Cheetham is such a fool.

This [the British Club] is a very exclusive club – the youngest member is 46 – I went to a ceremony, the donation of a helmet of Byron's to the National Museum by an American widow – and met all sorts of stray dignitaries including a Monsieur Caftazoglu, who made me a temporary member of this club – not only that, but introduced me to all its members – a horrible experience: 'Monsieur Petro Kokkino, Ministre des Chemins de fer en 1908' – 'Monsieur Papadopoulos, Ministre des affaires étrangères en 1853' etc. – and I shall never know any of them again. [. . .]

Best love and tell me when to write to Savernake again.

Love Bobs

---

1. Sir Milne Cheetham.

30 June 1926   Athens

Darling Mibble

[. . .] My labours get no less – as there are always a plethora of people whom I have to be going to *see* – I have made friends with a general Phrantzes, a famous Byzantine name, whose ancestors married the cousin of Constantine Palaeologes, last Emperor of the East, and who actually possesses a ring with Constantine's initial on it. This is a great discovery, as you know the old cry that there are no 'families' in Greece etc. I cultivate him assiduously – and hope to get a photograph of the ring. Luckily he was military attaché in London for years and speaks excellent English. He assures me that the throne is open to any Byron. We shall see whether it is or not after the book is out.

This morning I spent with Zervos at the National Museum, marking things to be photographed for my book. I have found a delicious set of Victorian playing cards (printed in Hungary 1829) in which all the court cards are portraits of the heroes of the Greek War of Independence. Very amusing.

On Sunday we went to Porto Raphti – which fell nothing short of my ideal – and allowed ourselves to be drawn through that delicious water on 40 feet of rope – I took 6 photographs so that I hope I shall be able to give you some idea of the place.

It has turned cooler today – the last few days have been appalling. I have spent them taking notes from the official dossier of the Smyrna atrocities – really *most* unpleasant. [. . .]

I am afraid my return may be delayed a week or two, as at last I have persuaded someone (Bryan Guinness) to come to Mount Athos with me – and he cannot get out here till July 28th. However he may not come at all – I don't know for certain yet.

I am suffering from bruised eardrums, the result of sea-water and shall have to wear a cap with flaps in future – isn't it absurd. Goodbye and best love – I am so longing to be home – yes of course the den is perfectly comfortable, if I could have a table which I could get my knees under.

Bobs

18 July 1926   The Merano, Piraeus

Darling Mibble

Thank you so much for your letter of the 11th. I am so glad to be able to write to Savernake again. [. . .] Please don't think that I should ever 'take office' *anywhere* abroad, unless forced to. Three months exile has already been quite enough.

Leonard and I are at last on the first stage of our journey to Smyrna – everything went wrong. It takes 2 days to get a Turkish visa – our boat went on Friday – on Wednesday I was ill with some odd food rebounding at the bottom of my stomach – on Thursday we decided not to go. Then I found that there was a boat on Saturday. We got a letter from the Turkish Legation to the Consul, whom I charmed with my manners and he gave me my visa. Then when we arrived at Piraeus, laden with luggage and parcels, the boat had not even arrived. We went and bathed, then came on board in time for dinner. [. . .] I must say I do enjoy getting on to a ship (this one is a large Lloyd Triestino and very comfortable) because one gets a real rest and having paid one's fare can really eat one's fill without thinking of expense. [. . .]

The smoking room is full of vast Germans shouting in authoritative voices. There is also a piano. I can hardly tell you how my music is improving, I practise a lot at our house, and there are sheaves of the best songs, you should hear me ripple out the Barcarolle. I shall do it tonight on board, as we glide amid the Greek islands.

My return home may be again delayed by a series of horrible intrigues which quite unwittingly Leonard and I have done our best to thwart. Some days ago there arrived a letter from Francis Rodd (Peter Rodd's elder brother) to the Legation as such, saying that he heard on good authority that a party of dealers were on the point of descending on Mount Athos with a view to carrying off its hitherto uncatalogued treasures. (It must be explained that the monks hate the government, which is always interfering and which purposes to catalogue the art-treasures in October and so might be willing to sell just to spite it.) Francis Rodd hinted that the dealers were American. Leonard and I then rushed off and made mischief, with the result that a circular letter of warning has been sent to all abbots and watch will be kept on the ports. No sooner was this done than another letter arrived from John Stuart Hay (John Lennox Howe in my book) – saying that he is arriving on the 25th for the purpose of going to Athos to *buy manuscripts and art treasures* – financed by the British and Sth Kensington Museums and Spink's (Byzantine things are in great demand and there are *none* in London). More than that – in the 3rd week in August Gavin [Henderson] and Peter appear in the Rodd yacht to take off the treasure! and the party [of dealers] as Hay proposes to join Bryan Guinness and myself. So that I *may* wait for the yacht or may not – I shall if it is punctual – but what the end of it all will be I don't know – Hay will be too angry to speak when he discovers what Leonard and I have done – yet it really was not our fault!! And then there is my own Madonna to get out – she is life-size, painted on a kind of adzed tree-trunk.

Smyrna I think will be amusing – there is a marble head, four times life-size, which we hope to smuggle out disguised as a pumpkin. The Turks are busy being nice to us now, owing to terror of Italy, so our stay should be pleasant. No – I don't think I shall be going to Rome with Zervos – as his negotiations are being very slow.

I am getting more immured to the heat – it has not been really hot yet, like last year, but I find that one has to take taxis and eat a lot – otherwise it is impossible to get anything done at all. [. . .]

With best love
from
Bobs

22 July 1926 Smyrna

Darling Mibble

We have just got back from Ephesus after a day of hideous heat and discomfort, though *extraordinarily* interesting. We left at 6.45 a.m. bearing a despatch case full of Conan Doyle, George Eliot and De Maupassant, 16 ham and tongue sandwiches and two cavernous bottles of Vichy water. The train took four hours to get to Selchouk – an English line built in 1869 – nevertheless everything is written in Turkish and we had difficulty in finding our station, much conversation with various guards who addressed us as *effendi*.

Selchouk consisted of a number of hovels clumped beneath an aqueduct, on each arch or pillar of which perched a stork on her nest. (Drawing follows.) It was really *very* like this. A car had been ordered by the railway company for us. The driver spoke only Italian. So we shot off into Asia Minor, and had not gone two miles when we left the road and took to the fields – not a *trace* of a road – and after finding a footpath and following it over hills and through thickets of unwholesome brambles, we reached Ephesus.

You could not have imagined such immensity – or rather such intricacy of workmanship combined with size, as the capitals, cornices etc., and *very* interesting from my point of view, as it shewed more than anywhere I had been, the transition from the classical to the Byzantine. Everywhere were lumps of exquisite marble lying about – I brought away a little piece of a porphyry column. There was a Christian church built by classical architects – and you can still see the grooves where the doors of the great temple swung back. [. . .] Leonard, who really knows about these things, saw none of them, as the heat was too much for him – midday in a low-lying *marsh*, so that one had difficulty in getting about at all. [. . .] Then after eating lunch and drinking our water we drove back to the station and drank Turkish tea, which is delicious, and fizzy peardropade. At 2.20 our train left and after the most *insufferably* hot journey, we reached here at six, having finished bottles of quinine tablets on the way, so that I hope we shall be all right. Tonight being the night before the Muslim Sabbath, is a gala night and this is the centre of Levantine smartness and society – so that they are brightening the lamps and the band is tightening its strings.

As you have seen in the papers, we missed the hanging of the conspirators by a week. A man, who had got wind of the time, described it to me – one of them broke his rope 3 times as they pulled the chair from under him – till at last he sauntered across and chose a stronger clothes line. Another pulled *his* gallows over altogether!

As for the state of this town – it is like Bournemouth on Christmas afternoon.

I prowl among the ruins taking photographs of things I dare not write. [. . .] No doubt you think all this caution absurd – but such awkward things do happen – and they were so suspicious of my landing at all. Besides which I wish to keep my pen virgin for a greater moment! As it was I had a fracas with a soldier up in the castle overlooking the town – I was taking a view of it framed in a nice Gothic archway when a soldier on a signalling tower began shouting and whistling – so that all I could do was to wave my arms frantically in reply until he began to descend, when I ran away.

The Turks are a *dying* race, literally dying as one looks at them, of consumption and less mentionable diseases.

Anatolia is very picturesque – camels grazing off willows – storks and cranes in the marshes – women in trousers – everywhere ruined houses and everyone diseased, malformed, more than filthy – and now robbed of the fez, without any excuse to exist at all.

Tomorrow we are invited to spend the afternoon in the house of a Russian Jew – naturalised Turk dealer – I hesitate at the prospect. We leave Sunday, arriving Monday morning when Hay will be awaiting us. Then I have just one more week to gather up the last threads – Bryan Guinness arrives on Sunday – and I hope we set off on Tuesday or Wednesday – a few days at Salonika full of interest ancient and modern, then Athos. I hate the idea of taking part in this marauding expedition, but I think that Hay will not want to come with us to the more inaccessible (and interesting) monasteries – and also I have written to Constantinople to try and get a letter of introduction from the Patriarch, which is the infallible key – and will distinguish an identity from that of Hay, to whom however I am devoted and shouldn't mind a chance of getting hold of one or two things for myself – but it is being financed by dealers that I dislike.

We have attached to ourselves a small Soudanese named Ali who is useful and attentive. It is so funny to hear people calling one another Mustapha, Tewfik, Ibrahim etc. and all with their appropriate titles of *bey* or *effendi*.

Goodbye – I shall be home as soon as is possible without losing any chances.

Love
Bobs

July 1926   British Club, Athens

Darling Mibble

Bryan Guinness *is* coming – so that I am afraid I shan't be home until about August 20th – as Mount Athos is a thing that I was very unwilling to miss and I feel triumphant having got someone to go with. He does not arrive till 28th.

Meanwhile I am busy collecting letters to the Governor of Macedonia, and to all the dignitaries of the church. We shall also take a cooking stove, as monastery food is not pleasant.

I am just going off to dine with the rich man. I forgot to tell you that our house has a piano – of the best and loudest tone and sheaves of the *right* kind of music. So I am very happy, in my spare moments – though I cannot sing for long in the heat!! All Greeks really appreciate my music, it is so *nice*.

Love
Bobs

29 July 1926   British Club, Athens

Darling Mibble

It is annoying to see your new hat and not know which it is. I arrived back from Smyrna yesterday at midday, to be confronted by a picture in the *Sporting and Dramatic* in which Sir Leonard's chin and Father's nose are the prominent features – while a bevy of hats leaves me in complete doubt as to which is you. [. . .]

I had a lovely time at Lidgie with the Whittalls[1] bathing and doing nothing – except learning a good deal about Turkey and the Turkish side of it all. We stayed Sunday, and left Monday evening, having most of the 50 mile drive by moonlight. The next day I sneaked into the Greek cemetery, when the porter was asleep, and had just got ten photographs of some nicely desecrated graves, when he came rushing towards me gnashing his teeth and shouting

'Tchuk! Tchuk!'

---

1. Members of an Anglo-Turkish trading family.

So I tchukked – luckily he never saw the camera, or else all my photographs would have been confiscated. I have taken over forty at Smyrna and can't wait for them to be developed.

Leonard's bronze statue which was being brought from Tarsus, was seized by the police on arrival – so that I was saved the embarrassment of bribing that through the customs, as Leonard had gone on by an earlier boat.

It is terribly hot here but not so shatteringly unhealthy as Smyrna, I don't think. As you saw from my letter, it was pure fiction that Ephesus needed an armed guard – we went quite alone.

Bryan arrives Saturday – and we leave on Wednesday. Hay went yesterday, in a great state of mind over the Rodd business. It is becoming increasingly difficult to go there (Athos) as the monks and Greek Government are quarrelling and each tries to keep strangers recommended by the other, out. So I am getting letters from the Foreign Minister, the Metropolitan of Macedonia and the Patriarch of Constantinople. It will be a terrifying business. One is given no meat at all, so that I am taking boxes of meat lozenges and 2 dozen tins of sardines – also brandy, pillow cases, insect destroyer, biscuits, quinine, phospherine, chlorodyne, cold mixture, novelettes, writing paper, 2 dozen films, tame canary (male), cooking stove, marching chocolate and emetics. If you think of anything else, wire to Salonika.

The drachma has suddenly fallen, and as I had a lot I have lost money. No, I don't think I shall go to Rome with Zervos. But if Gavin and Peter really are arriving in their yacht about August 20th, I shall wait for them, as I want very much to get some photographs in Rome and Florence – where are to be found the only really lifelike portraits and busts of the later Byzantine Emperors, and if I could get letters to the Director of Museums from Rennell Rodd, it would be a great help.

I think that the illustrations that I want are nearly complete except that I cannot think of a frontispiece – or a title. How does this strike you
'TO ROMEIKO'
It is really too hot to explain what it means – but we can talk about it later. [. . .]

Goodbye
Best love from
Bobs

Darling Mibble

At last, after a year's planning, I am here, and the suitcase. It is too wonderful for words – this long narrow peninsula – and a single wooded range of mountains stretching out into the sea – and ending suddenly in a terrific peak, six thousand feet high – with clouds wreathing round it – all around the fresh green of the gardens of the monasteries, the woods of planes and Spanish chestnut – and the sea, an ethereal silvery blue, like the wing of a butterfly, always visible.

Hay has met us. We arrived at Daphni, the little port, at six this morning – and were greeted by Peter Bonifacious, formerly Archimandrite of Jerusalem, who has a divorced wife in Athens, whom he visits now and then. Our breakfast consisted of liqueurs like fire, watermelon and tea – which he had already sugared! Then we got three mules, heaved the suitcases and the Gladstone bag – containing insect spray, 8 tins of sardines, 2 of tongue, 2 of paté de foie gras, marching chocolate, cooking stove etc. on to it – and getting on the others set off on a 3 hour ride to Caryes, the capital. A weird little town with beggars and half-witted monks lying about the tiny streets – one or two shops kept by monks, and not a woman or a child, not a hen, a cow, a dog nor female cat to be seen. Demanding Pater Adrianos we were ushered to the Government House, he being this year's head of the republic; vary fat and benign and terribly obsequious to me, *Byron*. Bryan's father's being Minister of Agriculture in our letters of introduction had no effect. He even did us the honour to walk down to the inn to see how our lunch was getting on – and was interesting about the political autonomy of the community. Hay has been here a week. We are now sitting in the school, a sort of guest house, waiting for the Holy Synod to reassemble at 4.30, to inspect our letters of introduction and give us a circular letter of recommendation to the monasteries without which they will show us nothing – as we discovered this morning on the way up.

We had the most fabulous time in Salonika – after a loathsome journey. The churches are very interesting, though the best were spoilt by the great fire of 1917. A friend of Hay's, Sultiel by name (one of the original Spanish Jews who emigrated there in the 15th century when they were turned out of Spain and still speak Mediaeval Spanish) – entertained us to dinner – we had a table next to Boubalis the governor, who had a sister-in-law – Madame Kotzias – and a vast Alexandrian Greek woman with him. Then we all went and danced elsewhere and never got to bed till 4, it was most depressing. The next day I explored the castle, Byzantine and Venetian, but most complete – and then in the afternoon we went to tea with Madame K. who is making terrifying plans for our entertainment on return. I can really speak French quite fluently now – though not as well as I should like. My Greek too is coming on. We had a very comfortable journey here in the boat – tonight we go to Vatopedi – another three hours ride – where there are the most exquisite things, a bottle made of turquoise among them. It is amusing to be back really in the 15th century – monks everywhere, flitting about with long beards, black robes and black caps – performing all the offices and very dirty and *smelly*.

Hay's business here is not prospering – I cannot say that I am sorry. [. . .]

Hay and I are just going out – Bryan is asleep.

Goodbye and best love from
Bobs

19 August 1926   Mediterranean Palace, Salonika

Darling Mibble

We are back, having arrived at 5 this morning, after waiting 24 hours for our boat. Luckily a friendly old monk Father Boniface, put us up – and we were glad of an idle day.

I cannot describe to you now how wonderful Athos was – but have decided to write 3 articles for *The Times* and try and get them onto that page with the leaders. If the photographs come out, they should be unique in some ways, as the synod did everything for us, put on their orders and veils, posed, trotted from shade to sunlight etc. At the Lavra, the biggest monastery, a Union Jack was flown in my honour from the guest house, and I had to march out in procession with the Abbot to a deafening peal of bells. I was *very* pompous.

But it was all infinitely more amazing than I had thought and in the heat of the mainland I cannot really tell you anything about it.

I am dreading going back to Athens as if it were the dentist – the heat of the mainland is now so truly awful – and I have so much to do there. Please don't write any more to the Legation but to Bryan Guinness in Paris. We shall leave Athens just as soon as I can get my things into my box.

Hay has got one superb MSS out of Athos – which Chester Beatty, the collector, has wired £500 for so he has to go back to get it. I can hardly wait to come home. Bryan is writing a letter in French excusing our not calling on the Governor.

I only wish I would find a letter in Athens, saying someone was dying and I must come home at once – not dying, no, but something imperative.

Goodbye and best Love
from
Bobs

1926   The Sea of Marmora

Darling Mibble

I can't describe the horror of the last few days – a sandstorm was blowing, howling round the house, sending great clouds of dust down all the streets, which filled one's mouth and made everything filthy – no bath – my stomach out of order – and millions of last things to do and people to see – on the last day I was up at 5.30 a.m. with a translator, trying to get the gist out of the Athos Constitution – and didn't go to bed until 1.30 a.m. the next morning, not having stopped for a moment, the Madonna having nearly killed us all. She is life-size you see and very delicate being painted on plaster, which is itself on canvas, which in its turn is stuck to two or three oak trees, which are roughly fastened together by two or three other oak trees.

Then there was the horror of getting her through the customs – I could get no permit, as the man was away – just as Nicola[1] had bribed one official the head douanier saw the enormous packing case and said that it must be opened – Nicola said that it was a painting by *me*! – and that it could not be opened – at that moment a boatman came up and staggered off with it. I hope to leave it on board at Constantinople and from there send it home by ship – otherwise there will be difficulty in every country I go to. I have got a famous wonder-curing ikon from near Trebizond, which Hay and I discovered in Salonika and which he thinks we may get £75 for out of Spink's – personally I should put £20 as the highest price – but we shall see – in any case we only paid £3 for it and also a piece of fabulously valuable Byzantine stuff, which is on approval – so that I hope to boost Byzantine art with success. The big Madonna I don't want to sell as it is *lovely* but if there really is a market, as Hay says, it would be worth it. Hay says that practically all the big shops, being overstocked with Italian and Flemish primitives, refuse to boost Byzantine art; but that Spink's, having none, are only too anxious to steal a march on their fellows. Certainly a few things of Hay's have fetched extraordinary prices.

It is very exciting approaching Constantinople again. This morning we saw the Dardanelles and the long peninsula of Gallipoli, as it was quite light at 4.30 a.m. when we passed through. We shall arrive at about 3 or 4 p.m. I think. This boat is Roumanian – there is a very jocular doctor. There are only 4 other 1st class passengers, and at meals they, the doctor and the captain all speak French out of politeness to us (although all Roumanian) – It is a very nice boat and I am feeling sick with over-eating and am lying up in the forefront of the ship in the sun – it is very windy and the paper is almost blown from my hand.

I have ordered the *Messager d'Athènes* to be sent to Savernake for 6 months so that if it comes do not throw it away like David's postcard! I have bought two pairs of shoes, a black and a brown for under a pound each – had them made of *very* good leather. Isn't it cheap. Zervos presented me with a bunch of bananas on departure. I had to bury his

---

1. Leonard Bower's manservant.

Dodecanesian pot and also the monument of shells and sponges – they were too unwieldy, I tore the best sponge off.

Atchley came back by the midnight train the night before we left – I just had time to say goodbye to him. [. . .] The Athos photographs are really very amusing though I don't know whether more than 1 or 2 are good enough for *The Times*.

Bryan has a very good camera – a German one – and those of his that have come out are wonderfully good – I do wish I had spent a little more money and bought a good one while I was about it. However I am sure that the *Graphic* and the *Ill. London News* will take them – only I want them published with my articles and I don't want to write the kind of articles that they would want. I think perhaps I can also sell the Smyrna ones for something, and even perhaps a few of Constantinople and Broussa – if we go there.

Though the breakfast is not out of my throat, the steward is now offering us bowls of soup. The Roumanian for butter is *wat!* [. . .]

Best love
Bobs

I am afraid you can't read much of this.

———————

After returning from Greece on 14 September 1926 Robert moved to London, maintaining himself by writing book reviews and articles but devoting his main energy to condensing the notes he had taken in Athens into the preliminary chapters of his Byzantine book. In the summer of 1927 he and David Talbot Rice formulated a plan to return to Athos to undertake a serious survey and to photograph the neglected frescoes belonging to the monasteries on Mount Athos and in Mistra. They proposed to study the whole development of later Byzantine painting, both the Cretan and the Macedonian schools spanning the early fourteenth to late sixteenth centuries. This research expedition for David to photograph the frescoes was based on Robert's expectation of gaining permission from each monastery, armed as he was with a letter of introduction from the Oecumenical Patriarch of Constantinople (Ardent suppliant of God) and head of the Orthodox Church. Further fortified by letters from the Greek Foreign Office, and from the Metropolitan of Athens, Robert set off on 12 August for Marseilles. He had also fixed up with Duckworth a preliminary acceptance of the travel book he was proposing to write as he moved about on Athos. Tom Balston, a Duckworth partner, begged him not to make it too serious.

After ten days in the great heat of Athens, an overnight train journey brought Robert to Salonika and to the steps of the Mediterranean Palace Hotel where his three companions in travel stood waiting, having themselves arrived by train only ten minutes earlier. There was David Talbot Rice, studious, competent, dependable, already an archaeologist (field director of expeditions at Kish and Constantinople), engaged to Tamara Abelson, who shared his studies. Next Mark Ogilvie-Grant, who had come along just for the fun of it, a delightful temperament, something of a naturalist, ready to burst out singing ballads of his beloved Scotland, already in demand for his pen-and-ink caricatures in fleeting outline of his friends. He was indignant at being described by Robert as a 'waft of artificial heather'. Lastly Gerald Reitlinger, an older man of independent means, artist and art collector and editor of *Drawing and Design*. Taking an overnight boat, the *Nausica*, they arrived at dawn at Daphni and from there set off on a two-and-a-half-hour ride to Caryes, the Athos capital: 'our luggage is enormous – but consists largely of food, films and plates'. The Holy Mountain awaited them.

Each of the four travellers required two mules to carry his baggage, mules being the only transport to the more inaccessible monasteries. They first made for the relative comfort of the Lavra, where, for five days, David photographed the frescoes entirely covering the walls of the church. On the sixth day they made for Kerasia and from there, palpitating in the afternoon heat, they achieved the summit of the mountain itself, which they could see spread out forty miles behind them. Ahead a precipice 'a mile and a quarter off the globe' presented them a view, to the east Lemnos and the coast of Asia Minor, northwards the coastline of Thrace, to the west Mount Olympus and the fingered coast of Greece. Retreat from such a prospect was hard. They lingered until the night cold drove them back. The party made its way down to Gregoriou. From there they climbed to Simopetra, perched on a mountain crag, the buildings strutted with wood to prevent them falling into the sea: on again to delicious Docheiariou, surrounded by forest, its courtyards punctuated by cypresses, and finally to the sophistication of Vatopedi with its masterly frescoes of the Macedonian school, thought to have been painted around 1312.

Besides bedbugs the party found the lack of edible food the hardest privation to bear. What food there was consisted of 'beans cooked in what tasted like train oil, little marrows which they christened "nails" because they were so hard and occasional salt cod from Newfoundland'

(Reitlinger). They never came across fresh fish or meat and an Athonite banquet triumphantly offered four courses of octopus dressed in different ways. Finally their stomachs could take no more and they fled on the first boat to Kavalla.

Thus after four weeks of incessant photographing and note-taking, most of their hopes and plans had been fulfilled. Returning to Athens, Robert and David doubled the size of their party by taking in Bryan Guinness and John Sutro and headed for Mistra, a Byzantine town.

To visit the ruined churches of Mistra was as important to Robert and David in their researches as their visit to Mount Athos. Robert had been there briefly the year before but then had only viewed the place as part of his impressions of Greece as a whole. From this visit he wrote later: 'The paintings of Mistra surviving in all the brilliancy and delicacy of their original colouring give an impression of freshness and humanism which is not to be found in the ascetic environment of the Holy Mountain.' These, or what was left of them, were their goal. Mistra, situated at the head of the valley of the Eurotas, was a ruined town. Villehardouin's castle and the houses in the narrow, steep streets which led up to it, were roofless. The churches of Peribleptos and Pantanassa, which contained the main frescoes, had no protection from rain running down their walls, and, as Robert bitterly remarked, the money being spent on a classical dig nearby might have been better employed preserving these frescoes of the fourteenth and fifteenth century: 'These churches contain the whole clue to the semi-oriental paternity of European painting. Their importance is not to be exaggerated.'

The large party of Robert and his friends stayed at modern Sparta and made their way daily up to Mistra where David photographed. With this accomplished the party endured a two-day mule-ride back to Kalamata.

Some inkling of the complaints of Robert and David as to the condition of the frescoes at Mistra may have reached Venizelos (the Prime Minister), whose family originated from there, and some efforts at better protection were made – a small museum was started in the palace of the Despots, earlier rulers of the dependency. But these efforts were not long-lasting.

---

13 August 1927   SS *Patris II*, Marseilles

At last I am on board after a hideous morning. I lost *all* my keys – they must have fallen out of my pocket – and have had to have the suitcase lock forced from the top – fortunately with no damage to the leather –

but it has been very annoying. The ship's carpenter on the Channel managed all the others with his own keys. I have wired to Harrods for a key – could you confirm it and make sure that they send it *at once – not* by Foreign Office bag, as that means delay.

It is delicious to be in the south again – even only as far as this – and smell the dust. I found that Gavin had reserved me a single sleeper and cabin at his expense, and it was too late to cancel them – I tried naturally – I travelled in the Train Bleu – a positive miracle of comfort with melon, trout, chicken and brown bread ice for dinner – the silver and glass shining as if the best butler alive were on the train – really extraordinary. The *Channel* was very rough and I watched people's faces with enjoyment. It threatens to be rough here, which will be hideous.

Things do not seem to be very cheap in this town. I am longing to get to Greece – I have already had my first row in the steamship office. As it is I keep thinking of Queen Victoria's words 'this vainglorious and immoral people'.

Even the locksmith, as we trotted round the town together, he an

enormous old man in a tattered shirt, must needs delay before a nude nymph on a fountain. He was convinced I was going to the colonies.

I must now start my book. Goodbye and best love.

Bobs

16 August 1927   SS *Patris II*

Darling Mibble

We reach Athens in the dawn – so I will have this letter ready to post to you. Really this journey has surpassed all horror that one has ever imagined. It was comfortable enough to Marseilles, despite the worry of the keys. I was so miserable when the suitcase had to be bored open, that I almost cried – but fortunately it was done by such an expert that when I have a new key and the top catch is replaced, nothing will be seen but the rather different screws to the others, the *leather* is intact – not even scratched.

Having left Marseilles, the heat has been growing more and more unbearable. For two nights I have been almost wholly unable to sleep – and I have one of the coolest cabins, and that thanks to Gavin, to myself. What the others must suffer, I shudder to think. In the middle of the day it is far too hot to sleep – I have played agonised chess in the brocaded and dyed sycamore 'ladies' room'. But of course once on land, it will be all right – one keeps the windows shut, the sunblinds drawn, and nothing of the heat gets in. I have wired from Marseilles for Nicola to meet me. I hope he will – and have Leonard's flat ready. I look forward *immensely* to seeing Alfred [Duggan]. I do honestly think he is one of the nicest people I know, with a perfectly stable character – I only hope, as he said in his letter, Constantinople has really improved his health.

Although literally *prostrated* by the heat most of the day, I have been full of energy. 'My book'[1] is up-to-date – most voluminous. All this year's solid writing has certainly oiled my facility – it is of the same inconsequence as *Europe in the Looking Glass* – but much better. After the infinite pains and thought that I have been contributing to the Byzantine book it seems trivial – but comes easily and is exactly what

---

1. *The Station.*

Duckworth's asked for – over and over again. Will you act as secretary and copy it all out?!! – as it is almost good enough to go straight to press – only illegible. However everything I do is always improved by being recopied – so I daresay it will be better to do it myself. Forgive all these details – only I feel rather oppressed at the moment with the thought of making a more successful book – and at the same time justifying my £67.17 – which I do think it was generous of them to give me.

The leader of the boat's festivities 'foxtrrott and scharlestonn' has just rushed in *'Monsieur Byron, voulez-vous venir en haut, pour les jeux de société?' 'Oui Monsier, avec plaisir après dix minutes. J'écris à ma mère pour lui ranconter ce que nous faisons sur le Patris II.'*

We are now in the Gulf of Corinth – having entered it at sunset. If you have ever read my book, you remember the description of Patras and our first bathe. We saw Patras in the distance and I felt emotional and reminiscent. Greece is so *much* more beautiful than anywhere else. All the colours become soft – the mountain ranges falling away in perfect tones – rosy grey and then as the sun sets, blue-black against it. But I can't really describe it. The air *does* become scented. I feel like coming home – and only wish you were here – though thank Heaven you are not. You would hate the heat. *One day*, directly I have made any money, we will go by land. I have taken a dozen photographs with my new camera for practice – very elaborate, with a colour filter to bring out the tones of the blue sky and sea – you know blue never shows ordinarily – and shall have them developed in Athens to see the result.

I find my French fluent. Greek I have not yet tried. I will write after a few days. I wish I was at home – and yet it is wonderful to be back here, and away from everything. You probably did not realise how terribly worried I was over Gavin's case[1] – as it might have had vile repercussions. Its fame has spread even to this boat. I heard an old bearded man saying: 'What I want to do is to set the Thames on fire like those young chaps. . . .'

I must go and join the *jeux de société*.

Goodbye
Love
Bobs

---

1. Gavin Henderson had set the Thames on fire at Henley after a party, damaging the garden of Phyllis Court, who sued him.

Greece

Darling Mibble

I should have written before, only haven't. The heat has robbed me of all power of action and thought. I am better now than at first when I lay down all the morning and slept all the afternoon. Athens *is* intolerable at this time of year – the thermometer hovers between 95° and 120° in the shade.

I was met at Piraeus not only by Nicola in a new hat, but also a naval officer, a bevy of sailors and a launch – sent by General Phrantzes, the commander of the President's military household – so that the vagabond who, to the horror of the very rich and overdressed first-class passengers had lain panting all day in nothing but an open-necked jumper and trousers, was whisked away off in state, while they had to remain another hour struggling with the doctor and passport formalities. You wait till you come to Greece with me! – though no one has been more astonished than yours truly. I found that a letter had come from the Patriarch of Constantinople for me to the Athonite Synod – so that was very satisfactory, as it may just make all the difference to our reception and the facilities granted for photographing.

Leonard's flat I found in such a state of filth – Nicola having let it to his friends of unmentionable profession [. . .] I have taken refuge with Hay. He and Alastair share a very charming cool underground flat – and as Alastair is away there is plenty of room. Hay, as you can imagine, runs a house to a perfection of comfort so that I am very happy. [. . .]

I leave on Friday or Saturday (today is Saturday) – I dread the journey, as the boats are *very* uncomfortable – films alone to take will cost about £6 or £7 – isn't it awful? I do hope that my pictures will be a success – it quite worries me.

I must go and dine with Zervos, a bore, but he is coming to England and I must make arrangements for his journalese reception. It is so nice to be back here – I feel as if I had come home. I think, if I can learn a few words on the way, that my Greek will carry me through on Athos all right.

Goodbye Love
Bobs

I have found the keys – they were *inside* one of the things that were locked.

Greece

Darling Mibble

We have arranged to pay a loose monk to go to Caryes today to fetch any letters – so that he can take them also – whether he will steal them or lose them I do not know – but I hope you will get this.

We are halfway down from the summit, having spent the night up there last night and got a *wonderful* view – a huge fire all night and more fleas than one would have thought would have existed. Now we are by way of resting and are going on to St Paul's this afternoon – I am rather tired after it all – but feel in *infinitely* better health since I have been here, it is doing me a tremendous lot of good. We have got you a tin of bulbs of huge spotted autumn crocuses from the summit – I don't know whether they will do in the garden.

The party is working very well – we have done the photographs at the Lavra – and they are a success – a great relief. All the beginning was very worrying as everything depended on us getting the letters from the synod and then at the actual monastery permission to photograph. Now I feel less concerned. It is very hard work [. . .] we are never idle – I am several days behind with my diary – and try now and then to sketch – I have done one rather good one of the Lavra – and another from the summit, which needs finishing. Also I have lost my spectacles which is annoying – but I don't suppose it will make any difference and perhaps at last I shall be able to give them up altogether.

It is of course more lovely here than words can describe and as we went higher, became quite autumnal, with brown bracken and hips and haws – everywhere I find monks I know, who greet me with shouts – do you remember the photographs of Bryan and Father Andréas at the top – he came with us this time. [. . .]

Forgive this stupid letter, but I am feeling very sleepy – it is midday and we have been up since 6.

Goodbye and best love – I think that I shall be home sooner than I thought – about Oct. 20th.

from
Bobs

11 September 1927 Athos Gregoriou

Darling Mibble

Tomorrow we pass Daphni the port and I shall pop this into the box of the tacky *dromeior* (post office) as I am too tired to write, having taken advantage of a quiet Sunday here with no frescoes to worry us, to get my priceless MSS on a little further up-to-date. The material is lasting out very well and I am full of plans now for the production of the whole thing and think it should be a success.

The lack of food is definitely becoming trying – you know how much I like to eat when I work – and there is nothing now – the foulest vegetables – I faint regularly every afternoon screeching for alcohol which arrives in the hands of an agitated guestmaster and revives me. Also both ankles are broken with the rocks. The only blessing God has so far showered on one is that fleas do not bite me – I feel them trying – but for some reason they never succeed – Mark is one weal from head to foot.

Reitlinger left this morning thank heaven – quite innocuous but a bore.

The sun has set – I suppose another tendril of octopus is waiting – Goodbye – and please don't expect letters as I have so little time and it is all so exhausting though my health continues excellent. Hoping this finds you as it leaves me – in the pink.

With best love
from
Bobs

1 October 1927 Actaeon Hotel, Cavalla

Darling Mibble

At last we are off that mountain. We all began to get so ill in Caryes – I had a frightful migraine and a sore throat of such horror that I felt sure it was the prelude to typhus, and David had dysentery and was sick, that we suddenly resolved to leave no matter whither, and rode down *in the dark* with all the things to Daphni the night before last. I can't tell you what it was like – the road being absolutely precipitous, and mules quite unable to see in the dark – the baggage mule fell into a gully – another ran off into virgin forest – David fell off and was sick on the way. I brought up the rear urging my mule by the ears away from the larger precipices and trying to keep our belongings together. When we arrived, there was neither bread, wine, fruit, or vegetables at the inn. It really *is* a mystery how Greeks live. But Mark pushed the man out of the kitchen and scrambled 2 dozen eggs which he found in a basket. Then we went to bed – at 10. At 11 I killed 46 large red bugs squirting blood over sheets already covered with vomit and by morning brought the score up to 95. Then we bathed, scrambled another dozen eggs and got on board a steamer at 10.30, which brought us here – taking all day in a *very* rough sea – so that the ship echoed in agony.

Here we find a clean hotel, very nice and Victorian, with lamp-post iron beds with muslin frills and all the wallpapers *identical* with those at Coulsdon. We dined *en pension* – a very good dinner – *how* we enjoyed it – and then actually found a cinema. This morning I write in bed, we motor to some place 30 miles away and get a train to Salonika and I trust to get on to Athens tonight, arriving tomorrow, Sunday morning.

If all David's last batch of photographs come out (we had not time to develop them and he felt too ill) we shall have been very successful – more so than I expected. Especially as we broke into one little chapel in Caryes (the man was away and there were four padlocked doors), which no one has *ever* photographed and which are quite unlike any others on the promontory – and earlier I think. I have got two-thirds as much written as my old book, and hope to make the completed thing a third as long again. I got a great deal of interesting information out of the Governor. I have also done one quite reproducible sketch – among about 6 or 7, all of which I hope you will like.

It has all been very hard work – it seemed quite extraordinary yesterday, when we got on the boat, finding that there was nothing to do. A sort of reaction set in, we became so tired we could hardly move – but that was dispelled by the motion of the boat.

I forgot to say that about 3 days before we left *Alfred* arrived with Hay and Hogg his keeper and Alastair Graham. They all went off as a separate party. But a most extraordinary thing happened. You know that I have always said that I *must* go to Crete as I am sure that the Cretan landscape will reveal why El Greco and the Cretan school of Byzantine painting use these terrific highlights and cold colours. Well I began to ask Alastair about Crete, and he replied in terms that might have been a description of an El Greco – he says it is too extraordinary, because, owing to the height and imminence of the mountains, the sun sets about 2 in the afternoon – with the result that there is the most extraordinary light and colour for the rest of the day. He described it, saying the landscape gets these livid highlights – and all without knowing *why* I wanted to know about it. So now I have decided to pay a flying visit there after Mistra, go on one long expedition to a deserted church with frescoes (2 days' walk without even a path) and then come home at once, curtailing my time in Athens [. . .] I really must do it because I always *knew* instinctively that the whole root and secret of Byzantine art lay in that landscape – and then somebody quite casually comes along and says so, without knowing it. Alastair is coming too and will act as guide.

I must get up now. We stay in Athens till Wednesday or Thursday, then go on to Mistra, when all our labours begin again. I dread it. [. . .]

Best Love from
Bobs

I am feeling very well.

6 October 1927   British Club, Athens

Darling Mibble

Why don't you write? I haven't had a letter for a week. We leave for Mistra tomorrow – and then go straight to Crete – catching a Lloyd at Kalamata at the bottom of the Peloponnese. We are an enormous party. Alfred, Hay (keeper) Bryan, Mark, John,[1] David and me – but only Bryan, Mark and I go to Crete; Alastair joins us.

The photographs really are very good, some of them I took, over 300 – I hope you will like them. I am really rather pleased.

Bryan and I then scurry back (about 23rd) to Paris by Orient Express

---

1. John Sutro, who delighted his Oxford friends with his impersonations and mimicry. Though trained as a barrister, he became much involved with the film industry in which he had financial interests.

– and I hope again to enjoy the comforts of his flat – incidentally doing a good deal of work there so shall be home easily by Nov. 1, perhaps before.

I must stop as I have so much to do – making all last-minute arrangements, letters to the Governor of Crete, Prefect of Sparta, etc. – and a lot of work. So Goodbye.

Love
Bobs

12 October 1927

Kalamata

Darling Mibble

For the first time since we have been out here, I am enjoying a long lie in bed after a 30-mile ride yesterday over terrific mountains – from Sparta down to here. The scenery was perfectly wonderful, I have never seen anything like it, so *enormous*. We slept the night before in a mountain village, having gone there by mule from Mistra and been met by the Mayor and president and police chief perched on a crag in the rain. A tumbler of marigolds had been placed in our room and we slept on mattresses and pillows of shavings containing the usual large red bugs, which were rendered inert, though not dead, by 'Flit' our chemical spray. Then we left at seven, going right up the Langada gorge, to the side of Taygetus, and eventually topping the pass at 4,000 feet, where it was bitterly cold and the banks covered with snowdrops and yellow, purple and white crocuses. We ate a tinned tongue for lunch at a weird little village where there was only bread and grapes – and were surrounded by a cat, a dozen dogs, a mule, and 3 pigs all trying to get at the food at once. We arrived here at 6 – very tired and had a bath in the public baths, very clean and hot – we enjoyed it. Then we discovered that the Lloyd which we are intending to catch to Crete cannot take us, owing to the international law forbidding foreign boats doing the coastal services of another country so now we have telegraphed the Legation and the Foreign Office to make the Minister of Marine telegraph his permission to the captain of the port – and are waiting – the boat goes this afternoon. For once, after 2 months incessant worry, formulation of plans and maintenance of them, I am wholly indifferent as to what happens. I don't want to go to Crete in the least except from the point of view of the book – for which it is *very* important. It will be exhausting and cost money. On the other hand I have several more things to do in Athens – and could then travel leisurely home and spend a comfortable and inexpensive week in Paris in Bryan's flat – which I should simply love, and get home earlier also. However we shall see.

The photographing is all finished – I think with great success. The arrival at Sparta had been heralded – I have yet to discover through whose good offices – by a telegram from Zainius the Prime Minister – so that we were given a sort of civic banquet by the Mayor and prefect – an appalling function, as I felt and was very ill in Athens, so much so that I had very nearly left the train on the way and gone straight back to England. However I got all right spending all day, even meals, in the open air at Mistra, and am now very perky as far as spirits are concerned, though physically rather exhausted, mainly I think, for want of congenial food. What I long for is not the exquisite food that any restaurant would provide, but the sort of food one has at home and regular hours. David, when we said goodbye to him had no stomach left at all.

I must write another letter – Goodbye

and Love from
Bobs

3

England and Austria
1928–1929

ROBERT SPENT the winter of 1927–8 at Savernake Lodge finishing his book on Mount Athos, *The Station*, for Duckworth and continuing his toil on the Byzantine Achievement, not yet named. The end of the winter brought an upheaval to the Byron family. Mrs Byron, appalled by her children's almost unbroken preoccupation with fox-hunting, beagling, rabbiting and forays into Savernake Forest, decided something drastic must be done. The family would go abroad. Mr Byron, always short of money (though the family, besides three indoor maids, kept a gardener and a groom to look after the two hunters), stipulated that absence must be for a year, thereby avoiding income tax. Mrs Byron opened out a large map of Europe and, extracting a hatpin from the hat she habitually wore, stuck it in blindfold, landing on Vienna. To Vienna they would go.

On hearing this news, Henry Yorke wrote:

Dear Mrs Byron

[. . .] I can't help writing again to say how sorry I am all of you are going. It really is tragic, for it was one of those things I thought would never come off. It is too dreadful to think of. Of course you will never come back. 'The Byrons of Vienna' we shall say with a catch in our voices. 'What do they do there? They live there. They *won't* come back.' Once a year a little pilgrimage goes to Mr Granville Barker to ask him to write another play, so a little convoy of people, eyes shining a little with hope, will get into the train, and be seasick on the boat and then go on in the train again – Brussels Cologne Frankfurt Wien all that way to entreat you to return. Think of their faces when they come back. They will do this every year. I hope you will find it so awful that you will come back at once, that is what I really hope, but still I wish the sea calm and the train calm and Vienna welcoming.

Yrs Henry

Having let Savernake Lodge for the summer, the Byron family, minus Robert, settled into a first-floor flat (No. 8 Schubert Ring) just five minutes walk from the Opera House which became their second home. On the nights when the family could only afford *Stehplätze* (standing room) Mrs Byron would take her shooting stick to sit on, much to the disgruntlement of the bad-tempered elderly attendants. But they could do nothing: their book of rules did not prohibit shooting sticks.

After many postponements on the part of Duckworth and much exasperation on Robert's part, *The Station* was finally published on 7 June. Robert wrote to Vienna: 'Really I think it looks too lovely in that jacket and so does everyone. It is such a success I nurse it all day long, like a mother with her baby. Osbert Sitwell has promised to send it to Arnold Bennett and I shall scan the *Evening Standard* impatiently.' That summer Robert began to earn a modest income by contributing to such magazines as *Country Life*, *Vogue*, and Desmond MacCarthy's new weekly, *Life and Letters*. And with articles on Athos, Robert began his long association with the *Architectural Review*.

Following Viennese custom the Byron family left the city in July and August for the Salzkammergut, having taken a flat overlooking the little square in St Wolfgang, later the set for the musical *The White Horse Inn*. Robert joined the family at the end of July and, though complaining bitterly about the peasant culture and the Prussian blue landscape, spent idyllic days boating, bathing and walking. Having followed the family back to Vienna, it was not until October that he returned to London and then went down to Savernake. Besides being welcomed back by the two dogs, Gerda and Ella, Mrs Clements the family cook was waiting to look after him. Of robust character and expression and a great talker, Mrs Clements's figure was the exact shape of a cottage loaf with her head perched in the middle as described by a friend who flew over the house when Mrs Clements happened to be standing in the garden. Nurtured by her cooking, 'Rabbit pie three days running', Robert settled down to complete *The Byzantine Achievement*.

Henry Yorke went to stay with the Byrons for Christmas in Vienna where he seemed quite happy to sit by the stove all day long and chat. He took his new book with him for Mrs Byron to read. Robert wrote: 'I am glad you admire his book – a great compliment I call it to be given it to read as no one else has seen it and it is sure to wreck the whole of England when it does come out – I feel rather jealous!! As for the "things not written about" well they are written about in these days so there's an end to it – but of course one doesn't know how long they will be. I do wish he had stuck to the original title *Works*.' The winter of 1928–9 turned out to be one of the coldest of the century. The temperature fell to minus 23° Fahrenheit in

Vienna where the family walked across the Danube on the ice floes; and at home Robert sat shivering with his feet in the grate, finishing one book and starting the first two chapters of *The Birth of Western Painting*.

[The first page is missing.]

[. . .] On Thursday I dined with Simon Elwes, a painter, whose wife [Golly] is Peter Rodd's sister. He knows all the Russians in Paris and said that Yusupov[1] was the most actively evil devilish man that ever existed. People, especially his wife, literally pale when he comes into the room. We then went to the Benjamin Guinness's which was rather boring except for a Hungarian band playing waltzes during supper, which I enjoyed. Babe [Plunket Greene] was easily the best-dressed person there – and as it was far from being a debutante party this was rather clever of her. Somebody described Lady Oxford as looking like a Dante carved in soap, which was rather apt. The next night I went with Olive Rubens to a *completely* Edwardian party – which I simply adored. I always think there is something fearfully sad about Edwardian songs – they are like a perpetual War Memorial, when one knows that nearly all the people who used to enjoy them were either killed or had their lives blighted. All the people at this were very musical – and for about 3 hours the whole room in tremendous high spirits sang 'The Belle of New York', 'The Merry Widow', 'The Gold Fish' out of *The Geisha* – and hundreds I didn't know. A Czechoslovak singer who was present said he was amazed to find such music in England. There were people at the party like Lady Violet Benson and Lord Carrisbroke. It was such a complete eye-opener to me. I believe that people *enjoyed* themselves before the war much more than we do. I always wish I could grasp a little more of the Edwardian essence – one gets it in old scrap-books – photographs of tennis parties standing on their heads. It is one of the things I shall certainly bring into my novel, when I write it. From that

---

1. Prince Felix Yusupov, instigator of the murder of Rasputin.

point of view (the novel) this place in London will have been of enormous value.

In the middle of all this strangely enough, I have done a lot of very good work – on the religious aspect of the Byzantine mentality – which is also very valuable for the Athos book, which Balston[1] begged one apprehensively not to make too serious.

Nina[2] has come to London – we are going to the first night of the ballet with her on Monday – also Michael [Rosse] and Bryan who are up at Hampstead theoretically recuperating before their schools. I had tea with them yesterday – lunched with John – as I thought I would take the day off then instead of today. Mrs Sutro is *most* anxious for you to see her house – she sent you hundreds of messages. [. . .]

I must go now and lunch. Goodbye –

What an *awful* long letter
With love from
Bobs

6 May 1928   6 Adam Street, Portman Square, London W1

Darling Mibble

It seems so long since I have written – I am so sorry – but I have been so busy. I moved in here on Friday, a most charming house next door to the Wallace Collection, kept by Mrs Wright, who has a host of children and a dog – the children help with the telephone and are very quiet and well mannered. The house is very clean and *tiny*, there is only one other lodger. My room is very pretty and if I had my own things in it it would be really charming – it is a little *too* Jacobean (Waring and Gillow) at the moment – but has a very nice brown leather armchair and sofa. It is oblong, very low ceiling, 2 large cupboards, and 2 18th century windows with thick struts to the glass like Knowle. My breakfasts are delicious. I pay £2.15.0. a week, which is not too cheap, but really it makes such a difference being *at last* in decent surroundings, that I work all the better for it. Mrs Wright had put a large vase of very

---

1. Tom Balston, a director of Duckworth.
2. Nina Caroline, Countess of Seafield.

expensive tulips to welcome me – which I thought was very touching. I wish you could see it all.

Thank you *so* much for the sketch, which I think is *very* good and very modern – just like Paul Nash's things if you know them. Do do some more – do a series of Viennese scenes like that, looking down on things – *how* I can *see* those trams one behind the other – what a joke abroad is. I should have thought you might have done some amusing architectural paintings – only I think, as in photography, the whole secret of making one's efforts *interesting* is to adopt peculiar angles. I should also very much like, in fact must have, *several* of the interior of the flat – so please start this morning when you have bought the sausages and arranged the gentians. I do so wish all the time that I was with you – really it is too annoying not to be – however I shall arrive somehow in the autumn.

I have been working fearfully hard making an index[1] of all things in the world. It has already taken me 2 days and is not done yet, I take 3 hours to do 40 pages – also there are the last proof corrections, and then there are the illustrations to fit to the pages, their titles to be inserted etc. I had no idea it would be such a business. The index is really very boring and I hate doing it.

I had a long talk with Desmond MacCarthy, his new paper is financed by a man called Oliver Brett, who lives in a palace in Hill Street, where D.M. has his office – it is going to be a *perfectly detestable* paper, of the type I most dislike, but will pay well and is starting a new kind of book review – that is, not an essay on the subject of the book, but a real criticism such as you would give to a friend. He wants them very short – and if the book is really bad, nothing at all. He has written for the books that I have asked for – so I really think he will take me on, which will be very nice, as although it is only a monthly, it ought to mean about £10 a month, *and* the books which are sometimes worth quite a lot. Also he has promised to give my new book [*The Station*] a review in it – so I have sent him a lot of loose proofs and cut up some of the illustration sheets. I would have been sending you all these things, but I think that you have had so *much* of it, that it will be nicer to see the whole thing complete and looking its best. The cover is to be *hideous* – but I can struggle with Duckworth's incompetence no more. It is going to be plain royal blue – I can't help it – it is the only good colour that they can

---

1. For *The Station*.

offer – and I will not have a bad colour, so there is an end of it. Anne's[1] jacket they have not yet had done – as they are waiting to know the thickness of the book. I shall be very excited to see the proofs of that. It is very lucky I didn't go to Ireland, as I would never have got any of these things done before I went.

Vogue has just commissioned an article on Spain for their special Travel Number. They offer 10 guineas – this will be very useful. Really I have almost an income now – I only hope it will last – but I think, when the book is out, I really shall be able to earn money properly. I have great faith in the book, as it has improved so much through the various stages of production – and I don't think the heavy parts will seem so heavy any longer.

Harold was much touched by your message – he is living in a huge Regency ballroom with a gilded ceiling in Warwick Square – I went to see him last night and he read me a little bit of his book on the Medici,[2] which is really very good, full of *facts* and information. Bryan Guinness has just got back from his month in the brewery – but I haven't seen him properly yesterday to talk about it. I shall go down to Mrs Clements[3] next weekend – on Friday this time – and have two whole days there. I feel I ought to be doing something about letting the house. Mrs Greene is going down there the week after next. Her mother[4] is absolutely mad now, and can't be left day or night. I dined with an aunt of hers, Lady Mary von Hügel, the other night – *most* extraordinary personality – they must have been a very remarkable family – the other sister was Lady de Grey – now all the sparkle has come to the Greenes and left the present generation of Herberts, who are very dull. [. . .]

I think I shall finish this now, as I shall be too busy tomorrow – I have worked from 10 to 6 with only 1 hour for lunch and still there are 50 more pages to index – so I shall be busy all tomorrow, and the longer I am, the more the book will be delayed.

So goodbye and best love to everyone.

from
Bobs

---

1. Robert's sister Anne designed all his book jackets.
2. *The Last Medici*.
3. The family cook had a cottage in Savernake Forest.
4. Lady Maud Parry, wife of Sir Hubert Parry.

24 May 1928   Portman Square, w1
Empire Day

Darling Mibble

[. . .] I went to tea with George de Patey yesterday – a sort of
reception of Central Europe at the house of some people called Alfred
Mulholland – it was really more than I could cope with. I don't *really*
find I get on with Central Europeans unless they have Jew blood – their
prejudices are so titanic, one can hardly talk on the same ground.
Anyhow I am going to ask de Patey to a meal sometime – next week – so
I hope he will do something for you when he gets out there. He
obviously can, as he is rich and knows everyone. I shall collect some
titles for him, as I suppose he is a snob like the rest of them.

I have just this moment finished the first big chapter of my book[1] –
copying it out – and as there is still an hour of the morning, and I
expected to use the whole of it, that is why I have time to write now.
Really, I think it reads rather well – I have read the whole thing through
again. It seems to me sober and learned, but I don't know. Anyhow it is
quite fun rewriting it – no great effort – and one gets a sense of creation –
which one doesn't in the first version.

John and I are immersed in a vast scheme – you needn't tell the
others, as I feel that it so nearly might come off, that I don't want
anyone to know about it till it has.

We – or rather *I* – conceived the idea of an *Empire* paper – to exploit
the Empire as an artistic, romantic, historic achievement never paralleled on earth – I can't go into the details of the form of the paper, but it
would be very soberly written, and *full* of valuable information –
illustrated too. Anyhow – John's father is the director of a printer's, and
we went off one afternoon to them to discuss estimates etc. These we
did. We want between £5,000 and 6,000 to start a weekly, and less
presumably for a monthly. John, you see, being rich, will of course
never bother to *submit* anything to any paper on chance – at the same
time he is dying to be able to write – so is Bryan, who if necessary will
put up £500 – so I think will John.

However it all seemed very chimerical, when I thought of the Empire
Marketing Board. I met Bob Boothby [MP] at the Guinness dinner –

---

1. Later to be called *The Byzantine Achievement*.

which was terrifying – 80 ambassadors and their wives seated in rooms like cowsheds lit by single candles and decorated with cow-parsley which fell out of pewter pots and caught in their stars and ribbons. We arranged to go and see him at the House of Commons. We went, negotiated 502 policemen before reaching 'Mr Churchill's room' – he is Churchill's private secretary – then learnt that the Empire Marketing Board is possessed of a statutory million a *year*, and doesn't know how to spend it. Bob is a great friend of the man who runs it. He is also a great friend of Harold Macmillan. Macmillan's, who made half a million *profits* last year – are the one publisher in the world who could distribute the paper, as they have branches all over the world. Then it transpired that Bob and H. Macmillan had themselves discussed founding a paper such as we suggest, but had given up the idea, as if they had done so, it would have been 'party', which would have been useless. So now we are waiting in a fever of excitement till after Whitsun. Bob seemed to think it the most natural thing in the world, and anticipates no difficulties over getting the money – why indeed should there be? So you may expect in a few months to find me seated in an office in Trafalgar Square waving at clerks. Of course it won't come off – but there is no reason why it shouldn't. *Wouldn't* it be fun if it did? The very summit of my ambitions. John would not be whole time at it, as he has his law, and has suddenly become inspired with the idea of being Lord Chancellor. Really it *must* happen – think of the power – such a triumph, to have discovered the Empire before anyone else. Bob says that the Mother of Parliaments is appalled at the country's apathy concerning it. However don't please expect anything to come of it – I don't for a moment – will let you know developments at the end of next week. [. . .]

I have a feeling I shall suddenly arrive in Vienna one day – so don't be surprised if there is a knock at the door – it seems so silly not to come. If only I could really make some money.

I must go to lunch –

Goodbye and best love from
Bobs

7 June 1928   Portman Square, W1

Darling Mibble

[. . .] Evelyn Waugh has come to live opposite – Evelyn Gardner is living on the ground floor at Upper Montagu Street – so they both spend all their lives in here – as their own rooms are so disgusting.[1] We learn from the postman that this street is *so* improper that during the recent election, none of the candidates dared canvass it at all. Outwardly it has such a demure appearance – but I have noticed an artist who will paint a Syrian model at midnight against an unshaded window. I explained all this to a charming middle-aged servant whom Mrs Wright keeps. She replied: 'Well, sir, in my opinion the proof of the pudding's in the eating'!!

[. . .] The most extraordinary things are going on about the paper. I really can't explain, it is all so long. Bob's (Boothby) greatest friend, a man called Charles Baillie Hamilton, has gone and bought the *Empire Review* secretly from Oliver Locker Lampson – and doesn't know what to do with it. Bob has told him he can't possibly run it in opposition to *us* – (as if we were already the *Daily Mail*) and we may arrange some kind of amalgamation. Meanwhile I have made out a vast and detailed scheme – very good I think – which I hope Bob will lay before the Empire Marketing Board. I have ransacked the libraries for books on Imperial Unity – and now think only of the Union Jack. If it is likely to come off really, I shall probably come out to you *straight away*, and then come back and work at it for the rest of the year. But it is all very much in the air at present. Somehow I feel that it will come to something. [. . .]

I have decided to give an enormous cocktail party in George's [Schurhof] house on Thursday week – the day of the book's[2] publication – and entertain all possible reviewers – and also Duckworth's etc., who really are taking a most tremendous lot of trouble about it, advertising, circulars etc. [. . .]

---

1. In a further letter of 25 June Robert adds: 'I am frightfully busy all this week, so don't expect another letter till the end of it – these weddings! It really is too awful – I have to *fetch* Evelyn Gardner to the church and I know she won't come.' Robert gave the bride away at her marriage to Evelyn Waugh on 27 June 1928.
2. *The Station*.

On Friday I am having my voice tested for the wireless – isn't it extraordinary the things one does? I want to discourse on Greek hotels – on travel in general. *Think* of the boredom. Now, if you knew how, I am sure you would switch your wireless set on to London. But I can't imagine my ridiculous phlegmy throat being satisfactory. [. . .]

With best love
from Bobs

15 June 1928   Portman Square, W1

Darling Mibble

It was so nice yesterday morning getting *three* letters, 2 from you and 1 from Father. [. . .] I am so *glad* you like the appearance of the book – after all, your opinions count with me so *much* more than anyone else's – I do think the jacket is such a success, don't you. It is a relief that you don't dislike the blue cover. Somehow I thought it was horrible. (I am writing in an armchair – that's why it has all gone up the page).

I gave my cocktail party yesterday – a feverish effort – in George Schurhof's house – about 60–70 people came – and most of them went away not quite as sober as when they arrived. Gavin made cocktails from 5.30 to 8.30 in 2 shakers – till all the drink was exhausted. [. . .]

The mixture of people was too extraordinary for words – ranging from shy debutantes like Oonagh Brassey to Osbert Sitwell and the Greek Minister,[1] the latter roaring about enjoying himself a lot. Henry was there *delighted* with your letter – he says you know just how to flatter him. Osbert said that Arnold Bennett happened to be dining with him the night my book arrived and he gave it him with his own hand and spoke about it and thinks he will do it. I am sorry to harp on this particular subject – but it is the best thing one can get from the selling point of view – a mention by him. Osbert says he has an 'eye for photographs'. Evelyn (Waugh) applied to the *Observer* to be given the book to review and was told that 3 people had already asked for it! So I suppose there is some interest in it. I enclose a circular, 2,500 of which

---

1. Demetrius Caclamanos, Greek Minister in London since 1918.

arrived on someone's breakfast table yesterday. I have been much complimented on the get-up of this circular. And as a matter of fact, I wrote most of it – and arranged it. Do you like it?

One review has already appeared – half a column in the *Daily News*. It says I border on the vulgar and quotes bugs and spittoons. It is headed 'Mr Byron returns to Greece'!!! Anyhow it's calculated to arouse interest, which is the great thing. Mark is *furious* – and has drawn the most hideous caricature of me asleep, which Patrick[1] says he is going to publish in the weekly *Despatch*. He and Nina and Henry are coming here at twelve – and we are all going off to [Henry] Lamb's studio (Lamb painted Lytton Strachey) as Nina has been given £60 by Grant town to have her portrait done, and I am trying to arrange that Lamb shall do it.

I went to an awful dance for Prince Potenziani last night at which Lady Rodd[2] was acting hostess and there found Simon Elwes who offered to paint my portrait free – it would be so funny I think, as he is almost as chocolate box as Laszlo – and I can't think what the result would be like. [. . .]

Now as to my plans – I can't work in London any more. That is I can do my little jobs like book-reviewing, occasional articles etc. – but I can't get on with my big book at all. The truth is that I am so excited by this one's coming out, that it has made me restless. I feel I have earned a holiday not from work, but mental effort. So what I have in mind at present is this: to take all the notes, in museums etc., necessary for my monograph on the paintings[3] – then come out to you and write till I have finished both the big book and the monograph – *that is*, of course, only if something permanent doesn't turn up in the meantime. I may get a job – I am always asking for one – but you see there is no doubt that, when this book has had its full effect, and the other two are in the press, I shall be in a very much stronger position – a position in fact really to earn money. And it would really be cheaper to write out in Austria – where I could probably make an occasional penny by sending articles and photographs home. Also I want to take the opportunity of getting a working acquaintance with German. Nearly all the standard works on art history are in that language.

---

1. Patrick Balfour, later 3rd Earl of Kinross.
2. Lilias, wife of Sir James Rennell Rodd and mother of Peter Rodd.
3. *The Birth of Western Painting*.

My plan then – again supposing nothing offers here – (the Empire thing is no further, but it may still be quite feasible) – is to come out at the end of July. But of course it depends on what you and Father think. I know you want me to get a job. But you will agree that the sooner the things I have on hand are finished, the better. Also I do really need a little mental food – there seems none here. I long for music and so on. Also I must begin to make plans for a new creative effort – and can't here. Of course if anything like *The Times were* to offer I should take it at once, I think it quite likely will. But I am saying this in case nothing does. Further if I am coming out, I shall naturally try and get definite commissions beforehand, to do things in Central Europe – even a correspondentship. These will need arranging.

Will you let me know what you think of all this? My plan is to join you at Strobl for a month and then return to Vienna. I might come straight away, were it not for those notes on the paintings. All my Russian idea has fallen flat, as apparently books on Russia are at a discount – so Curtis Brown say.

I may say, incidentally, that by being here personally, I have done a *very great deal* with regard to the book's reviews. It may have made all the difference. [. . .]

I have got some more work out of Desmond MacCarthy – also a *dreadful* article in *Vogue* – and have done one or two reviews for Locker Lampson. So I suppose guineas will go on arriving. [. . .]

With best love from
Bobs

How lovely that mass in the cathedral sounds.

4 November 1928   Swinbrook House, Burford, Oxford

Darling Mibble

I should really have written before – thank you so much for your letter. I spent most of last week in London, got *nothing* done, at least a good deal really, but there is still more, and then motored down here, with Bryan who is grotesquely in love with Diana Mitford (who is very beautiful) and goes red whenever she comes into the room. The Mitford family are very amusing – especially Nancy and I enjoy being here – the house is modern, built in fact the other day, square, of Cotswold stone, commanding, as they say, a lovely view. Yesterday we went for a nice mild ride on nice well-behaved horses, and I enjoyed it very much – a *lovely* October day with everything turning and an occasional *minute* wall or bank to hop over. Now I am very stiff. On the way down we stopped at Eton to give lunch to Randolph Churchill, a third generation of brilliance, who was very nice but I don't know how brilliant – and also at Oxford, where I found Roy Harrod, who tells me that a certain Professor Dawkins, who for twenty years has been the only Byzantinist in England, is so angry over my book that it has injured his health. Plainly the next one will kill him. That is shaping very nicely now that the corrections are being put in. I enslaved Mrs Hourmouzios[1] for a whole afternoon to help with different versions of the poem with which it ends and which I myself shall render into English. Tell Father that I had to pay £7.17.0 for entering the London Library and it is a crying shame. I have been busily poking about for employment, and have received a nebulous offer of a post on the *Egyptian Gazette*, with a little *Times* corresponding also – this however is not yet concrete. I suddenly hear that Michael is to become attaché to Lord Lloyd[2] – so we might settle in Cairo together – but as it is the most expensive town, without any exception, in the world, I have my doubts. However there are other things on hand and I may know more in a week or two.

Lady Redesdale makes £100 a year out of 500 laying hens – deducting all expenses, including a whole-time man. She says it is no good doing it unless you are an expert. She never sells an unwashed egg – supplies all the smart London clubs.

I went to tea with Cecil's grandmother[3] who is just eighty and very bitter – also to see his house in the slums, which is dramatically squalid. He finds his colleagues infinitely tiresome and is now much less of a parson than before. It is very satisfactory. He seems very happy. There seems no news. I enjoyed being at Savernake so much, did lots of work and am longing to be back. [. . .] I have lots of books to review – and

---

1. A Greek lady who helped Robert translate the poem with which he ends *The Byzantine Achievement*.
2. High Commissioner for Egypt and the Sudan.
3. Mary, Dowager Duchess of Abercorn, who considered that Cecil was wasting his time taking Holy Orders and devoting his life to the poor.

things due out in *Country Life* and the *Architectural Review*, so money will keep on coming in.

Best love from Bobs

24 November 1928   Savernake Lodge, Marlborough

Darling Mibble

Thank you so much for the letter which I found waiting for me on getting back here. [. . .] The wind is terrific again – Hillier [the gardener] prognosticates that the telephone will be out of use again tomorrow. I am feeling slightly deranged, as the gramophone is broken and I have no cigarettes. However I hope both matters will be repaired tomorrow (Saturday). I met Aunsssy[1] in Oxford today whither Mrs Sutro had motored me, as she was going down to see John take his M.A. degree. Then she sent me on here in the car – so I arrived in extreme grandeur. The wind was such on the way that the chauffeur could scarcely keep the car on the road and we had to crawl. I only hope a tree did not destroy it on the way back. There seemed to be trees down every 10 yards from the other night. Wasn't the telephoning extraordinary? There was something uncanny about it, in the middle of the forest with the wind in the trees and Mrs Clements and the dogs long in bed. I ordered the call for 11.15 and I didn't think it was more than 11.30 when it came through. It was the only time we could be sure of you being in. It was funny hearing the Viennese exchange arguing with Father, and then asking Daventry who I was and Daventry asking me. I hope you enjoyed the conversation. [. . .]

Mr Alfred Knopf has bought 750 copies of the Byzantine Succession [later Achievement] in advance, on trust, without having read it. So I almost detected a suspicion of satisfaction in Warburg's voice on the telephone. I go to see Mr Knopf next week – also to have a free photograph done by a rather soppy photographer called Lenare. I am trying to get a Frank Brangwyn etching of S. Sophia for an illustration to the book, tomorrow I begin to plan that with the paintings.

---

1. Gertrude Baker, an aunt of Robert. Aunsssy was regularly spelt thus.

I have seen a lot of Michael Rosse in London, who is rather disgruntled with Spain. He has gone to Wilton this weekend to meet its Queen and is, I hope, coming over here on Monday if he can cast off the Infantas. Hugh Lygon is permanently in Packard's shop in Piccadilly and drives about in vast limousines when he wants the use of them. The Sutros were most kind when I stayed with them. Mrs Sutro even sent me off in the car with a big box of Fortnum and Mason chocolates. Poor Bryan is assailed with plain speaking [on his marriage]. Michael told him the other night that now he would *have* to spend some money. While David painted eons of hopeless misery [. . .] I have a letter from Ward Price[1] confirming what he said about reviewing for the North-cliffe papers and asking me to write again in January – so I hope something will come of it. Patrick has now got the *Daily Sketch* gossip and £1,100 a year for doing it! Still one can scarcely be envious, in view of the odium attached [. . .]

Now I am going to bed.

Best love to all from Bobs

2 December 1928   Savernake Lodge, Marlborough

Darling Mibble

[. . .] I am afraid it is a long time since I have written. I spent last week in London and can't remember anything that happened there! On Tuesday I went to see Mr Knopf – an American Jew of no words – a type with which one is unaccustomed to deal. The insides of his nostrils shewed for miles and looked as if they had been burnt with acid – do you know that kind of face. He said 'Come to the Carlton' – so we went there – he produced a cinema from his bedroom, we went out into Pall Mall and having reached the Crimean monument, he waved his hand at the Duke of York column and the Athenaeum and said 'I guess this is the nearest thing to Byzantium we can find around here' (just like a book) – whereupon I struck a Napoleonic attitude between Florence Nightingale and Sydney Herbert and he danced round turning the handle.

---

1. A Director and chief foreign correspondent of the *Daily Mail*.

How you would have laughed – a ring of gaping errand boys – however I was filled with admiration for a man who could afford to stay at the Carlton and yet was enterprising enough to do his own cinematograph-ing in a London street. Feeling I was expected to look like an author I had dressed like a guardsman in a stiff collar (though without any thought of this) – he said he used the film to show to critics – he took *hours* of it – hat on and off. I should love to see it!! However, there is no chance of that. He said *The Station* hadn't done at all well in America – but as I gathered it had sold 200 copies without any reviews *at all*, I don't call that so bad – I hope to get some reviews soon. He wants me to change the title of *The Byzantine Succession*, I am thinking of calling it *The Mediaeval Greeks* – do you dislike this? Beyond this the week was an unbroken sojourn in the British and the South Kensington Museums and the London Library, mainly getting illustrations – it is so *awful* having the sense of wanting to do things as well as possible – once I really got on to the illustrations I felt I had to see every single print, map and *objet d'art* available in the world and literally I had out about 30 books a morning – till at last I forced my way into the attics of the British Museum and insisted on examining the maps and panorama department myself – even now they are not done, hundreds of French and German publishers have to be written to – and I have only got the notes down here from which I shall make a final selection – then they must all be photographed and I shall have to consult the museum photographers, but still it *is* fun finding things that have literally never been seen before in any country. I now think they are going to be an important part of the book – the MSS has actually gone to print – I shall get proofs in about a fortnight, which will really be exciting – I will send one lot out to you if you like. It will be a ghastly moment – I feel the whole thing is imperfect and immature. I am gradually coming to the conclusion that my book on the paintings[1] is going to be *really* very interesting and may arouse a large interest [. . .] However you must be sick of the subject. [. . .]

I had a very amusing letter from Lucy the other day – it made me laugh a lot – she is maturing tremendously – and though you had better not tell I tell you – does not seem at all happy at the prospect of coming back here to devote her brain to chickens. I do wish you would try and formulate *some* plan – you know what always happens when people of active mind are imprisoned in the country – they reach the town eventually and plunge into extravagances (I don't mean financial necessarily) which are very tiresome and take a long time to outgrow.

I dined with Charles Sutro and went (and a party of his friends) to a ghastly entertainment organised by Lady Rodd and Olive Rubens to benefit the Conservative party. John and I were turned Labour for life. Peter Rodd was Vulcan and Simon Elwes some other disgusting God – Bettine[2] was among the audience dragging her husband about like an inconveniently large handbag. The next night Patrick [Balfour] gave a party to a lot of smart people he didn't know and on Friday Babe celebrated her 21st birthday with a perfectly terrific party which I enjoyed very much – it went on all *night* but as I was going home next

---

1. *The Birth of Western Painting.*
2. Elizabeth Valetta, Countess of Abingdon.

day and had decided to take two days off (the first in three weeks) I stayed till the end. [. . .]

I have no more to say and it is 11.30 – so goodbye

and best love

from

Bobs

December 1928   Savoy Court Hotel, w1

Darling Mibble

[. . .] I have just got back from Highcliffe – Nina, who was staying with Mark's sister nearby, motored me up which was very convenient. I enjoyed my week-end very much, except for the detestable journey to London on Friday to buy Father's nibs! General Stuart Wortley[1] is the most wonderful type and his conversation like a book of all the things that memoirs never publish. He said, like Grandpa, that the Kaiser could be perfectly charming, and that he once said to him in his own dining-room at Highcliffe: 'Mark my words, one of these days the war-party in Germany will get the upper hand.' That was about 1910.

The King[2] is less boring now that the first hysteria has subsided – I don't think there is any chance at all. London is full of rumours about how his doctors won't let proper specialists go near him, out of professional jealousy. Everyone is agreed that trade will be ruined, even my photographer at the British Museum. For the moment, however, every black hat and coat is sold out. I was in two minds about yours. I hope you got it all right – and it is what you wanted. I thought it looked quite nice. [. . .]

The Labour party hate the Prince of Wales according to Arthur Ponsonby. The new Archbishop of Canterbury[3] officiated at Joan Talbot's wedding – is a *repulsive* man, blithering and slavering like a

---

1. Major-General the Hon. Edward Stuart Wortley, a champion in colonial warfare since the Second Afghan War. Sometime Military Attaché in Paris.
2. George V was seriously ill of a lung infection.
3. Cosmo Gordon Lang.

village demagogue – and with the skin of a newly weaned rat, the kind that the very good always do have.

I hear that my book has had a very large and successful press in America, but the agents say no cuttings have come through, so I suppose one can only wait. Harold told me this, and he is naturally so jealous that he would have concealed it if he could. He and William[1] have taken a gigantic house in Lancaster Gate and are furnishing it with really good Italian things – which they will sell off as people come along and replace by others. They both say that space is the great thing in London and when one has it, one doesn't want to be out all the time – I'm sure it's true. [. . .]

I do hope that you will have a nice Xmas – give my love to everyone and best wishes to Henry – Afterwards, as you say, it will only remain to pack. Auntie Eva is descending on you at the end – I am trying to kill her first by sending her to out of the way places in Greece, but don't suppose I shall succeed.

Goodbye
With best love and wishes
from
Bobs

20 January 1929   Nore, Hascombe, Surrey

Darling Mibble

I am so sorry to have written you such a skimpy letter for your birthday, but I was in rather a hurry, just going off to the country. It is very nice here, very comfortable, most delicious food, and really Mrs Howard[2] *is* rather touching. I hadn't seen her for ages, since *The Station* came out – she said at once, directly we got alone 'I'm so proud of you Robert' – it is always rather astonishing, when people whom one has always regarded as rather remote, suddenly display a proprietary interest. Harold told me that it has had a very good press in America,

---

1. William Acton, Harold's brother.
2. Brian Howard's mother.

and that his mother has actually *quoted* reviews in letters to him – so I shall move heaven and earth to get hold of them. But I am quite sure that one will never do anything over there, till one *goes* – so I am going to do all I can to find a financially feasible way of going in the autumn. Mrs Howard says, if one takes the trouble, one can get to New York for about £15 – in discomfort of course – but that wouldn't matter – I really know a good many people there. [. . .]

Brian spent a lot of time with Siegfried Sassoon in Paris, who liked *The Station* very much and regards me as 'of promise' – I hope this will please you. I have sent the proofs of the book to J. Mavrogordato[1] – a fearful imposition for him – however I rang him up the other day and he was very nice about it – and is going through them. You must *admit* that there is something rather daunting about publishing a book of some pretensions without *one* single soul having read it – because not even Warburg or anyone in Routledge's have – as one of the partners has been ill – so I shall be glad to have his opinion. All the accessories are going to be very good, Warburg liked the illustrations enormously – well he might considering the labour they have been. I have about 50 letters at home of permission, from strange professors in Paris and elsewhere – even the other day arrived one from Alan Cobham![2] including aerial photographs of Constantinople. However a German company provided a much better one as you can imagine it would.

Brian is playing Beethoven's IX symphony – do you remember when we heard it together? It reminds me both of Vienna and the spring at Savernake. I saw Henry the other night and have also seen a number of his friends – he really did enjoy himself in Vienna very much. Of course I can see he is most fearfully wrought up about his book[3] – I daren't say anything – because I think he feels that all this time he has been sacrificing his youth so to speak in the dungeons of Birmingham in order to make a real success – so I only hope it will have one – though I have no doubt it will. It seems likely to be delayed till the autumn.

---

1. John Mavrogordato, from an Anglo-Hellenic family, an expert on Greece and author of *Modern Greece: chronicle and survey 1800–1931*, etc. He gave Robert a favourable opinion on *The Byzantine Achievement*.
2. Sir Alan Cobham, aviator; pioneered air routes to Burma in 1924, South Africa and then Australia in 1926.
3. *Living.*

Hermione Tennant [Baddeley] who is here is really very charming – she is a really *good* actress, apart from such things as *On with the Dance*. David Tennant is odious and frightfully selfish.

I have ordered Bryan a book plate in gothic, with on it:

THIS BOOK

HAS BEEN

STOLEN

FROM

BRYAN

AND

DIANA

GUINNESS   do you think it funny?

They have got the most *charming* house in Buckingham Street – very large – and are setting up housekeeping with innumerable servants, chauffeur etc. – Nancy says that he has £20,000 a year settled on him already, but I don't know if it is true. However I can see that his marriage is going to change him very much – they are going to Sicily for a honeymoon.

Now I must go out for a walk.

> Goodbye
> and Best Love from
> Bobs

24 January 1929   Savoy Court Hotel, W1

Darling Mibble

It is your birthday and I do wish I was with you and could give you a present. However I am sure it will be nicer when you come home. [. . .] How quickly the time is going. Everything seems to be happening in such a rush. Routledge's have telephoned to say the page proofs and illustrations [of *The Byzantine Achievement*] are in. I dine with John Mavrogordato tonight to hear his comments on the proofs – and am going for the weekend to Sachie and Georgia Sitwell at the house which they are forced to live in in the middle of Northamptonshire, where I hope to correct them and even get a little advice. [. . .]

Alfred's engagement is off – huge posters everywhere. I feel it is a personal affront. My publicity becomes more and more – Evelyn Waugh referred to me in an article in the *Evening Standard* as one of the five writers embodying the spirit of my generation – and as an art critic! Patrick never ceases – but I never see any of it. Tomorrow I am getting hold of the organiser of the B.B.C. entertainments and hope to do some more in that line. I have just rung up *Country Life* and that article is coming out soon. I haven't heard from MacCarthy about the long thing I sent to *Life and Letters*. I am afraid it must have given him a shock.

I dined with Patrick the other night, who gave one the most *expensive* dinner, 1919 champagne, *canard à la presse* etc., all free because he had once given the place two paragraphs and the manager was too delighted and said it had done him a lot of good – this without even mentioning its name.

I am absolutely obsessed by the idea of going to America, I believe it would pay so. However. [. . .] Mrs Hourmouzios says the Greek colony over there is fabulously rich and would organise one's life. It would amuse me very much to go to New York and Chicago and see no one but Greeks. This next book may make it more feasible – but I can never find out *what is going on*.

Now I must go – I am supposed to be going to a Fancy Dress lunch at the Trocadero, a bogus wedding party in Trocadero clothes, i.e. 1921. But the humour is too elaborate and I don't know that I shall.

Goodbye
With love from
Bobs

31 January 1929   Savernake Lodge, Marlborough

Darling Mibble
[. . .] Bryan's wedding was quite fun, the bridesmaids very pretty for once, with wax gardenia wreaths in their hair instead of Russian crowns or Parma violet toques. I succeeded in not ushering a single person!

Bryan had had his hair cut. They both want to plan an expedition to Cappadocia this time next year. Bryan has bought that icon – did I tell you? I feel rather unhappy about it, but am giving him a reduction. Michael made a rather butlerish best man and Lady Evelyn was frankly bored, receiving Bryan's parting kiss with 'Oh good gracious!!' I saw [Brendan] Bracken, who introduced me to Ward Price, and he said the Northcliffe thing was coming off all right and I may have to go up next week and see about it. I have also suggested doing a weekly review of the London cinemas – though how that can be accomplished from here I don't know. Bracken is standing for Parliament and I have a feeling he will be Chancellor of the Exchequer one day. He is in Eyre and Spottiswoode's, the King's printers. On being asked by a female elector if he supported the new prayer book, he answered: 'No, it supports me' – which I think is rather neat. [. . .]

Knopf has written to say that there have been no press cuttings in America except two, which he sends – very dull – I call it bad management on his part. However I shall write to Beverley Nichols[1] about it and see what he can do. It really is insupportable to be ignored!

I went to the Dutch exhibition[2] and felt quite ill – partly perhaps the crowd. I have come to the conclusion that Vermeer is a loathesome painter. Rembrandt's *Chief Rabbi* was very fine – but only in a rather aggravating dramatic way. The Van Goghs were the most interesting. There were two portraits by him that were superb. Sachie Sitwell said that he didn't suppose such a gigantic collection of bad pictures had ever been got together before, and I have no doubt he is right. I have at least one supporter. There is to be an Italian exhibition in two years' time, which will be more interesting.

I have now removed to my own room and it is very much more comfortable. Also there is room in bed for Gerda [his dog] in the morning, so that she can put her arms round my neck. Mrs Clements is in triumph over the stove which now burns beautifully. [. . .] It is extraordinary how delicious Mrs Clements's food seems when one comes back to it. [. . .]

I am going to London to address the Anglo-Hellenic society, poor

---

1. Popular author of novels and sentimental essays describing his country cottage, e.g. *Down the Garden Path*, *A Thatched Roof*, etc.
2. At the Royal Academy.

things, on the subject of El Greco. In fact Miss Thring[1] is giving a party for it. I do wish you could meet Miss Thring. You would so enjoy her.

I really must go to bed and listen to the rain – it is raining so hard that I shall have to move all the books off all the window sills.

Goodbye
with best love from
Bobs

2 May 1929   Savoy Court Hotel, W1

Darling Mibble

Thank you so much for your letter – yes – the *Daily Mail* was very good[2] – it is supposed to pass through the hands of eight million people daily so I suppose some of them saw it. I wish some others would hurry up. People seem to like it who have read it and the most surprising people too.

I have been very busy with all my schemes – Longman's are still sitting on a thousand fences – so yesterday I told them that if they paid me 2 or 3 hundred pounds to write them a novel, it would alter the face of the earth and I would go and live abroad for a little and do it. Yesterday afternoon I spent wandering from person to person in the B.B.C. – they adored my talk – and I am now in every hope of fixing up a series of six at the beginning of next year – biographical – which ought to bring in £60 to £90 straight away.

Last night such a good example happened of how one's life is altered by just *being* in London. Rather, in fact, very unwillingly I joined Patrick and a girl called Wanda Holden for supper and then went on to a night club – knowing all the time I ought to be in bed and resenting it. Daphne Weymouth,[3] whom I literally haven't seen since she was married came in – and said that Beaverbrook (the owner of the *Daily*

---

1. Member of the Anglo-Hellenic League.
2. The *Daily Mail* printed a review of *The Byzantine Achievement*.
3. Daphne, Viscountess Weymouth, later Marchioness of Bath.

Express and *Evening Standard*) had been given my name as a promising young writer and was anxious to know more about me. *That whole day* I had been revolving in my mind how best to approach those two papers to do things I want – now I hope it is all in train – so you see.

It will be delightful next Wednesday – we will lunch together. I dined with Henry and Dig[1] and Mrs Yorke – very amusing. Dig is *so* nice. Henry very cheerful, hair brushed and accepting invitations to all kinds of dances!! [. . .] I am leaving here today to go and stay with Patrick. [. . .]

Love from
Bobs

---

1. Adelaide Mary Biddulph, engaged to Henry Yorke.

4

India and Tibet
1929–1930

ROBERT LEFT for India on 27 July 1929. A chance invitation to Sikkim from Gavin Henderson had aroused again his ambition to visit Tibet, which he had nurtured ever since making the acquaintance of a yak in his first alphabet book. The problem, having little money, was how to get there. His encounter with Daphne Weymouth gave him the opportunity. Hearing that her friend Lord Beaverbrook was looking for new writers, Robert begged her to arrange an interview and, on confronting Beaverbrook, assured him of his passionate interest in the Empire and suggested that the new airmail to India, recently inaugurated, would surely strengthen our imperial ties with the east. After some weeks of discussion on Empire Free Trade, Robert asked point-blank for his fare to India and was always grateful to Beaverbrook for agreeing to such exploitation. They both knew that five articles in the *Daily Express*, covering the five days of his flight, hardly rated the cost of a single fare, which was £126.

At last the 'dream of my life' was becoming a reality. Before Robert left, the possibilities of travelling in Tibet were explored. To visit Lhasa was forbidden but thanks to Sir Charles Bell, who in 1921 had won permission from the Tibetan authorities, certain travellers, approved by the Indian Government, were to be allowed permits as far as Gyantse. Michael Rosse, who had decided to join the expedition, now weighed in with representations to the Viceroy's secretary, who passed them on to the Indian Foreign Secretary, who informed them on their arrival in India that permission must be obtained from Colonel Weir, Resident in Sikkim and liaising with Lhasa. Weir, a practical man, had no objection but warned them of dates so that they would not be occupying the rest-houses when his officers were on the move. October was late in the year for travelling in Tibet but the opportunity had to be seized.

After Robert's arrival in Karachi and his outcast dinner (he had brought no evening clothes), he was determined, with Gavin Henderson, to see the

Dravidian temples and they made their way down to Travancore, taking in Goa and Kandy on the way. Back in Calcutta they moved into a flat, 4 Elysium Row, found for them by a friend David Fyfe, a Burmah-Shell executive. Awaiting Michael's arrival they busied themselves ordering warm clothes, such as riding suits made of green felt, and stores for Tibet. A menu for each day was carefully planned and written out but in fact their trouble was wasted. The right travelling box was never found available on the right day.

It was this catering, relying as it did entirely on tins, which made Robert on subsequent journeys insist on buying what food was to be had locally. He found scrawny chickens, bread baked on hot stones, curds and local cheese more sustaining than the luxuries of Messrs Fortnum and Mason or the Army and Navy Stores.

The three weeks that Michael, Robert and Gavin spent in Tibet were perhaps enjoyed more in recollection than in actuality. The ferocious cold and flaying winds were worse than anticipated and it was an exhausted and frozen trio who finally descended on the Residency in Sikkim. Nobody could have been kinder than the hospitable Weirs and a lasting friendship was formed between Thyra Weir and Robert, brought together by their common interest in sketching.

Instead of returning home from India after Christmas as he had planned, Robert consented to take a job with Burmah-Shell running a nationwide publicity campaign for three months. This enabled him to travel widely in India and to enjoy a regular salary for the first time since working for the *Daily Mail*. At the beginning of April he left for home, stopping off at Cairo and at Athens, where he was eagerly welcomed by old friends.

---

30 July 1929   Athens

Darling Mibble

We had the *most* lovely trip yesterday, right over the heel of Italy, lunch at Corfu, and then across Missolonghi and down the Gulf of Corinth – the pilot allowed me to stand right astride the cockpit – the most wonderful sensation – to feel oneself moving very pompously and slowly through the sky in this vast machine, with the whole of Greece below one. Today he has promised to fly over the places I went to in Crete. Now we are just off. I am feeling ever so much better than when I started, though a little tired this morning after being up at 5.30 a.m. yesterday to type my article and staying up till 12.30 a.m. this morning with Zervos, Leonard, Hay, Gallop and Pallis – I do wish I wasn't leaving.

Could you send me the articles (*if* they appear)[1] by *air mail* – as I want to know as soon as possible how they are received and what prominence they are given. I shall do another today and post in Alexandria tomorrow.

It is fearfully hot – but I am in my Moss Bros and the jumper is a great success both for looks and use. Tonight in Tobruk I believe will be awful – sleeping in an Italian hospital with mosquitoes! but I don't know.

I had a lovely evening in Naples with the Rodds – they have the most beautiful villa overlooking the whole bay. We bathed and had dinner afterwards – then I went off in a *pony cart* back to Naples, as their car had had 3 punctures that day on the way from Rome. Simon Elwes and Golly were there seemingly very cheerful despite their baby's death. Another is on its way.

Our party is reduced to three – the journalist, Sir G. Salmond (that important man, an air marshal) – and self. Now the pilot is here and I must go – such a nice man – there is a delightful atmosphere about the whole of Imperial Airways.

Best love to everyone from
Bobs

31 July 1929   Tobruk

Darling Mibble

[. . .] This is Africa, quite extraordinary, and *quite* unlike anywhere else – very ramshackle little Italian colony where no one ever comes at all. I have just written *quite* a good article for the *Express* and have had 2 bathes, one here and one in Crete. I flew all over the island in the cockpit and the pilot said it was a severe test of nerves for a novice, as we flew

---

1. Robert's articles on his flight to India were published in the *Daily Express* on 11, 12, 13 and 17 September 1929.

through a pass and it seemed just as though we were going to hit it. I recognised every *house* and bush of our trip two years ago – from 4,000 feet!

Dervishes and dancing outside, but I must go to bed, as I am fearfully tired and we have to get up at 4.30 tomorrow – when we leave our lovely flying boat for another beastly land machine – it has all been too heavenly.

Love Bobs

3 August 1929   The flight over Baluchistan

Darling Mibble

I haven't written since Tobruk as this will get to you before any other letter that I could have written, as it will catch the airmail back tomorrow. We have about two hours more of the journey. It has all been too wonderful and I can't really describe it, till I have assimilated it a little more. I feel *very* well – my eyes cured, and I have just written my fourth article for the *Daily Express* which I shall post with this. Heat seems not to affect me, as the flight across the desert from Gaza to Baghdad was really devilish – the air was like hot flames, and in Baghdad all the bath water, though meant to be cold, was boiling hot, and the paper shrivelled as I typed. But I found no difficulty in sitting down to do an article as soon as we arrived. I do *hope* they publish my articles, as I think really they are quite amusing and quite interesting.

We should not have stopped at Baghdad – but I am glad we did as I saw something of the town. The next morning we had to get up at 2.30 – it was awful – I must say I am looking forward to a whole night's rest, though I think flying rests one, as though one is always tired in the morning, one perks up in the afternoon. Yesterday we flew 1,070 miles – Baghdad to Jask – all along the Persian Gulf. You never saw anything *like it*, so desolate and terrifying – and the places we came down to refuel at, with all the natives in extraordinary costumes – one sees quite wonderful types among them exactly like Persian and Indian minia- tures, down to their very movements.

In Alexandria I had lunch with Mr Casselli, the Dodecanesian cotton millionaire, who met me with his car and drove me all round the town and afterwards to the aerodrome at Aboukir. He lives in an enormous palace decorated in the Victorian Arab style – I have never seen anything to equal it. That afternoon we flew over the 'wilderness' of the Bible to Gaza – next morning over Jerusalem, Bethlehem, the Dead Sea, Jordan and Moab. The night at Gaza we took a car to the sea and bathed – it was *far* too hot to be refreshing.

A man paid me a tremendous compliment at lunch in the desert by saying that he didn't think I had at all an Old Etonian manner.

I find it so refreshing to be among efficient people doing something and not just sitting in offices doing things they aren't interested in. I think I have enjoyed that part of the journey almost more than any – the organisation of the route – there is something creative about it. Of course I want frightfully to come back this way stage by stage, and shall try and get a free ticket this time by offering to write a guide book of the route – but I don't suppose the idea will come off.

I am sending some photographs to the *Daily Express* by the next mail, and am asking them to return those they don't want to Father. Will you ask him to try the *Sphere*, and then the *Illustrated London News* with them – anyhow I shall probably write in greater detail about them, it depends how good they are. There is really something daunting about the prospect of getting back to land, with so much to do again. However I shall have four easy days in Karachi, writing up the trip.

All the things I bought have been splendid – though I do rather regret not having a tidy suit to put on when I get there, as my Moss Bros. is now filthy and crumpled. It was awful in Baghdad – we had a sort of party with the Airways people who would say to the waiter 'Give the Sahib another whisky' and talk about their Memsahibs. 'Social laife' they told me 'was absolutely delaightful – there was one club where you'd faind no one but Britishers' – I literally dread India in this way, and wish I were landing at some remote spot and could just go off alone.

We are flying actually in the clouds all the way, as we got into the monsoon at Jask last night. It is deliciously cool but rather bumpy. I haven't felt the least ill the whole way, everyone else was dying across the desert. [. . .]

Best love from
Bobs

August 1929   Sind Club, Karachi

Darling Mibble

[. . .]We got here 10 minutes early – I found a letter from Lady
Rosslyn's friend, who turns out to be High Commissioner here and is
frightfully grand, and also two people from David Fyfe's company,[1]
who have installed me in this temple of Sahibdom in a suite of three
rooms with bath – the terror is worse than one's first day at Eton. I have
done the one *unforgiveable* thing by not bringing a dinner jacket and am
obliged to have dinner in my room as a result. It is really too awful to
arrive in India and find the outskirts of Balham, with camels walking
along an asphalt road – an old ghoul is creeping round me now – he
never leaves my room! I have no clothes but fortunately it is very cool
here at the moment and I can wear that awful grey suit. My feelings are
quite indescribable – so I had better stop.

Will write by the next airmail.

Love from Bobs

23 August 1929   The Adam's Peak Hotel,
                                                          Ceylon

Darling Mibble

I wish you could see my surroundings – an extraordinary little hotel
stuck away in the hills, the centre of social life for the neighbouring
tea-planters' bungalows – 1 peroxide 'brown cow' and 1 bald foreigner
dining by the fire – 1 over-eyebrowed planter making conversation to
the peroxide – a vast pink manageress with a twisted mouth making
conversation to me – electric light of unearthly brilliance, slightly green
– a life-size map of Ceylon on the wall, together with several hunting
pictures – and a gramophone wheezing out a Hawaiian waltz – self in
shirt sleeves and the reception clerk's shoes at 9 p.m. waiting for the
night mail to Colombo.

I have just climbed Adam's Peak, where Buddha left his footmark, a

---

1. Burmah-Shell.

gargantuan imprint now covered by a ramshackle little temple. It is a very famous place for pilgrimage and you will find an old print of it in one of the *Broadway Travellers* dealing with India – I can't remember which – it may be Ibn Battuta – probably is. If you can imagine the Hundred Steps at Windsor, twice as steep going for 3,000 feet through dark woods, with a heavy rain coming down them & occasional hair-raising interludes on cliffs, where one clings to wire ropes – that was my afternoon – deep in cloud, so that it was half dark, and most of the time pouring with rain so that my lovely topee is a pudding. The burberry was excellent – in front ran a guide, hugging a bottle of soda water and a lantern in case we were benighted – and all the time I thought of Athos and wished I were there instead. But it had the same atmosphere – little resting places etc., only Buddhist architecture is more inextricably complicated with corrugated iron – so that Orthodox has the advantage! Anyhow I enjoyed it very much, such a relief to be on one's feet again after all this travel. At the top, which is scarcely bigger than Athos, there were the most delicious rhododendrons, just the shape of old twisted thorn trees – all lichen and moss grown – with lovely deep red close bunches of flowers – and also the most lovely clumps of great big montbretia.

I can hardly write as the foreigner has now started to tell two planters how he lost £1,000,000 in 1921.

We have done a tour of the buried cities, which were very interesting, though I *loathe* ruins – but the Singalese appear to have reached an extraordinary civilisation before Christ – at one place, Sigiriya, there are the most *lovely* frescoes – or really sketches, ready to be finished, dating from the 5th century A.D. Their position is too extraordinary – in a sort of fold of rocks on a cliff about 700 feet high – why they are there and how any one got there to paint them, no one has explained. The present approach is horrifying – the last 30 feet are ascended by means of a swaying rope and wood ladder hanging *outwards* – I arrived at the top all trembling. However it was well worthwhile, as I now feel so assured in my appreciation of painting – they are far the most interesting things I have seen so far, *except* the English people out here who pass all belief and gradually cease to be funny.

I get back to Colombo early tomorrow morning, and then at last I hope there will be letters – and some cuttings from the *Daily Express*. I am sending them another article on Sunday on the Perahera, the ceremony of Buddha's tooth, which was very picturesque till an entire torch made of burning coconut rind fell out on our feet – an interminable procession of elephants of all sizes, with extraordinary dancers leaping about to drums and pipes, rows and rows in the same position down to minute children. I can't write any more now – am too tired but will continue from Colombo, where I hope to have got a letter. [. . .]

25 August [?]   Colombo

[. . .]We leave tonight, to see the southern temples and to make a fantastic pilgrimage to the Monophysite Christians of Travancore, which means going 70 miles in a bus and sleeping in the girls' school at the end of it. Gavin's servant Nadjibullah hates these adventures – especially as he is unable to speak the language down here and can't get his food cooked in the manner proper to a Mohammedan. [. . .]

Photographing in India is very difficult – the light, for some reason, is quite awful, especially in this cloudy weather. But a good many of mine have been successful, and I hope to write some articles round them when we get to Calcutta.

[. . .] Now I must go down to lunch and so goodbye – I am so longing to hear from you – practically a month without a word.

I have at last planned my 'nice little book' on England – to be called, I think, 'The Pompous Island' 'Vol I. Essays' 'Vol II. Stories'. Do you like it? It will be partly 'nice' and partly quite excessively nasty. [. . .]

Best Love from
Bobs

1 September 1929   Trichinopoly Station

Darling Mibble

I can't remember when I last wrote – Colombo I think it must have been. Since then we have had such an interesting time and at last *got away* from our beastly countrymen. We had a fascinating time in Travancore, travelling about in the most extraordinary Ford buses (fortunately Gavin has run out of money, so we are travelling cheaper than ever) – and saw the Syrian Christians, who have existed there since the 4th Century – the old Athos atmosphere again, even the same coloured priests and delicious old creatures in beards – in the intervals we lunched with the Salvation Army and attended lectures at the Y.M.C.A.! Such is the cause of culture. I discovered an icon, a triptych of St George, in the Indian style, very attractive 18th century, St George an Indian in spotted muslin trousers – most interesting. Travancore is lovely, all wooded and hilly, quite unlike the rest of India – with its own style architecture, eaves like cat's ears. Nadjibullah the servant got roaring drunk to the horror of the town which had never seen anything like it. We hurried out to try the drink with which he had been so successful, coconut milk in process of fermentation – it tasted fantastically nasty, a mixture of sewage and toast.

The great Dravidian temples, with their tapering decorated towers, are *magnificent* – one had always thought them too awful from photographs – I am writing a great deal on architecture, which will give people a very different idea of India, if they ever read it.

We are assailed in this station (we sleep over it) by hordes of monkeys who stole somebody's false teeth the other day, with the result that there was a police court case, when suddenly a monkey was observed with them in its hand. They also will get into the bath, according to the proprietor – but this pleasure we have so far avoided.

2 September
Yesterday we spent out at the temple, about six miles away, and the largest in India, containing a whole town within its precincts. We took lunch, which was quite incredibly nasty, like sandwiches always are – and the beer was fizzling with heat. I did a sketch of a gopura – one of the towers thus the whole thing fantastically decorated. I never would have

believed that anything constructed by human hands would have been so difficult to draw. As a matter of fact I succeeded in drawing it rather well. But the architectural detail defeated me and I could only sketch it in. However the whole thing is not bad really. I also made the ascent of one – the usual conspiracy that the white man is a maim and halt creature – of course the steps would be far too bad and difficult – it was dark etc. In fact there were a number of perfectly solid flights of stone stairs, a little steep but nothing more. It was rather dark and I was terrified of snakes, having discovered some in a tower I was about to go up at Ramesvaram, another temple. However everyone in front was in bare feet, so I didn't think there would be any danger. They produced a torch (in the mediaeval sense) eventually – the top was petrifying, as I got out onto the roof, a thing like an inverted boat (as you observe), and clutched one of the flame-like ornaments which I have indicated by dots, upon which it almost came off. However it was all very interesting and what I don't know about the architecture of gopuras isn't worth knowing.

It is growing rather hot – yesterday the amount of iced soda water I drank made me almost burst – but I like the heat I find – one is so comfortable in only a shirt and shorts – I haven't had a coat on for weeks – the only thing is that one is apt to leave little pools where one sits, and yesterday sketching I had to protect the book from my knees. Of course I was surrounded by hundreds of Brahmins and people, urchins, and beggars till at last the temple elephant, an enormous tusker all painted to make it look like a mantelpiece ornament, came and stood *just* in front. Then a beggar began to snort and spit with such violence (everyone else was speaking in whispers in order not to disturb my prowess) that we all burst into hoots of laughter. The Indians have a great sense of humour – they think I am rather comic, I find. We bought a mechanical bird in a cage in Kandy, price 1/9 – it sits between 2 dog roses, while a mechanical cat batters on the outside – whereat it twitters. This inestimable *objet d'art* has followed us everywhere in Nadji-bullah's careful hand and I scored a great success by presenting it for customs' examination on the boat from Ceylon. Here is Nadjibullah and the cage – brown frock coat, white trousers, bare feet and umbrella [drawing follows]. I must say, if one liked Indian tea, it would be delicious here, as it always tastes of the flower. I sent the *Express* a note on the Ceylon tea-trade – and shall do them an article on the Syrian Christians. This will complete my obligations. Then, if the cuttings are satisfactory or even exist, I shall launch new schemes at them. I want them to send me down to Rangoon by the Dutch postal aeroplanes – and then back across India.

At the moment we are stuck here completely without money, as there is no bank to cash my letters of credit – however I have hopes of persuading one all the same, otherwise we shall be in the workhouse. We reach Madras in 3 or 4 days time, taking in the old *Danish* settlement of Tranquebar on the way, and possibly Karikal, which is still French – and at Madras I know there are letters waiting. We are both looking forward to getting to Calcutta, as Indian travel is not particularly comfortable – the *food* is almost Athonite. We had the most extraordinary evening in Travancore in a native hotel, eating native curry – incredibly nasty it was – but I enjoyed it very much as the whole of India is one enormous conspiracy to make one imagine one is in Balham or Eastbourne.

Goodbye.

Give my love to everyone and a kiss to Gerda and Ella, I am always wishing that Gerda's nose was suddenly on my shoulder.

Love from
Bobs

18 September 1929   4 Elysium Row, Calcutta

Darling Mibble

Such a pleasure to get your letter this morning by air-mail – I was miserable when nothing came by the boat mail on Sunday. How lovely everything sounds at home – with all the fruit ripening and cubbing – even though you are surrounded by communists [. . .] I *do* regret the Great Dane, having always wanted one more than anything. Can't you still get it? [. . .]

I am afraid the articles have been an awful bother and expense to you – I am so sorry – but you have *no idea* how relieved I was to get your wire saying they were published. I have now written screeds to Beaverbrook suggesting he should send me to Java, Northern Australia, Mosul and Mt Sinai, so I hope to get home somehow, even if he only falls in with a quarter of my plans. My finances are not too bad. I am still owed £60 in England, am earning a certain amount here, and hope to get £100 advance on a travel book immediately – so that if I can get my fare paid home, I don't think I shall be much out of pocket, even before I have started to do my English articles and broadcasting on the East, which should bring in a lot and of course I am hoping for a job from Beaverbrook too. I only hope *he* approved of the articles. [. . .]

I have done two really first-class sketches (in my class) of Dravidian temples, and am having them photographed (and thereby much improved) to send to the *Architectural Review*, 9 Queen's Gate. If you find yourself with nothing to do in London, you might like to see them. Of course they please me more than anything else. Quite a lot of the photographs are good too.

Meanwhile I am working frightfully hard, as usual, typing all day, articles and millions of letters and telegrams about our trip. The whole of central Asia is in a fever on account of our advent and there is scarcely a human being within a hundred miles of the Himalayas that has not been circularised by the Viceroy or the Government of India. There is *already* 3 feet of snow in places, but this apparently is due to disappear. The storms sound quite awful, but as the wind blows all ways at once, one is no sooner flung from the saddle, than one is in it again. We are having Jodhpores made of carpet and are taking horse-rugs to sleep under. There is a telegraph the whole way, so I shan't be out of touch – there also appear to be adequate posts – so you may get letters – but *don't expect* them. If you want to send an urgent wire, David Fyfe will always forward it and I will pay him back for the expense.

The prospect of staying in Government House appals me, we are expected to attend the 'Darjeeling Knight Errants Ball' in full evening dress – *imagine!* On the other hand it would be very useful and entertaining if 'Lord Rosse and party' are invited to the Vice Regal lodge at Delhi – a great economy, and one would be staying in the new Lutyens building, which has only just been opened and furnished.

I have had a wire from John to say that he has popped off the boat at Port Said and gone to Cairo – so Michael will arrive alone. I shall be here to welcome him, and will then go on to Darjeeling a day or two ahead, to make arrangements about coolies, mules, ponies, food etc. We have got special permission to visit monasteries beyond the ordinary limits – but are not allowed to sleep beyond Gyantse.

I am enjoying Calcutta very much, though I never go out, as I have too much to do. The flat is charming. It is now pouring with rain and there are occasional terrifying thunder claps. One can't walk at all without becoming absolutely soaked through. I go in trams, the only white person to do so since they were laid down.

We spent the weekend at a Jute mill up the Hoogly, with one of David's friends. It was very interesting, as one has always heard so much about Indian sweated labour. This afternoon we are going dropping cards in people's boxes (such a lovely habit) – Indians, *not* English – it will be amusing when Cooch Behar[1] comes out, as then we shall meet a lot of Indians. The English out here disapprove of her beyond words. [. . .]

With best love from
Bobs

25 September 1929   4 Elysium Row, Calcutta

Darling Mibble

[. . .] What a bore those letters getting burnt in the air mail. Can you remember, was the one from France a Frenchman or an Englishman. One can always tell by the arrangement of the address. If by any chance it was from Millet, it might have been rather important.

It seems so odd to think of you penetrating the fastnesses of the *Daily Express*. I am afraid it must have been such a trouble. Aren't newspaper offices *loathsome?*

Our Tibetan preparations are almost completed – and I have skilfully got a $12\frac{1}{2}\%$ reduction on all stores, by promising to mention the Army and Navy Stores here in my book – thereby saving about £5. Michael arrived, a little deranged by the squalor of the East. He disapproves of people sleeping on the pavements. We have purchased the most incredible clothes. I am having a suit of Jodhpores made of native carpet, a rich blackish green, by a native tailor – costing almost nothing – I have also bought 4 native blankets, vermilion, for £1. We have windproof

---

1. Princess Indira Gaekwar, the beautiful and witty Maharanee of Cooch Behar, was an ornament of London society.

waistcoats, as supplied to the Everest expedition, and gloves with no fingers. Also balaclava helmets and sweaters. No wind can possibly get near us. I leave tonight for Darjeeling. The others come up on Saturday. We start on Monday morning, and thereby miss the 'Knight Errants ball' that I told you about, a great relief to me.

The whole of Tibetan social life is bound up with the presentation of ceremonial scarves. In order to buy some, our teacher took us to a Tibetan Colony here, living in the top of a vast house, unutterably filthy, with refuse all over the floors, everyone covered in sores, pockmarked and sweating – utensils lying about with the dregs of yesterday's food and drink. Having allowed us to drink in these details (it was Michael's first morning and he was extremely unhappy) our teacher said: 'Of course in Tibet the houses and shops won't be clean like this.' Thank Heaven there are bungalows the whole way. During the conversation about the scarves, I found I understood quite a lot – and even uttered a remark! *Could* anything be more impressive?

I haven't really any news – we went to a Parsee theatre on Saturday night, being given a free box and free drinks and ices by an employee of David's firm. He brought his daughter, who sat between us in an apricot sari embroidered in silver. How Indians can wear anything else passes my belief. The play was two plays given in alternate acts. One might have been H. Irving in *Hamlet*, the other George Robey in *Wives for Two*. It went on till one, but we left at twelve. There was a great deal of Indian music and singing, which is very peculiar, but quite indescribable.

Tea Time

I find I must finish this in a hurry as I have to pack – frightful rush all day – we lunched with a minor Indian prince, to the fury of all the Europeans in the restaurant. One can't be seen with natives. How *awful* they are! I have just extracted £12 from the *Statesman* here – a great help. The Army and Navy Stores, besides the rebate, have secretly presented us with a whole case of whisky, which has gone off to Darjeeling and will need another mule – a great bore really.

Will write from Darjeeling –

Love from

Bobs

29 September 1929   Government House, Darjeeling

Darling Mibble

What a letter I could write you about this place, were it not for the effects of the height, a cold, a migraine, the ceremonial meals and the worry of getting off – all of which have left me in such a state of exhaustion that I can barely move. It is 7,000 feet up – imagine Bognor and Southend roofed in corrugated iron and reassembled in the form of an Italian hill town! and that in permanent cloud, which, when it is clear, reveals mountains so high that there is no sky at all. Just the same hideous Wolfgang colouring – Prussian blue – but the snows are lovely. I went for a long ride this morning on a prancing polo pony and it was too lovely really Kinchinjanga rearing up to such an incredible height one could hardly believe it – 21,000 feet above one. The colour is bitterly disappointing – but I hope that the bleak wastes of Tibet will have a little more.

I must say Govt. House has its virtues – we are in a guest house in the garden (a garden rather like Coulsdon on a mountain spur about 30 yards wide with drops so deep that you can't see the bottom on either side) – we have fires all day long, masses to drink, unlimited rickshaws (which are pushed by 5 men – Michael and I had ten yesterday who all fell down in a heap which wasn't a great help) – and horses. The whole procedure is preposterous, one assembles for dinner – an A.D.C. then fetches the Governor (known as H.E.) and Lady Jackson – 2 A.D.C.s precede them into the dining-room – we follow – a horde of magnificent men in beards, red and gold robes and blue and gold puggarees salaam – an invisible band strikes up some incredibly idiotic tune (you know the kind that English bands always play, generally an adapted nursery rhyme) – one jibbers at H. E. or her for an hour. H.E. then gets up and says 'The King-Emperor' – the band accompanies, everyone stands like teddy bears with their glasses of port clasped to their stomachs and all shaking at different speeds – when the band has finished everyone grunts or pipes 'the King-Emperor', the A.D.C.s then hurry out, followed by H.E. and Lady Jackson, and ourselves. A few more sweet nothings – and then they are shoved up to bed – last night however the house caught fire. Lady Jackson, apprised of this fact in a state of nudity, refused to allow it to put her out, lest her bedroom ceiling should be discoloured. We all rushed outside, to discover the Governor standing in a cloud by the front door beneath an umbrella, saying plaintively: 'They keep on whistling, but the guard doesn't come.' One guard then came and fell in. Meanwhile the fire-brigade, summoned a quarter of an hour before, had telephoned to ask if there really was a fire. Michael and I were then discovered by H.E. in hysterics in a corner – at length 120 servants and a dozen helmeted firemen rushed into the hall and stood there. Gavin found a fire extinguisher and insisted on squirting it up Lady Jackson's chimney – she was now clothed – in order to see what noise it made. I then developed a migraine and went to bed. I haven't laughed so much for years. If it is what the Government of Bengal is like in the country I only hope that Michael will be able to cadge us an invitation to Vice-Regal Lodge in Delhi!

The preparations for the trip have been too awful, I feel quite ill with exhaustion – while the height makes it not only impossible to walk up a flight of steps, but brings on a kind of permanent depression so that one wakes in the morning with such a load of misery and worry that it might be one's day of execution. As the whole of Tibet is exactly twice as high, I don't know how we shall survive! Michael is in splendid health, though a little fussy about snakes and other imaginary dangers. Gavin has a streaming cold and a red nose. We leave here tomorrow. I have engaged a cook called Ah-Chung and a sirdar called Ah-den. Upon their arrival having learnt it up, beforehand, I said in fluent Tibetan: 'Can you speak Tibetan?' upon which they almost collapsed with astonishment. We have unlimited food, and a *case* of whisky, besides odd bottles of rum. This Gavin and Michael ordered clandestinely, as they knew I should disapprove. The reason is that we want to have a Tibetan party given for us in Gyantse, and must return hospitality. I also hope to buy a trumpet 16 feet long, which will be a pretty ornament in the drawing-room. The Dalai Lama takes in the *Illustrated London News*, I wish we could get to Lhasa and see it. If you want to know what we are doing get Sir Charles Bell's two books: *Tibet Past and Present*; and *The People of Tibet*. Both are very interesting. We learn that the monks in the monasteries stab one at the slightest provocation, that all the villages are full of mastiffs which tear one from one's pony, that in fact the whole expedition is a form of elaborate and painful suicide. However I am looking forward to it *tremendously*, and am *thankful* that all the preliminaries are over – Calcutta was dreadful, so sticky and humid and this has been little better, being so exhausting. But one gets over that fairly soon.

It is so interesting too to get among *Mongol types* – and away from

India – half the people here are Tibetan and wear the most lovely and fabulously expensive jewellery, though otherwise in rags.

Now I must write my own diary, the others have gone with H.E. to the cinema, a fashionable afternoon pursuit, conducted, doubtless with becoming ceremony.

Goodbye With Best Love
from
Bobs

There is a post from Gyantse so I will write all the time – letters may be delayed.

5 October 1929 Kapup

Darling Mibble

Here we are, about a mile and a half away from the Tibetan frontier, held up in a two-roomed bungalow by a frightful storm which is turning to snow in one night, and whitening the pass that we have to go over. This is 14,000 feet, and we are now at 13,000 and you can imagine the cold! Fortunately there is plenty of firewood here, though it is above the tree-line. Also, by the Grace of God, I bought an aluminium hot-water bottle in a pink vest (you shall have it when I come home, as it is the ideal hot-water bottle) – so that with that, 4 blankets, grannie's rug and the green overcoat, I managed to spend a pleasant night – though interrupted by an appalling headache which I contracted the afternoon before, owing to the height. It was an awful headache, the kind you always get I think, due to excessive blood pressure. However it is better this morning, and will be all right tomorrow I hope – as the whole of Tibet is this altitude. It is annoying to be held up here, as we have got a letter to a high Tibetan official at Yatung, the next stop, and he is reported to feed one on Chinese sea-slugs and rare Chinese wines, which we now shan't have time to stop and taste.

The suit of green carpet Jodhpores which I told you about is now very handy. I have also got a Tibetan hat, richly embroidered with gold on the outside and having fur-lined flaps on all four sides – generally worn thus – but in bad weather the whole effect is this:

Yesterday we climbed from 6,000 to 13,000 feet, doing almost the whole of it in about four miles. The tropical forest with its astounding vegetation and astounding butterflies (one herewith) gave place to woods composed wholly of rhodo-dendron trees of all size of leaf, from those about two inches long to those about a foot long – as they were all the same shape (you know how they grow) and all a lovely bluey colour which one doesn't see in England, the effect was perfectly beautiful. Then we  got into a kind of country like the Scotch moors – with great expanses of dank yellow grass, dead flags and streams, and occasional trees, silver firs etc., but all very battered by the storms. The sides of the hills were covered intermediately with small plants whose leaves were a gorgeous autumn red – and also with masses and masses of dwarf rhododendrons, about two feet high, growing like gorse, so that the hillsides were alternately this rich pinky red, dank yellow and bluey grey, all very dark and rich, with black rocks cropping out, and the tops hidden in clouds.

It is heavenly spending all day riding, and even Michael, who was not too happy at first, as he was run away [with] and then thrown over another pony's head, is now very cheerful, and enjoying himself, especially collecting seeds etc. Gavin is growing an adequate beard, which is more repulsive than you can imagine, but strangely Chinese in shape.

Such Tibetans as we have seen are weird figures. One emerged out of a cloud yesterday thus: [drawing] – they use their stomachs as pockets – he was dressed entirely in rusty vermilion. And red lips and highly coloured pink cheeks on yellow gave a curious painted effect. Many of them wear Homburg hats, which they perch on top of their heads and tie on with their pigtails.

All the way through the mountains, the path is cobbled – it is really an important trade route, and we meet enormous caravans of mules, sometimes 100 at a time, carrying packs of wool. Also the single telegraph wire to Lhasa comes along here. Even now we are only four miles from a telegraph office, which we passed yesterday – so by no means cut off. We have masses of food. The cook was ill last night, but has recovered. I bought him a sweater and boots in Darjeeling.

There is really something rather frightening about the Himalayas, which I have never felt before. They are *so* enormous – one looks down such vast distances as one's path negotiates a mountain corner and the pony slips. The snows are seldom visible, except in the early morning, as there is always cloud.

I am thinking of spending the day writing an article for the *New Statesman* on America. This seems so exactly the place to do it from. I heard from them the other day that they were about to publish one on education that I originally wrote for the *Pall Mall*. Have you seen it yet? [. . .]

With best love to all from
Bobs

The dogs here are so heavenly – Lhasa terriers, like Peter, only brown and white, Afghan hounds and Tibetan chows – I wish I could bring them all home.

10 October 1929   Phari, Tibet

Darling Mibble

I am sure this is my last letter on earth – having woken up this morning with a face so blistered that it felt like a flame – and is now pouring liquid – the result of the Tibetan wind and snow-glare. We had an awful journey yesterday, digging the mules through drifts and wondering whether we should ever get through – now, however, we have reached the Tibetan plateau proper and all should be plain sailing – but the physical discomfort is *awful*. We are now 14,300 feet up and my head throbs perpetually – however it is all *so odd*, and the landscape so extraordinary, that it is worth anything. This morning at 6, the two Jongpöns here, that is the custodians of the Jong or castle, arrived bringing a raw sheep and a number of eggs – we are to pay them a return visit in a minute – one of them wears a turquoise earring six inches long. The light is quite extraordinary and yesterday in the snow I had to wear two pairs of glasses. All the servants are getting ill! It was too exciting to see people riding on yaks through the snow – they are so odd, with huge bushy tails. My pony has now gone lame, and the Jongpöns have provided us with another that looks as though no human being could control it. I can't write any more as there isn't time – but will from Gyantse – if – we don't turn round!

Love from
Bobs

17 October 1929   Gyantse, Tibet

Darling Mibble

The last time I wrote was from the highest inhabited town in the world – at least we believe so. Words can't describe the horrors of our journey here. Every morning I used to wake up with the most *ghastly* headache from the height – and could hardly eat, and only suffer myself to be ambled along with a pony like George, only smaller. Our faces dripped and peeled and dripped and peeled – mouths swollen and purple and covered in sores – I really can't tell you what it was like. One morning at 14,700 feet I really made up my mind to turn round and go home – so however did Gavin – upon which I insisted on going on!

Now here it is too heavenly, I am feeling very well and enjoying every moment of it. This is 13,100 feet. Lovely weather, blue skies and hot sun – though cold at night. Yesterday I went for a long ride over the hills alone – it was too gorgeous – all the hills and the Gyantse plain on such a *terrific* scale – one could get nowhere, as everywhere was so far away.

We are living in a round of wildest gaiety – and attended a wedding feast the other day, drinking out of lovely jade cups and adding our own present of a box of gingernuts to the others. The costumes are *fantastic*, Chinese only odder, and the only place now I suppose where they survive. Yesterday, the great official of the place paid us a state visit, bringing sheep and eggs – wearing a yellow hat, much embroidered and surmounted by a blob of coral – a buff velvet jacket, woven with that *awful* bamboo pattern which you see on screens (think of seeing it in natural surroundings), a purple silk flowered skirt and boots like canoes of untanned leather. Today we lunch with him off Chinese food, and tomorrow we ride out to lunch in a country house 6 miles away. I want to stay here for *months* – but suppose I shall have to go back with the others, owing to the expense of the caravan. We shall only have a week here altogether. I have done one sketch and hope to do another this afternoon in the monastery after lunch. I am also buying a Buddha! – an old painted one on paper, very attractive – and a monk here is making me a mask. You have no idea how wonderful it is to be in a *huge country* as mediaeval as Athos, one gallops about everywhere and everyone does the same – so amusing in the streets of towns and not a wheel in the whole country! Also I imagine, though I don't know, that this is now the only country where one can see anything of the old China – as the modern has become so westernised, according to all accounts.

Michael and Gavin have made perfect travelling companions – as anyone's temper might have been tried by our sufferings. We are having masks made to go home with.

I see in a copy of the Calcutta *Statesman* that the *Daily Express* have printed the whole of my 5th article on the airmail, a general one, non-descriptive – which makes me hope that Beaverbrook will put up the money for my homecoming. I plan, if he does, to be back about February – as there is still much I want to do and see in India. I have a lot to do in Calcutta, while the others are in Burmah, besides, as I think I told you, perhaps getting some kind of temporary job. Anyhow, if I don't I can make a certain amount of money by writing out here and for English papers. I am dying to be home, but feel it would silly, till one has done what one should do.

The telegraphist here managed to develop one of my films, fortunately the camera seems in order so I hope my photographs will come out – if they do they ought to be *marvellous*, as the light up here is so incredible.

I feel I can't go on, as I shall never stop, so goodbye

With best love from
Bobs

24 October 1929 Tuna, Tibet

Darling Mibble

Tomorrow we reach a post office again – though we hear that the mails can't get through at the moment owing to the snow. We have been riding all day at 14,700 feet in thick snow – anything from 2 feet to 2 inches according to where the wind has caught it – across an interminable plain, dotted with a herd of wild ass – and all around the glass-like mountains, that might be in the moon. One of them, Chomolhari, rising 23,000 feet – a vast crumpled sugar-cone filling all the sky as we get near it – a sky an intense greenish blue – and the glitter from the snow such that to look at it for five minutes gives one a headache. My clothes today consisted of: 1 Tibetan fur hat, 1 green silk mask, 2 prs of dark spectacles, 1 coat, 1 sweater, 1 windproof waistcoat, 1 jumper, 1 shirt, 2 vests, 2 prs of pants, 1 pr of shorts, 1 pr of Jodhpores, 1 pr of stockings, 1 pr of Cretan boots, the scarf you knitted, and 1 pr of fingerless gauntlet gloves. Please note the lunch in saddlebag also containing whisky, also note how smart stockings turned down over boots look. We hear that we can't get beyond Phari, which we reach tomorrow, after 21 miles over the snow – but it is thawing during the daytime now and should be better. We also hear that there is 6 feet of snow on the Himalayan passes that we have to go over – but it may have gone.

In a way I am sorry to be on the homeward journey – but it is lucky that we have not delayed any more, as the winter is really beginning and the cold is no joke. Last night my sponge turned to ice in its bag, in a hermetically sealed room which we had all been sitting in with a fire – the fires all of yak dung – which makes one wake with a sense of nausea – however tomorrow we ought to get some wood again.

I have ridden on a yak, I ordered a riding one at one halt, in *Tibetan*! it was brought from miles away, you steer it by one rope through the nostril, which you fling from horn to horn. Their motion is just like that of a horse. All the bungalows have lamps without glasses that go by clockwork, KRANZOW is the name – an American make – I am sure Father would like to try one. They give an excellent light and must save a lot of labour.

I want so much to tell you all about our stay in Gyantse, but feel that once I begin I should never stop. The *meals* we had, 30 dishes eaten with chopsticks, frightfully good food, the visit to the Tibetan country house, its little garden of trees – courtyard with stables all round – private chapel with lamas intoning, then a lunch party of 20 people given by a *nouveau riche*. All the officials were in gorgeous Chinese silks playing a kind of domino-bridge, one was in contact, socially at least, with a completely assured, sophisticated way of living, *absolutely unwesternised* and unconscious of the west – probably the only place

one would find such a thing – exquisite manners, and everywhere a real love of beauty. Exquisite jade and porcelain cups, vases etc., no taste in arrangement, but appreciation of being surrounded by beautiful things, a music whose tunes are exactly like Scottish folk songs, they can play our tunes if they hear them.

Of course it may all be just watered Chinese – but then from all accounts China is becoming so very westernised and in Tibet there is no trace of it. I spent lots of time in monasteries and if my photographs succeed, they ought to be marvellously interesting – I have never done anything so worthwhile – one could never I don't think love the country – it is too terrific – those awful plains, tearing biting wind, huge mountains and gorges, fierce sun etc., but I feel I shall come back to it. I wish I could go to Lhasa. Fortunately I am now inured to the height – the journey up with those headaches was really a nightmare, but I don't seem to be feeling anything now, & here we are at our highest halt.

We get to Gangtok, the capital of Sikkim, in about a week – if the passes are open – and there stay with the Resident, who will have our letters waiting for us. [. . .] I am longing to be home and am really feeling rather tired. Yesterday we did 26 miles in fearful cold – today 15 in the snow. I only hope the masks will save our faces from their fate on the way up. Gavin has a huge permanent moustache. We daren't shave and shan't for another 3 or 4 days – or wash, except the eyes – anyhow it is much too cold in the mornings. Apparently no one except those obliged has ever travelled the road at this time of year before. We have masses to eat, but are running out of tinned milk. Ah-Chung, the cook, makes delicious scones every day. Michael and Gavin are at the moment drinking hot rum. I find alcohol doesn't really agree at this height. The height has such odd effects. One is sitting quietly in a chair and suddenly finds oneself out of breath. All the tinned things one opens emit a great hiss of British air.

I hope Lucy got a letter for her birthday all right – I sent her a present (not a real one) naked from Gyantse – did it arrive?

Goodbye – dinner is ready, I think.

With best love
from
Bobs

30 October 1929   Kampajong, Sikkim

Darling Mibble

[. . .] I last wrote, I think from Phari. We had an appalling ride down the Chumbi valley, on a tiny mountain lodge blocked with huge avalanches – then Yatung, where I got your letters, 9,900 feet – no snow really (I saw two men cutting up a human body on the way) – then up again to the Nather La pass 14,300 – we only *just* got over – in places I was up to my waist in snow and then was by no means touching the bottom – the pony disappeared practically – all on a steep precipice – and of course every movement made one *frightfully* out of breath – my mask going in and out of my throat. Recent tracks were wholly covered, but fortunately we had the British Trade Agent in Tibet with us (weighing 16 stone on a black mule), whose Tibetan clerk knew where the path ought to be. At Yatung, quite accidentally I bought an enormous green and gold Tibetan banjo very highly decorated – horse's head handle – which had to be carried over this pass in pouring snow – so that its musical capacities are now somewhat less, as it is too big to wrap up – about 4 feet 6 inches long. How or whether I shall ever get it home I don't know. It really is very pretty.

The Weirs,[1] with whom we are staying here, are really very nice – Mrs Weir frightfully 'brown cow', but has done most excellent drawings and gouache paintings of Tibetan buildings – so we compared sketches, she thinks mine frightfully good and regards me as a professional artist! Looking at them again they aren't too bad – but I shall have to wait for you to tell me how to finish them off. Unfortunately, they are not as good as the ones I did in Southern India I don't think – but I had so little time – and one can't choose one's composition in a hurry. I am in an agony of suspense over the photographs.

Sikkim is a tiny little state – and this morning we got to shake hands with the Maharajah, who is a brother of the owner of the country house near Gyantse where we lunched. This afternoon his other brother, an extremely holy lama, comes to tea. Tomorrow we are off again on our ponies, spend one night in a bungalow and then get a car down to Siliguri, and train that evening to Calcutta. I have nothing but feelings of regret that it is all over – but realise that I am frightfully tired, as I wake up aching all over every morning. It has been most exhausting. But of course I am dying to go back and would start this moment if there were any chance of getting to Lhasa.

[. . .] I think I must write a book – as I have done so much that is interesting – and Calcutta won't be the least extraordinary of all when I have finished with it either!

The joy of getting into a house, and drinking beer etc. – we even had a cocktail last night – rather ineptly made by Michael and Mrs Weir.

As you suggest, Michael has found the experience of discomfort rather odd – but will enjoy the retrospect he says. No letter from Beaverbrook yet, but I hope there may be one in Calcutta.

I must get up – I *hear* a hot bath arriving – what joy!

Love from
Bobs

This second air-mail accident is dreadful – Stone and Pembroke (wireless operator and engineer) were both on my boat going out – I became the greatest friends with them – the pilot was different, but I can't help thinking it was the same machine.

---

1. Colonel Weir had the rare distinction of being invited to Lhasa by the Dalai Lama who sought his advice on how to proceed against the already impending menace of the Chinese.

28 November 1929   4 Elysium Row, Calcutta

Darling Mibble

I write in such a hurry and have so much to say. I am coming home by Lloyd leaving Bombay Jan 16th arriving Venice about Feb. 2nd or 3rd – where I may stay a day or two to see the Byzantine things, which I have almost forgotten. [. . .]

The Tehrings, Jigmed and Mary,[1] have arrived from Tibet and I have had a gorgeous time with them – took them to dine in full regalia at Firpo's the smart restaurant – people nearly died – Jigmed in a cinnamon brocade robe with a scarlet sash – then of all things to *Journey's End*[2] – they had scarcely heard of the war before – it was most peculiar. The theatre was also extremely surprised. They live in a ghastly Caravanserai in Chinatown, filthy, where I go and rout them out. Then I set on foot a tremendous intrigue and got them asked to lunch at Government House, much against the will of everyone there – I felt like a mother getting her children to their first party – and only hoped they arrived on time and looked nice. Tonight they are going to Buddha Gaya on pilgrimage, and I am going too! I think it will be amusing. Buddha received enlightenment there. They are a heavenly couple and quite helpless here. They had an appalling journey down – tried to get round by Everest, got completely blocked, and had to sleep out in deserted stone huts at goodness knows what height. Mary wore a flannel mask, but Jigmed lost his face, which was a comfort. Mary being a Lhasan, is very interesting about Lhasa – all the houses have electric light. Ours will very soon be the only one in the world that hasn't. Pray God it never does.

I have sold my old camera and bought a new one like a box – absolutely enormous – it takes no bigger photographs, but the actual picture, actual size, that one will take is reflected in a bit of ground glass – and one focuses by eye – so that I shall be able to take proper portraits with it. I wish to God I had got it before instead of having so many spoilt. I have been frightfully busy with my book, articles etc. I am

---

1. Son and daughter-in-law of the Rajah Taring, of the royal house of Sikkim, and Robert's host at his country house near Gyantse.
2. A play by R. C. Sherriff based on his experiences in the trenches during the First World War.

really rather glad that the decision of coming home by ship direct has relieved me from all sorts of temptation to stop on the way. [. . .]

Love from
Bobs

5 December 1929   Calcutta

Darling Mibble

I hope you and Father will have a very happy Xmas and New Year – another apart! How queer it seems. However I am delighted at the prospect of coming home so soon [. . .]

I went on my pilgrimage to Buddha Gaya with the Tibetans – it was really very pleasant. There was no food, but their servant cooked in the bungalow. They insisted on going to a cave on a mountain top beneath a huge mimosa-tree, where Buddha once slept. The local dignitary lent us an elephant, furnished only with a small red mat – it sat down, we all got on, Mary's very fat Tibetan maid clinging to my waist – then it got up – an appalling sensation – there was nothing to hold on to at all – and ran up a flight of steps. We went for miles across country, all rather hideous like the river at Culham, only sand and pampas grasses – no colour – reached the cave and came back in the dark. There was a pony with us which the elephant would try to race.I never thought they felt like that about the lower animals. Then of course it tried to go into its own door instead of up to the bungalow and when prevented literally pirouetted on one foot and galloped up the village street.

I have done quite a good drawing of the temple except that it is slightly out of drawing and I shall have to resquare the paper. I have now done six sketches altogether which are really a great advance on anything I have done before. I notice you don't express any interest! It is difficult to get the right verticality, when all vertical lines are convergent, and in addition one is looking up at a thing.

I am coming home by Agra and Delhi – Lutyens[1] is at New Delhi and I am half hoping to get a bed out of him – but don't suppose I shall. I had

---

1. Sir Edwin Lutyens, the greatest British architect of the twentieth century.

a letter from Michael saying they have discovered two new kinds of monkey puzzle in Burmah. I trust he is bringing seeds of both. Wouldn't a variegated one be lovely? My book is getting on – we are in Tibet in it. Do you think 'Plains of the Moon' a good title?

I am sorry not to be able to send you a present – but I am bringing you and Father back some Tibetan paintings, which I think you will like when framed. They are *not* like Chinese or Japanese and the colouring is lovely. Lucy and Anne's masks should arrive the first week in January and will come down by rail of their own accord.

With best love and wishes – I shall be home so soon now.

from Bobs

How *ghastly* Anne must have looked as a bridesmaid!

10 December 1929   Calcutta

Darling Mibble

[. . .] I went to the wedding, looking more Roman than anything in the world with a kind of frilled muslin skirt. It was too pretty for words. An enormous wedding – about 700 guests – the *cream* of Bengal including Lord Sinha, the only Indian peer. I was the only English guest – would you believe it? One prominent opponent of the British rule almost wept with joy when he saw me thus clothed, and of course the English people here are so *appalled* when I tell them that they just look away as though something indecent had been brought to their notice. You can't think how lovely all the women looked, in stuff absolutely clotted with gold. Except that it took place in a marquee it was just like an English wedding, the priest had the voice of an English parson, the choir also, the Sanskrit tunes might have been A. and M. Afterwards there was an enormous meal (I forgot – an Indian band played *Lohengrin*'s wedding march!) at which I managed the curried prawns, but found the junket difficult to eat with the fingers.

I have been very busy and have no news. My book is nearly half done already – and I have done a lot of articles on Tibet for the *Express*, who wired for them. Incidentally, have my *other* travel articles on Ceylon and the Syrian Christians come out?

I have just been asked to spend Xmas in a native state, where the

Nawab, who has a million pounds' worth of jewels and wears them, is giving a Xmas party. It would be rather fun but it depends on what plans the others have made. I am getting rather tired of Calcutta – it is so lassifying – people pour in to see me – you would laugh – some of them are very nice I must say – the nice ones feel the horror of it all so, which depresses one. I am calling my book[1]

THE BRITISH EVENING

IN THE

MORNING-LANDS

The last two lines as a sort of sub-title – doubtless you recognise the allusion to morgenland (east). *Don't dispute* it and *do* say it's a good title – you had better wire – otherwise I shall have no peace of mind. [. . .]

Best love from

Bobs

Only a month more by the time you get this. I am so longing to be home. I am glad Gerda hasn't forgotten me.

Xmas Eve   The Palace, Rampur

Darling Mibble

You can't conceive what this place is like – some vast hotel – very comfortable – band playing all day – 60 guests including the Dunsanys – sparkling claret – sacramental wine instead of port – Liberty silver – vast landscapes of the Farquarson and Marcus Stone schools – charming old Indian pictures – very cold and cloudy (I am in thick tweeds) – a smell of stale central heating – a gigantic ballroom – the Nawab like a tortoise – his sons wearing vast diamonds in their ears and talking about racing cars – huge expanses of pseudo-lawn interrupted by municipal fountains and beds of cannas – avenues of lamp-posts like Oxford Street at midnight. If I ever write a novel, it is going to be about Indian princes. Cooch gave a dinner just before I came away for a mass of them, including Jodhpur, who is very grand – all in turbans – the table was one large hiss of 'Highness'. They Highness one another. 'I hope your Highness will come and stay with me in March for a shikar.' 'I should

---

1. *An Essay on India.*

like to, your Highness.' 'Could we settle a date, your Highness?' 'I think perhaps it would be best if I came round to your Highness' home to talk it over.' 'Certainly, your Highness' etc.

I travelled to the circus afterwards in a Rolls draped in purple like a Second Empire bed with orange lights belonging to the Maharajah of Dharbanga, who has a *private* income of £800,000 a year. However I can't stand it for long, and am going to Delhi on Thursday. Lutyens asked me to stay the first week in January – but owing to my new job I have to go earlier and he can't put me up then, which is rather a disappointment.

This job is too extraordinary. David's firm [Burmah-Shell] suddenly got an order from their London headquarters to embark on a press campaign in favour of their political integrity. The managers (each receiving £10,000 a year) were *quite* helpless – and suddenly thought of me. I arrived back from Puri, full of excitement at the thought of getting home and having only 2 more days in Calcutta, to be confronted by it. I said I wanted £100 a month – and they threw in the 1st class fare home as well (with £90 – the best that can be got P. & O.) – so I accepted. I am to travel all over India to their branches, expenses paid at all hotels, plus those of a servant, and accompanied by a special inspector. It will be very amusing and very easy work, I think – but oh the boredom of three months' waste of time. I put off the B.B.C., which will infuriate them, I begin on January 2nd and end the last day of March and shan't stay one day longer if they offer a million pounds a month. I feel as if I were caught in a trap – I take no interest in money and don't want it and if only I had £500 a year of my own would never try and make a penny more – but this at least has provided me with a release from financial worry for the first time in my life and I am grateful to that extent. I shall more or less pay off my overdraft and shall also be able to come home the way I want, by the Gulf, and across the Syrian desert to Damascus – then either up through Asia Minor to Constantinople or by boat to Athens [. . .]

Puri, where Michael and I went for the weekend, was lovely – or rather the temples – the best Hindu things I have seen, by a long way. Now I am in the Mahommedan–Moghul area and everything is *entirely* different. I shall spend 5 days at Delhi photographing and making notes on the new capital for the *Architectural Review*, from whom I got an urgent letter about it the other day. I doubt if Moghul architecture can be good – always this [drawing], so ugly I think.

Everyone in a great fever about the Viceroy's bomb.[1] Doubtless the beginning of the 'New Mutiny'. [. . .]

The disappointment about not coming home was dreadful, I could hardly bring myself to accept the offer – but it will save me and, I think, probably you, a lot of worry – so I look forward to the tulips and the honeysuckle (if the canary will let one get near it) and I shall never go away again.

I hope the masks have arrived.

With best love
from
Bobs

30 December 1929   Hotel Cecil, Delhi

Darling Mibble

I got your last letter at Rampur on Xmas day, with a mass of others from unexpected people, which was very nice. No, I didn't have to pay on any of the presents the week before. The cold has been *awful* and I haven't left off the jumper, or for that matter Father's green coat, which grows prettier and prettier, and even then with my tweed suit (the new one which is very thick) and the sun shining brightly it is colder motoring than I have ever known it in England. [. . .]

Christmas day at Rampur was even odder than the others. I drove to church, bitterly cold, as it had no glass to the windows, everyone coughing and sneezing like Eton chapel in February. In the evening a state banquet, the Nawab in British grey velvet and many orders, all the rest in uniform of some sort, very magnificent. I acquired a bottle of champagne and spent the evening talking to the librarian, an old sage in a white beard, who unlike most Indians, knew something about his job.

Then came on here – disgusting hotel but they are all very full. I have spent all my time practically in New Delhi, at *vast* expense, as I have to have a car for the whole of every day, but as the *Architectural Review* has commissioned me to spend up to £20 on photos alone and as my own are *extremely* successful, I shall send them a list of expenses.

---

1. An unsuccessful bomb attack by Indian terrorists against the Viceroy, Lord Irwin (later Foreign Secretary and 1st Earl of Halifax).

I can't *describe* to you how beautiful it is – nothing but the Piazza of St Peter's can compare with it. The work of an Artist triumphing after 17 years' struggle over every stone, bush and drop of water with official India. The Viceroy's House is the first real vindication of modern architecture, it *succeeds*, where all the others have been only attempts. It is *really* modern, not quite cubist, or skyscrapery. My admiration for Lutyens is unbounded. His versatility is so astounding – every niche and ornament of the inside is his, every flower in the garden. It is so fantastic too, a lot of it – fountains all over the roof – gold dome – glass star 15 ft high on a column (this isn't up) – pillar of smoke from the top of the War Memorial Arch. And the *size*, miles of waterways all coped in the local deep red sandstone, a delicious deep red with a cream in it, while above the foundations the buildings are of cream stone from the same quarries. I could go on for ever about it. People don't *realise* what has been done, how stupendous it is, and such a work of beauty, so unlike the English – one would never have thought of them – it will be a mystery to historians. Such a triumph, to have created this to leave behind us, when no one talks of anything but 'welfare' and 'our Mission' and the King Emperor and all the whole damned rot. Not content with not realising what has been done, people of all kinds and opinions set out to crab for all they're worth – what a waste of money when there aren't enough midwives – 'Modern' too, why weren't the arches pointed? Why have anything Indian about it? Why move the capital from Calcutta at all? It makes one sick, and what Lutyens must have endured to get it done at all passes belief.

He is a *heavenly* old man, the only one who takes India as a joke and sees the officials as they are. He has been most kind to me and I have lunched and dined with him daily, he likes talking about it all, and seems genuinely glad of one's opinions – obviously it is his life's work and I think he and all the people connected with him (of which there are a great many) feel that not enough notice has been taken, in which they are right. He has such enormous knowledge and is so completely of this generation in his outlook and taste. It astounds me to think that he designed the Viceroy's House before the war – it's like the setting of a German film in its convergent (Athos-Tibetan) perpendiculars, and yet with none of that stark industrial feeling which distorts so much that would otherwise be good. He is so essentially aristocratic in outlook, and such a master of his material, he pours stone about. He tells me that when Lord Halifax and Basil Wilberforce visited the Taj Mahal in the

70s they sang 'How sweet the name of Jesus sounds' in 'mellifluous unison' over the grave of its inhabitant. Lutyens has been thwarted at every turn, largely owing to cost, but also by sheer perversity and wish to annoy. He had to call in Baker[1] to design the Secretariats and Council House – miserable things – but his own scheme and layout for them is so good that they survive and look quite lovely inspite of themselves.

I lunched with the Viceroy on Sunday, he was *extremely* nice and seemed to know all about my writings and was interested in what one was doing. There was none of that grotesque pomposity of the Calcutta Government House. One was simply lunching in an English country house and Sir Edwin says it is always the same except when there are official guests, but he is by no means merely the English country gentleman as everyone is inclined to say – a man of great charm who is interested and interesting about everything – and I should think very competent.

Lady Irwin was very nice and took me all over the house. Fortunately she is a woman of some (though not perfect) taste and is really going to get it very nice – to begin with hanging all the pictures *low*. It is almost completely unfurnished at the moment and magnificent in the extreme, a great deal of marble which I love and gorgeous inlaid floors of terrific coldness, if only they had had Italian workmen to do them, but they are superb. Lady Irwin said that the princes always commiserated with her at having to live anywhere so plain! She has the right ideas about India, finds the south more interesting than the north and knows about and remembers everything, such a relief after the halfwittedness of people like the Jacksons. Irwin said 'I suppose you left Calcutta in a whirl of gaiety.'

I said 'Yes – a little depressing I found it.' Upon which he laughed with feeling, having held a court there in the winter before. They have no illusions about Anglo-Indian opinion and that sort of thing. But one couldn't very well pursue the subject.

I hope all this hasn't bored you, but I was so delighted to find at least one sane spot in the whole country, and that in such a superlative setting. It has really given me the first ray of hope since I caught sight of the church spires of Karachi. I know my point of view is fundamentally

---

1. Sir Herbert Baker, architect and uncongenial partner to Sir Edwin Lutyens in the building of New Delhi.

that of the artist rather than that of the district nurse, but it is my point of view that counts in the long run, whatever the temporary benefits of the other.

As for the Mogul buildings, they fill me with horror as I knew they would. I trotted round mosques this morning, my servant carrying the camera and in fear of his life being a Hindu. (One can't travel without a servant and as I am to have his expenses paid by Burmah Shell, have engaged him now.) I also went to the fort. There are moments of beauty but it is all so *bad* fundamentally. Out beyond New Delhi, the Emperor Shah Jehan's daughter (17th cent.) has a tiny marble sarcophagus with a little lawn on top according to her wish that nothing but grass should grow on her grave. Rather touching I thought.

Tomorrow I go out to the Kutub Minar,[1] and then instead of on to England, back to Calcutta to begin my loathesome job the day after. However it is only three months and the money is consoling.

My photographs[2] are really marvellous, some of them. I have taken about 150 of New Delhi, practically all successful. I *wish* I had had my new camera in Tibet, such false economy it was, and all round the south and in Goa. I will send you some specimens, as soon as they are printed. *The Times* have commissioned an article on Tibet, 1,800 words. I shall want Father to send them a selection of these photographs, but will write when ready.

Best love from
Bobs

2 January 1930   Calcutta

Darling Mibble

I wrote today in a dreadful hurry by the ordinary mail and suddenly remembered that I never thanked you and everyone for the Xmas wire –

---

1. Ruins of one of the earliest mosques of the conquering Moguls; built in 1193 by Kutb ud-dîn.
2. Lady Irwin wrote to Robert on receipt of his photographs: 'They are excellent and quite different from any I have ever seen which is a great charm – such nice unexplored bits of the house – I tremble to think where you climbed to take them from!'

which made me feel wretched at not being at home. However I thought of you all on Xmas night at that preposterous banquet when the Nawab got up and croaked out 'absent friends' and everyone said 'absent friends' in a grotesque chorus and slobbered into their glasses.

Nor have I thanked you for your 3 long letters which I can't bear getting as you say you are so glad I am coming home. Another vile day this has been – I sit in the office hating and hating – though fortunately (and strangely) there is a certain amount to do. *What* an insight into the occupation of half the world – I can't tell you how I DESPISE it – a living – but why live? My novel is germinating like a mushroom bed – this completes it. No wonder past generations despised 'trade' – well they might. People feel so creative about it too – to me it is literally like being in a Bedlam, for though I now understand how 'business' is conducted (which I never did before) – I *cannot* understand why? It seems to me entirely irrational that people should be devoting their lives, efforts and intelligences to – nothing. They are like puppets with a drunken man at the strings. Thank God I was firm about the 3 months – even so I automatically have £9 income tax deducted from £300.

Mark [Ogilvie-Grant] has gone as attaché to the Loraines[1] in Egypt – so I may stop there and at Athens on my way back – I feel Greece would be a little bit of a rest and a holiday before the rush of things there will be to do in England. Anyhow my passage is being booked in the *Ranchi* leaving Bombay April 5th. This will give me time to see that Taj Mahal.

Don't expect long letters any more – and if I miss a mail, it will be because I am travelling and have miscalculated. Anyhow I shall be out of Calcutta for about 3 weeks almost at once – but still immersed in the company's filthy products – the very horror of it makes one gloat – I never really suspected before how stupendous must be the gulf between oneself and the ordinary man – it is the one thing in the world (or out of it) that I have ever met, which I know that I cannot, and never shall be able to understand – BUSINESS.

Best love from
Bobs

---

1. Sir Percy Loraine, High Commissioner for Egypt and the Sudan since 1929, and his wife Louise.

9 January 1930   4 Elysium Row, Calcutta

Darling Mibble

This detestable career having begun, I now have no time to write at all, and have got up early to get this off before I go to the beastly office. *How* the next 80 days will pass I don't know. Yesterday I spent at an oil installation down the Hoogly – an unappreciative audience I am afraid – lunch with the manager – then conference with the general manager of the whole India branch as to the expenditure of under £500. I exaggerated when I wrote before – they are only spending from £2–3,000 at the moment. I must say that the Scottish are the saving grace of business. They have some wit – though I am thinking of learning Gaelic in order to understand them. How loathesome it all is – but so interesting to discover what business really consists of. I have always wondered and wondered and wondered. This will absolutely make my novel. I sit at my desk wearing Martyr's Crowns and thinking that Henry[1] did the same thing, only much worse, for 2 years. I am going off on tour almost at once for about 3 weeks – Delhi, Karachi, Bombay – then back here and down to Madras. I am quite looking forward to the travelling, *so long* as I can stay in hotels and am not engulfed in the lavish and refined hospitality of branch managers.

My stomach is growing enormous and I always go to sleep after dinner. I am going to give up eating.

My Delhi photographs are *extremely* good. I will send you one or two, when the next lot are printed, they have cost goodness knows what, but I hope to get it back easily and anyhow for the moment, thank goodness, it doesn't particularly matter. I am suggesting an article for *The Times* again on this. People are so *frightful* about it – so contemptible. I asked quite an intelligent person the other day what he thought. He said: 'New Delhi (a town of about 12 square miles)? You should see Lady Irwin's bathroom, it's like a mortuary.' How vile the English provincial mind can be – petty and mean – it makes one ill. What Lutyens must have had to contend with! [. . .]

It is dreadful the way one looks forward to weekends now, as one did at school. And lunch is so awful – seated at a long table making conversation to strangers, when one is tired and would like to be silent.

---

1. Henry Yorke spent two years in Birmingham working in his family firm of Pontifex.

What a disgusting invention the communal table is. I am sorry to hear Lucy has grieved you with her book. You don't, and never will, understand or acquiesce in the modern novel – so there it is – but as one can't hinder one's artistic instincts for anyone, do be a critic rather than a censor. At least when I write my novel, otherwise it will have to go to press without you seeing it and *then what would happen?* [. . .]

Best love from
Bobs

15 January 1930   Lahore

Darling Mibble

Do look this place up on the map. I arrived here this morning – bitterly cold – I huddle over a fire in a deserted ruin which is called a hotel (the outside is just as you see above) – having spent the day interviewing the proprietors of local papers, one Indian and half-witted, the other English and wordless, and traipsing through the bazaar seeing how the company's stinking oil is distributed to that mysterious entity known as the consumer. Lahore is very different from Delhi – masses of very narrow streets and tall old houses – a vile confusion beneath – all rather like pictures of India, while the South, being India, is not.

I had a pleasant time in Delhi and saw something of Lutyens, also dined with 2 lesser architects. New Delhi seemed even more beautiful – though as a business man (engaged in observing the excellent effects of 'spraymex' on the roads) I felt a pariah and almost averted my eyes. Now I am bored beyond belief and have bought books. *Do get* E. M. Forster's *Passage to India* – that is if you *want* to know what India is like. Now I read it again, I can see what genius it is. I have also bought a very amusing bit of 18th century painting – 3 Maharajahs prancing along on piebald horses with umbrellas over their heads. I felt I could afford to buy one thing! I must say it is nice being able to have some comfort without a conscience – fires for example which I shall certainly charge to the company, though I have no doubt they would be glad if I froze to death. When in Delhi I saw a man called Miller, a ponderously important figure in the firm and afterwards accidentally saw a confidential note from him to the Branch Manager in which he described me as a 'good fellow'. One's business laurels! He suggested that if the present campaign was a success, I might be induced to stay out here longer. A spasm of nausea flew down my spine. The only possible inducement would be if you could *all* come out and I would pay for it, bringing you overland, which would be great fun. I feel confident that if I tried I could get a really good job out of them. But as I am not yet ready to commit suicide, it is out of the question. However, to have launched a publicity campaign of this size may prove a useful credential in England, if one could work this sort of thing as a sideline. More I will not do, though I know it's selfish. I go about with a kind of empty feeling, as though I were denying both God and the world by this sudden futility. I don't mind writing the stuff, or even organising the campaign. But having to take an interest in it and collect material is dreadful. What is so strange, though, is how easy it is. I find my mind automatically jumping to the essential points of the business and am positively astonished at the profundity and hard common sense of my conversation, still more so as I see it impresses my superiors. It is such a pity to think that one might so easily have been a business genius, you loaded with diamonds already. I am sorry to talk so much about it, but I have nothing else, except wishing the time would go. My servant has a cough – I don't wonder. I am wearing all my underclothes and thick winter tweeds. In 3 months' time it will be 110° in the shade all day and about the same at night. It is awful to think that originally I should have been sailing tomorrow. [. . .]

Best love from
Bobs

23 January 1930   Calcutta

Darling Mibble

I have *no* time to write at all, I work day and night, day at my office, night at articles – tore back here from Lahore, 38 hours in the train – and now off tomorrow back again via Delhi to Karachi and then down to Bombay. It is so strange the way one *always* goes back to places. I am feeling less resentful of the whole thing now – as long as I have a lot to do, I don't mind, but sitting in an office trying to fill in time is awful. It is *so like* you and Father not to have a word of congratulation for the first money I ever earn! I am *thankful* that you realise how futile it is. As for *his* remarks about my going to the wedding in Indian dress, and *yours* about the colour bar, they merely seem to me to belong to the first ten years after the Mutiny, in which apparently the whole of England still lives. It is that kind of attitude which makes it so difficult not to wish that the English could not be turned out of the country altogether. Coming down from Lahore, I couldn't get a reservation and travelled with 2 married couples. The 1st an English officer and wife – he shouting and incredibly rude, banging everything about, then suddenly apologising and telling me his life story – she growing more and more *cowed* at the prospect of another man in the carriage at night, till eventually I got out and found another train. The other couple were Indian nationalists by their dress, evidently very rich. Their courtesy was exquisite – every movement a pleasure to watch, as they squatted on their berth eating a Hindu dinner. Eventually without a tremor the woman retired into the lavatory, and emerged in a charming white linen sari edged with green in which she crawled on to the upper berth, looking dignified even there. The man read to her part of the time. *What a contrast!* If I had been an Indian in the other carriage I can't think what would have happened. If I lived out here, I think I should go about disguised as one, just to see what did happen to one. [. . .]

I am persuading the general manager to start a £3,000 All-India photographic competition illustrating the use of 'our products'. I have already let them in for £3,000 elsewhere.

Tomorrow is your birthday – how I am longing to be home and wish I were there [. . .] This letter is very short, but I must have breakfast and go to the office.

Love from
Bobs

A minute more. I forgot to tell you about an estate we went to up in the Punjab, a man called Vanreven (?) who breeds horses and runs his place like an old colonial plantation – large English country house – family have been in India for 146 years and then they came from the Cape. The horses were very interesting, each stallion with its harem and children –

most picturesque to see them all frisking together. He had several mares out from Oliver Dixon,[1] all of which had been failures. [. . .]

I am feeling rather tired this morning having got up at 6.30 to finish an article – but otherwise everything suits me. The enormous train journeys make me tired – afterwards – which with me takes the form of depression – that is why my last letters have been rather morbid. It is so difficult to get enough to read on them. David and Gavin get all the new books. [. . .] Henry tells me he is writing a book whose setting is entirely Victoria Station. [. . .]

    B.

30 January 1930   Sukkur

Darling Mibble

[. . .] This place (you have doubtless already rushed to your atlas) is on the Baluchistan border, or thereabouts and they are making the biggest dam in the world here – a mile long as the river is a mile wide. I made my way across it yesterday – very interesting, with its various canals going off from either of the upstream banks to irrigate 9 million acres. However I can't describe it to you as I am not an engineer. But it is the sort of thing that has made the Empire famous.

I am most exhausted and literally have *not been able* to catch the mail. I left Calcutta Friday night, reached Allahabad Saturday morning, mingled with the largest crowd in the world at the confluence of the Ganges and the Jumna (anything up to 3 million – it only happens every 12 years) – where Burmah Shell had a stall at the fair[2] – caught another night train to Delhi, spent a day of indescribable gloom there except that I motored out for one last look at New Delhi and dined with the Shoosmiths,[3] got up at five, and caught the aeroplane to Karachi. It was wonderful to be in the air again – I didn't notice the noise this time, as I did before, and it all reminded me so *vividly* of the journey out, which I

---

1. A well-known horse dealer.
2. The Kumbh Mela, a religious festival of great antiquity.
3. A. G. Shoosmith, assistant architect to Lutyens.

really think I enjoyed more than anything I have ever done. At 10 o'clock we landed at Jodhpur, where Gavin and Michael were staying. They met me in a chocolate Rolls allotted to them alone for their stay. We tore to the palace, snatched up a packet of sandwiches and a bottle of beer, said good morning to Allenby[1] who was there also (as Gavin remarked 'one's only Field-Marshal') (Lady Allenby asked if I was flying to England. I answered no, my parents had demanded written permits – she said 'Are you *so* precious?'), dashed up onto a hill to catch a view of the old town and the fort, which is simply astounding, and whirled down to the aerodrome where I precipitated myself into the aeroplane with many goodbyes to Michael whom I shan't see out here again. We flew all across the Sind desert, 400 miles of utter desolation, tiny bushes in sand, and got to Hyderabad (Sind), a town where every house is surmounted by a wind vane – so that it is literally a town of windmills and from the air looks as though it had been constructed by a German film producer. Another hour brought us to Karachi, which filled me with strange emotions – I never thought to go back there. The ugliness was worse than before. I felt terribly tired after the flight – about 700 miles (it takes 36 hours in the train), I can't think how I did a week of it before. But it still seems the only rational way to go home. However I won't, you needn't worry. My passage is definitely booked for the 5th of April – I shall be home about the 19th or 20th, if I don't stop in Egypt. Thank God a month has gone but for one day.

[. . .] Last night we motored out to a village (to study the village light) and were received by the headman and taken into his house – it was most interesting, great mud room – the woman crouching over a little fire in a corner – they didn't dine till eleven he said. We went into smaller houses too. The headman salaamed to our feet and presented us with sugar-cane, in fact he asked us to dinner – but I can't face Indian food even in palaces.

Everyone here is sewn all over with looking-glass. The little boys wear caps like Norman helmets, covered with it, I am trying to get some in a remote state called Khaipur where we are motoring today. The women wear bodices of it which are most beautiful. But all the embroidery with it is done at home – so the stuff is difficult to come by. I

---

1. Field Marshal Edmund Allenby, 1st Viscount Allenby, was on a visit to Jodhpur with his wife.

am travelling with a Burmah-Shell man I knew vaguely at Oxford. We dined last night with an engineer. The B.S. man said that he didn't like Von Stroheim's *Wedding March* because it shewed two old men drunk and that was bad for Indians. I lost my temper for once and told him just what I thought of him and Anglo-India in general. Oh they are contemptible. It makes me quite ill with rage, and as for New Delhi *nothing* is too bad to say about it.

Love from
Bobs

6 February 1930   Taj Mahal Hotel, Bombay

Darling Mibble

I suppose we shall have to get used to one another's typing – as it is so much less labour than writing. I should have thought you must have found it such a pleasant change to be able to read my letters – *if* you ever open them. I am here in this mausoleum of a hotel again – after an absolutely frightful journey from Karachi – two days and two nights in a tiny metre-gauge train with the dust of the Sind desert covering everything, and clogging the typewriter on which I was trying to compose prose poems on how Burmah-Shell considers the needs of rich and poor alike. The railway officials in the goodness of their hearts had had the sort of leather mattresses on which one sits and sleeps extra-sprung – so that with every jolt one bounced out of reach of the typewriter or fell heavily on top of six letters at once, all of which caused considerable surprise to a Jodhpuri motor dealer opposite, who said he had been the first motor-dealer in Rajputana ten years ago, that everyone had laughed at him, that he consequently made a fortune, was just going round the world for pleasure, and was going to stock aeroplanes when he got back. In the dining-cars on this line – which were attached solely for me – there are 'complaint books', in reality albums of praise. I copied some of the entries:

'Food genuine and very neat – Fellow of Bombay University'
'As the great lexicographer says "A good breakfast is worth a king's ransom"'

And then the inevitable British officer: 'Cheese toast very cheery'

On the way down from Sukkur I spent a morning in Hyderabad – which really is the maddest place on earth, as every house has a wind-vane to catch the breeze – it is as though one had got inside one of those rather *bad* cubist pictures. I have also bought yards and yards of cheap printed stuffs, with the most amusing patterns on them – and shall have a curtain orgy when I get back.

This hotel is fabulously expensive – rather more than the Ritz – it is such a comfort to think that the company is paying. I have also *made* them take a ticket for me back to Calcutta on the P. and O. blue train that leaves tomorrow – also at an enhanced price. But I believe it is incredibly comfortable, and I am so tired with travelling that I need it. I was working out that by the time I get home I shall have travelled 30,000 miles, of which only 12,000 will be accounted for by the journeys out and back. I do wish I could fly back – it seems so stupid not to, when I am so rushed – I am now bitterly regretting that I can't spend a fortnight more here when my job is over just to see one or two more things and possibly Gandhi – but I don't think it can be managed – having today received Papa's wire re completion of book. As a matter of fact only yesterday I wrote out a wire to him asking him to cancel all negotiations, as I had decided to do my novel first – but then thinking it over, I came to the conclusion that I have accumulated so much material here for a series of *essays*, that I should want to do them anyhow – and as I want some money at once, I might as well do them first. The air and the Tibet pieces, which you will have seen, are to be the only bits in diary form – that is chronological – and even those will be much cut down. The rest will be definite essays on different subjects. I think this will be best – as a diary of all that I have done would fill the *Encyclopaedia Britannica*. I am very anxious to hear what you think of the bit I have sent – if you DARE criticise it – still if you must, remember that it will be considerably pruned, and made as concise as possible.

As for my novel, I am really getting rather excited about it, I intend it to be the first book into which I put all that I can put, all that I have been collecting in my mind since I came down from Oxford. I intend it to be most perfectly constructed – if I have any power of construction. It is to be called *The Viceroy*, and the setting is to be largely New Delhi, but with a good deal of England. I intend to plan out every paragraph first on a vast bit of paper – as I have got so tired of the ill-put-together modern 'slice of life'. I am longing to get at it.

If it wasn't for Europe I should be very happy living in India. There is no one to talk to, it is true. But it is such an *interesting* country, as one can study both the east and the west at the same time – and everywhere one goes is different. I don't think there can be anywhere in the world with numerically so many interesting things to observe – the variety is almost grotesque. But of course there is nothing civilised in the European sense of the word, and one starves from mental inanition. The English are not really a civilised race – though their efficiency is almost a work of art. Some people think that a revolution really is likely to break out any moment. For the time being there is a railway strike here – and they have been trying to derail the trains. So my blue train tomorrow will probably be upset. [. . .]

I hope your cold is better. How heavenly it will be arriving home when I do – just at the very best time of all – I hope you will meet me! Send me a snowdrop or something in an envelope. I shall now be stuck in Calcutta for the rest of the time – but by the time you get this it will be more than half over. Have the masks arrived?

Best love from
Bob

10 February 1930   Calcutta

Darling Mibble

I was so delighted with your letter about New Delhi and must answer it at once. I had no idea you had any feelings about it. To me it was always merely nebulous, and I went there rather sceptical. It is so much greater than anything of Lutyens' in England. However I can't begin all over again about it. But the whole thing is just what you describe it – romantic. My last view, from the air, with the dawn just beginning to gild the towers and domes, was like a mirage of European genius set down in this forbidding country. Poor Lutyens – he has been aged and really wounded by the struggle to get it done – and then so imperfectly according to his plans. His voice became really tragic when he described how the chief aim of the lay-out was frustrated by Baker, whom he called in to help him. The man who was with him described to me his almost unbearable excitement coming out this year, as the train approached to shew him the dome for the first time; he began looking out of the window eighty miles away! Lutyens wrote me a very interesting letter about the 'field of New Delhi covered in lost possibilities'. I will enclose it if I can find it – also one from Lady Irwin. Please keep them.

I also enclose an article I have sent to the *New Statesman*, though in another more polished version. It strikes me as miserably inadequate, and even so is really too long for them to publish. *What I cannot understand* is how the ordinary person can be so insensitive to it. It has the two most obvious beauties, as obvious as an opera setting – colour and size. In the article, I changed the phrase 'as emotional as an opera' to 'as emotional as Brahms and Beethoven in their grand moods'. This very well describes it, I think, or rather the effect it had on me. I do wish we could be there together. It is the only thing I should really like to bring you to India for. If you *care* to motor through Persia and sleep in a tent we can do it one day. [. . .]

I have decided to give you another Christmas and birthday present, now that I can momentarily afford it. I know it isn't usual for children to send money to their parents. But your remark about the Italian Exhibition really terrifies me. 'I hope I shall see it,' you say. I don't think you realise what it is at all. To see the *Birth of Venus* is an experience that will never be repeated in anybody's lifetime. But I know what those awful Wednesdays in London always are. So will you go with Lucy as a present from me on *Friday* the 5/- entrance day, when there won't be a crowd, and in addition spend a *comfortable* day, doing nothing else, and lunching in comfort at the Ritz (which I think costs 7s. 6d.). You might order a table beforehand on your way from the station, but I don't think it is necessary.

What has really driven me to this pitch of excitement is that I suddenly learn that they have brought over some of the sculpture from the Bargello. One *can* see Italian pictures outside Italy, and get a very good idea of them. But never the early Renascence sculpture. There is nothing so lovely in the whole world. And they have got the best of it all – Donatello's *David*. Look at this and then you will see how futile the ancient Greeks were. I regret not being able to go to this exhibition with you more than anything else about not coming home. It is an exhibition of all the things that transformed me from an idiot into a person when I went to Italy with Lord Beauchamp seven years ago (how much longer it seems). If you feel annoyed at my sending the money, I will keep all the things I am bringing home for myself. But for God's sake go, and go in the way I ask. If you don't I swear I shall fly home. And anyhow you owe it to Lucy.

I had a very comfortable journey back. The blue train is magnificent – white carriages labelled in gold 'Indian Imperial Mail'. There were roses in pink bowls on the dining-tables. Every coach was filled with soldiers armed to the teeth, as they expected trouble owing to a strike. But unfortunately nothing happened. Now I am very glad to be back. Intensive travelling in India is very exhausting. My servant is worn to a tooth pick.

Thank you so much for the snowdrop. How dreadful that it should have come up without me [. . .] Yes – Nancy [Mitford] has called herself engaged to Hamish[1] for a long time. It appals me, as I am devoted to her, and he, though charming, is more typically Rosslyn than you can imagine – not immoral, but without morals, which is always frightening. I am afraid that she suddenly felt herself becoming spinsterish when Diana [Guinness] married after her first season. Nina's [Seafield] young man I don't know. Yes I quite agree with you about Shane Leslie.[2] There is nothing more unspeakably loathesome than the confusion of sex and religion. However I must admit that I have always observed it as one of the chief characteristics of Anglo-Catholics of the Oxford brand (Clonmore excepted). That is why I so dislike them – or one of the reasons.

My article in the *Burlington* seems to have caused some interest. I had a frantic letter from Frank Rutter, the art critic of the *Sunday Times*, asking permission to use my two pictures of Mount Sinai in a book of his on Greco, to appear in the spring. I wired back that I was unwilling – which I think was reasonable, considering the tremendous labour involved getting them. And they are, after all, one of the strongest points of my case, and the case in question is entirely my own idea and has never been put forward by anyone else. I hated not letting him have

---

1. Hamish St Clair-Erskine.
2. First cousin of Winston Churchill, he aspired towards a drawing together of Catholics and Protestants in Ireland. Author of *The End of the Chapter* and biographies of Cardinal Manning, Mark Sykes, Mrs Fitzherbert, etc.

them, as so many people have been so very generous to me with their materials. But I think I was justified. The proofs of the illustrations have arrived – or at least some of them. They have done very well with the bad photographs – but not so well with the good. However I think they will be all right and am feeling more confident about the book.[1] I set great store by it – as it is my first really original bit of work in the intellectual sense and will, I hope, be a definite addition to the history of European art. But I foresee a great labour getting it out. [. . .]

It is still very cold here after Bombay. I went to bed in the train with the fan on, and woke up four hours later to find my breath freezing. I have lost the Lutyens' letter – a pity – it was amusing. [. . .]

Best love
from
Bobs

20 February 1930   4 Elysium Row, Calcutta

Darling Mibble

[. . .] I am glad you liked the MSS. I myself read it over again – it seems quite amusing I think and fairly interesting – but a lot wants cutting out. There are far too many sententious passages. I shall get on with it on the boat.

The illustrations for the other book have begun to arrive from Routledge – they have really been very successful with them. I wish it was out.

I am now stuck in Calcutta permanently and it is getting hot and I am thoroughly bored. There is a holiday on March 3rd – a Monday – so I shall try and get away on Friday night and go down to the Black Pagoda, near Puri, taking my food etc. There is a small bungalow there which one can get the use of – otherwise nothing but this gorgeously beautiful temple – did I tell you about it? I could spend 3 days there all alone and should enjoy it. *Far* the best thing in India. [. . .]

I am getting so fat I can't turn over in bed. It is too awful. I pine for

---

1. *The Birth of Western Painting.*

Mrs Clements's cooking in order to take it off. I hope you still have nothing for lunch.

I went to Tatanagar this week – one of the biggest steel factories in the world – great seas of molten metal dropping from the ceiling or popping out of the floor at every turn – most exhausting. My servant, carrying the camera, became so alarmed that he refused to come any further. I went to see our tin plate works nearby – most advanced – they do it in so many days, whereas every other factory takes so many more. Run by 2 Welsh-Americans, whose fathers were South Wales tinplate workers – a kind of tinplate dynasty. One cannot help being struck by the American idea of living. This man, that is the Manager, had worked for 20 years as a factory hand in America and his wife was of the same class – yet they gave one better food and had far pleasanter rooms etc. than the average so-called English gentleman out here. The whole visit was very tiring, a day among molten metal with furnaces of 4,000 Fahr. fizzling about one's ears, in between 2 sleepless nights in the train.

We have a new friend in the Rajah of Nilgiri, a feudatory chief of Orissa, who ascertains the truth of murder cases in his state by going about in disguise like the Caliph Harun al Raschid and distributing oranges and sweets. Fortunately he is not a Highness, so conversation proceeds smoothly. He has a passion for the cinema.

The Carl Rosa Opera company has arrived. It did *Maritana*.[1] Do you remember that song:

> 'Now let me like a soldier DIE
>   Ti tum ti tum ti tum
> 'My breast expanding for THE BALL
>   Ti tum ti tuum TUM'

Gavin and I laughed till we ached, to the embarrassment of Nilgiri who thought opera was serious.

I have been reading Bertrand Russell's *Marriage and Morals*. It is a pity you don't – a very good, sincere, and witty book, like all his books. It would explain to you the modern outlook on such things – even if you didn't agree with his arguments. I don't ask you to alter your attitude,

---

1. Opera by W. V. Wallace, 1845.

but simply to *understand* the other and not to regard an outlook which is not based on Christo-Jewish hypocrisy as merely filthy. Otherwise my novels (if I ever write them), and I should imagine Lucy's too, will have to go to press without your corrections – which would be a disaster.

I am determined now to fly to the Cape. When does the service start? I see that Beaverbrook has linked himself with Rothermere – hopeless – I thought he was better than that.

> Best love from
> Bobs

26 February 1930   4 Elysium Row, Calcutta

Darling Mibble

Thank you *so much* for your birthday letter and all its wishes. Today it is – a little cooler, and February nearly up. In fact after getting this, you won't need to write here again I don't think. I shall leave Calcutta D.V. on the last day of March and either go to Agra to see that Taj or else to Ahmedabad to see Gandhi. As the latter seems to be planning his own arrest, it may be too late by then. But on the whole I feel he is more interesting than the Taj and shall choose him if he is still at large. I have already started to make arrangements.

The sketch book and pencils have arrived after a delay at the customs. Thank you so much. I am afraid I shall have scarcely any chance to use them now – but hope to get down to the Black Pagoda next weekend for 3 days – draw it – one *could* make something lovely out of it [drawing follows] a long building supported on wheels with a horse at the end – exquisite it is – but it may be rather difficult.

You say you are spending money on me for my return. I am longing to see what. But don't do anything to my two rooms, that is as far as decoration is concerned, as I have bought a mass of stuff out here for curtains and I am planning them entirely done up in my own way. [. . .] I would much rather you didn't do *anything at all* till I arrived – for as I say I want to furnish my own rooms and our tastes do not agree. In any case I *pray* you allow me to come home to plain walls. In fact I shall wire from Athens to find out and stay there till I know!

I am glad you were going to call on the Guy Wyndhams.[1] I can't imagine why you didn't before. Her mother is the most incredible old woman called Ada Leverson, with tight pink curls all over her head, who used to write for *Punch* in the 90s. She is a great friend of Harold's [Acton]. In fact they are scarcely ever apart.

My first articles for Burmah-Shell are now in proof. They look rather well and are full of poetry. The whole thing is becoming an awful effort – as I have to do it all single-handed. My elderly brown typist now talks about 'we'. 'We must get so many articles out today' – 'We can't sit here with such a draught' etc. – I employ him in the evenings as well to dictate from my notes on New Delhi etc.

One of my Eton fags, by name of Walsh, has arrived out here and apparently told someone that I was the only possible person in the house, apart from the fact that he was deaf and played the violin I can't remember anything about him – but have asked him to come and see me.

It will be heavenly coming home to the spring. Oh! this country – how people can live here – yet it has its advantages over England in the matter of pay. Anyhow I shall return home a fully qualified advertising consultant.

Yes – the Waughs – I had a letter from Evelyn poor creature about his divorce – he is still paying for the furniture in the flat now inhabited by the other Evelyn[2] and Heygate. Heygate, I remember, you liked *so much* when he came over – in contradiction to Evelyn. As a matter of fact he is quite harmless and the most irresponsible person in existence. But they have both behaved abominably. Evelyn's book *Vile Bodies* he says is making him rich and famous. [. . .]

Nina's husband is a drunkard, a bastard and an adventurer. He beat the secretary out of the house and compromised her into marriage. So every letter says that arrives. I don't suppose it is true. But he is evidently quite awful. I suppose that there will be another divorce.

I am writing in the office. My typist has arrived, very smart in a blue collar. I must get to work.

Best love from
Bobs

---

1. Colonel Guy Wyndham and his wife Violet. Her mother was Ada Leverson ('The Sphinx'), a great friend of Oscar Wilde's.
2. Evelyn Gardner (Waugh) had left her husband for John Heygate and was now living with him in the flat in Canonbury Square rented in her name.

26 March, 1930   Hongkong House, Calcutta

Darling Mibble

This, God willing, is the last letter I shall ever write you from this inferno of sweat and boredom. Today is Wednesday. I have a plan to leave on Monday night, reach Agra Tuesday night, spend two days there, catch the boat mail early Friday morning and embark at Bombay on Saturday morning. The journey will be *awful* sharing a cabin and very hot – but I am looking forward to Cairo and still more to Athens.

Really this month has been one long stretch of misery – ending up last weekend with a disgusting cold, which even now prevents me from breathing. The heat is vile – I feel utterly exhausted and can't even take my Empire building walks in the morning. I shall never become a permanent resident of India – though I believe all this ill-health is caused by boredom more than climate. However my eyes are better, which is something and I think they will get quite all right, next week – except what is one to do when travelling but read? The Nationalist press has called me 'a propagandist with a fat emolument'. Its representative appeared this morning offering to insert an apology, if *we* would insert our advertisements. I asked him 'wasn't he a blackmailer and didn't he mind his paper appearing so foolish to its readers.' 'Besides,' I said, 'you called me a propagandist with a fat emolument,' and burst out laughing. He was rather embarrassed. They are so stupid [. . .]

Thursday
Another filthy sweaty day. I am pursued by the ten plagues, last night at 1 a.m. in spite of a mosquito net, a small beetle crawled down my ear and started flapping about on the drum. I had to wake Gavin and induce it out with light and forceps. This morning I have something in my right eye, which isn't there at all of course but causes the most acute irritation.

I heard from Mark that I am expected to stay at the Residency in Cairo, *if* the Prince of Wales doesn't arrive at the same moment blast him. If he does I shall turn Republican even before Princess Elizabeth ascends the throne, Mark is having the time of his life, an orgy of royalty. It will be amusing to see him in that atmosphere. He says that Michael remarked a new note of command in his voice.

It made me too unhappy for words to think of not seeing Ella again – just once. As you say there never could be another such dog. When you think of how one's whole life in the forest has been bound up with her, and all those sticks and stones, it seems like the end of a phase – and probably is. She was the reflection of all our characters. I am sure the spaniel is odious – do get rid of it. Send it to Northumberland. We don't *want* a spaniel. They are such caricatures of dogs. [. . .]

The *New Statesman* have returned the article on New Delhi not unnaturally. It isn't good really. *Of course* Lutyens has a grievance – it has soured his whole life.

I have nothing to say except that a number of Indians that I have made friends with will be in London this summer. Nice ones are so very nice.

I am longing to be home – and can't think why I am stopping on the way – except that I really feel I want a holiday before beginning the struggle with new work in London. They tell me that I must certainly call on Shell in London. This really has been a very big publicity campaign – and it is now in full swing – I don't know what effect it is having, but there has been nothing like it in India before and people are rather surprised. Indians find the articles rather interesting as articles. I will bring home a complete set for you to laugh at!

Best love from
Bobs

I suppose the snow has destroyed all the flowers.

11 April 1930   SS *Ranchi*

Darling Mibble

[. . .] How any sane human being can ever go on this kind of voyage for pleasure is beyond comprehension. The BOREDOM!! When I left Calcutta, my eyes went wrong again, rather badly – so that, although I read nothing while at Agra, I was still debarred from using them when I came on board. For the first two days I nearly went mad, and became so ill with sheer rage that I eventually decided to go blind rather than die and started correcting my proofs (of the book on paintings) – with the result that I was immediately restored to health, and have had no more headaches since.

Fortunately, Lady Guernsey is on board, chasing home after her son Aylesford, who left clandestinely by the previous boat to marry an adventuress called Amber. She is very amusing and can at least talk one's own language, and so has made all the difference to the voyage. Miller, one of the lights of Burmah-Shell (the very name makes me feel sick, like Wolfgang did), had very kindly arranged for me to sit at a table with the social lights of Bombay, to whom he introduced me. It was so awful that I just left it after two meals, with the result that they have all cut me since. The whole management of the boat is that of a boarding-house in 1889 – vivid communal life – bridge tournaments – deck games, for whose prize-fund I had much pleasure in not subscribing – no smoking in the dining-room – and everything done as a favour by the stewards. With great difficulty, I have managed to get a very comfortable and large single cabin to work in in the daytime. Lady Guernsey had it. But it was next to that of the Afghan minister to Egypt, whose five brats and God knows how many women emit the most bestial noises, punctuated by loud screams when they are very properly beaten, night and day. She moved – and I got the use of it for nothing. But – a table – such a thing had never been heard of. Eventually I built one out of boards and string. My companion in my cabin proper is named Camps and travels in cycles. He hums getting up in the morning – the sort of tune which is played when Princess Mary opens a maternity home on the Pathé Gazette – and also eats oranges and Pepsodent at the same time. Blood, whom we came to like so much at Gyantse, is on board but second-class, where I spend most of my time. He is very nice. But I dread his wife.

The other passengers include Kapurthala, with whom I had a long conversation in the 'we princes' vein, and Sir Dorab and Lady Tata, the richest couple in India. The Maharajah of Rajpipla, who has 'a bad reputation with white women', has offered special prizes for the sports, and is consequently much sought after. There are numerous knights of the Albert A. Biggs type. In fact, as you can imagine, it is a very cheery crowd and most people are enjoying themselves fraightfully – at least they were till we got into the Red Sea – today and yesterday have been fearful – everyone mopping themselves at meals, and half the women collapsed – but I don't mind it as much as others, and having been at work haven't really noticed it. I am beginning to think that I have lost the capacity for leisure – though I plan to do nothing but enjoy myself in Cairo and Athens before starting again in England. [. . .]

The more I read my book, the better I think it, and am longing to get it out. The illustrations have really been extraordinarily successful.

I disembarked at Aden, and saw the stuffed mermaid – and also went for a long walk on the surrounding hills. Just as it got dark, the path ended. I could not possibly have found my way back. So I dug my heels into the mountain, and slid a thousand feet, bringing most of the mountain with me.

Agra was very interesting, and I am glad I went there. The Taj is beautiful in spite of itself. I went to Fatehpur Sikri, Akbar's capital, and did quite a good sketch, which has compensated for the failure of the Black Pagoda one. I am so looking forward to shewing you my drawings – I can't imagine why, as they are extremely uninteresting and have no merit – but I feel they convey something, to you at least, which nothing else does.

I can't tell you how ill and wretched I felt when I left Calcutta – reaction I suppose – HOW I hate that place – I really can't think of it, or of the products of oil, or of business in any form. I didn't know I was hating it all so much at the time, thank Heaven. Had I left an afternoon later, I should never have got my train owing to the riots that broke out. It is really rather unfortunate to have left India at such an interesting moment. I feel I shall have to go back. How delicious it will be arriving just as the trees are coming out. That plane just opposite Sir Robert's is the one that always greets one on the way from the station. Having said this I suppose it will have blown down. [. . .]

I must now go and join the eternal cocktail party that never ends. I will say for the boat that drinks are cheap. They also have matches like trees, and excellent Stilton. Otherwise there is nothing to be said at all – except that I have now had rows with so many people that I shall be spared a number of expensive tips.

I will write from Cairo, and let you know definitely from Athens when I get back. [. . .] Will you or will you not meet me in London? Don't if you don't want to. It will be just as nice to see you running out of the porch. But it would be very pleasant if you did, all the same, though possibly not worth the money. However I *may* arrive on a Wednesday. But I think I shall be back before that. It depends how much I spend in Cairo and Athens.

Best love from
Bobs

The Afghans are at it again.

15 April 1930   The Residency, Cairo

Darling Mibble

I arrived here to find your letter waiting, thank you so much – I am so sorry about the decoration and my alarm – but I really have a terror of wall-papers. However your description of my room now sounds really too delightful, and thank you so much for having had it done. I am sure I shall like it.

I am enjoying myself here very much, having luckily forestalled the Prince of Wales by 3 days – very comfortable and *such* a relief to get out of the Anglo-Indian atmosphere and off that filthy boat – a dreadful drive from Suez at breakneck speed, 70 miles – as all the others were having the day of their lives in Egypt before rejoining the boat at Port Said – and were consequently in a hurry. The High Commissioner is in London – but Louise[1] is here and *very interesting indeed* about Egypt and the Lloyd regime. They have had an appalling time here obstructed at every turn by their own compatriots.

The pyramids and the Sphinx lie in a suburb surrounded by advertisement hoardings. One would never have believed them to be *so* uninteresting. No doubt if one had come on them in the midst of the desert, all alone, they would have seemed very impressive. But the pyramids are no more interesting than Silbury. The mosques here are very fine. I haven't yet seen the Museum of the Tutankhamen things but am going this afternoon, also to call on the secretary of the Archbishop of Mount Sinai – and David Rice's brother who is here in the Welsh Guards.

I still feel very tired and exhausted – a kind of reaction. Caselli[2] has asked me to stay in Alexandria and says that he may fetch me in his very fast car – which would be heavenly. I am just trying to telephone to him. Anyhow I shall leave tomorrow to enable the servants to prepare for H.R.H. and stay two nights there. It is an interesting place. [. . .]

I don't feel like a long letter as I shall be home so soon – how lovely it will be.

Best love from
Bobs

---

1. Lady Loraine.
2. An Alexandrian Greek businessman.

21 April 1930   Athens

Darling Mibble

Three letters waiting – thank you so much. Thank God this ought to be the last I write. This journey has really cured me of all desire to move out of the forest for years. I feel absolutely worn away, and even half an hour's conversation leaves me absolutely exhausted. My eyes are still very tiresome – but I think it is just general debility, and will get all right as soon as I am in the garden with Gerda to play with and you to talk to.

I had a very interesting time in Alexandria. We went for a long drive in the desert, and I had an audience of Meletios the Patriarch. The crossing here was *awful* – very rough, a very small Rumanian boat, reeking of stale scent and filled with men whose faces were azure with powder and German women whose faces looked as though they had been polished with a wire brush.

Everyone in the world is here, including the Sitwells, who arrive back from Delphi tonight. They have just been to all my pet Byzantine places so I am longing to talk to them. Leonard [Bower] is here – also Miss Kephala, whose dog-tooth is longer than ever. Zervos has produced a vast book about nothing, and is giving me a copy bound in gold, together with a basket of coffee and doubtless a sponge. Everyone is very nice, and I seem quite well known! I am going round the Byzantine society people tomorrow to tell them how sensible I am of the honour conferred on me. As a matter of fact it is rather distinguished, as the only other honorary members are the most notable scholars, with world-wide reputations.

Of course you *wouldn't* like my memoirs. I *told* you that they are meant to be rewritten, but I had no time to do it before I sent them off. *I* think the first one is rather well-constructed. Don't, will you? Please tell Father that they are to be published at once.

I think it is very funny your having to sign that assurance about my not performing the banjo. I hope you do like it. The painting is really rather a commonplace thing – but the banjo is very rare, as Tibetans themselves told me. However I shall soon see for myself whether it does look nice about the room – if it doesn't out it goes. I think some of the stuffs will amuse you – though they are of very poor quality.

Unless you hear otherwise, please meet the 7.35 on *Monday* the 28th. Don't meet me in London, as I am not certain which way I am coming. [. . .]

Goodbye, how wonderful it seems to be coming back – I really have got the never-again feeling (but have no doubt it will wear off).

Best love from
Bob

I don't think B. Russell has a dirty mind – rather a dirty wit, which I enjoy. No, I don't know whether I agree with him particularly, I have no view on social subjects – but I like his attitude.

5

Russia
1932

ON HIS return from India in the spring of 1930 Robert spent the rest
of that year at home completing the text of *The Birth of Western
Painting*, which finally appeared in November. He also gave much
time and effort to refurbishing his impressions of New Delhi, the masterpiece of Lutyens whom he admired with such fervour, accompanied by the
denigration of Herbert Baker, architect of the buildings flanking the
Viceroy's palace. The following January the *Architectural Review* devoted
a whole issue to Robert's lyrical exposition of Lutyens' design. His
descriptions of the architect's triumphant use of native forms and materials
are almost as vibrant as the buildings themselves. This fanfare of praise, so
rare with Robert, was accompanied by the best architectural photographs
he ever took, using the wide-lensed camera he describes in his letter of 28
November 1929. This number of the *Architectural Review*, often quoted,
has since become a classic. Robert concludes: 'But above all, in every rib
and moulding, in every block of stone, he has revealed and given life to that
perfectly balanced sanity and proportion which is the distilled essence of
beauty and which Europe calls the humanist ideal.' Lutyens wrote: 'Your
article in the *Arch. Rev.* cheers, heartens and amuses me.'

In February 1931 Robert took a flat in York Buildings, Adelphi. G. M.
Young, who lent him furniture for it, described the street 'as where David
Copperfield played as a boy'. Robert was still working for Shell and he
instigated and wrote the catalogue for the Shell exhibition held in June,
which gave Shell an opportunity to display their patronage, under publicity manager Jack Beddington, of such artists as Paul Nash, Algernon
Newton, Mcknight Kauffer, etc., who had all designed posters for Shell.
The success of this exhibition enabled Robert to keep his job until the end
of the year.

Robert's other effort, a short book entitled *An Essay on India*, met with
little success when published in April 1931 except among the 'Young

Europeans' of India. His main contentions were that in spite of Gandhi, whom he admired, self-government must come eventually and that the British, though he admitted their genius in administration, could not maintain their racial superiority and lack of social contact with Indians indefinitely. The fact that this essay made so little impact could be attributed in some degree to the deepening financial crisis.

After covering a Byzantine exhibition in Paris for various periodicals, Robert set off in July on a lonely expedition to Epirus in the footsteps of Lord Byron and later Robert Curzon. Besides visiting the monasteries of the Meteora he explored and photographed the fortress of Ali Pasha. Robert seems to have been annoyed by the chauffeur lent him by the local Governor, from whom he received this letter in reply to his complaints:

Dear Mr Byron

I thank you for your letter. It was by the help of Mr Atchley that I managed to read it. I would be very happy had I been able to send you, as a present, the head of your chauffeur. But unfortunately we are very far from the time of my predecessor Ali Pasha. I called my chauffeur and I reproached him. If it will be repeated I shall send you his head as well as his feet.

Sincerely yours
G. Modis

This brief excursion hardly lifted Robert's mood of depression and restlessness. 'Existence in London is merely a form of suspended animation and, as soon as I can get away and do something worthwhile I shall do so', he wrote to his mother. But first there was the growing financial collapse of the country to consider, which was absorbing people's attention to the exclusion of all other problems. A great many families, Robert's included, lost up to half their income as shares slumped, in many cases never to be recovered. Firms like Shell reduced their employees' salaries by a quarter, others were made redundant. In September, for the first time, the pound lost its gold backing. With this shock many thought the whole social order in danger; indeed Bob Boothby told Robert that Lloyd George had remarked to him 'that to his mind the peril of 1916–17 is as nothing compared with that of the moment'. Robert urged his father to organise at least some self-sufficiency in growing food for the family, so grave did he consider the crisis. Michael Rosse wrote: 'I can suppose farming will be the one thing that will pay if the pound does collapse. I shall make a fortune out of my ears of wheat on my much complained of farm in Yorkshire.'

The crisis was international. Robert's project of an exhibition of Greek panel paintings, in collaboration with Eric Maclagan, Director of the V. &

A. Museum, was reluctantly turned down by collectors in Athens who were unable to support the expense involved in the shipping and insurance of the panels. Relieved of the work of mounting this exhibition, Robert began to concentrate on a visit to Russia, collecting commissions for articles and enlisting the help of Stephen Gaselee, Librarian of the Foreign Office. Through him Robert made contact with the British Ambassador in Russia, Sir Esmond Ovey, who was cordiality itself, and on 30 December 1931 Robert left to stay with the Oveys in Moscow, in the hope that Michael Rosse would follow him later. Another friend, Adrian Stokes, took over the lease of his flat in York Buildings.

Robert's chief concern in visiting Russia was to avoid all political controversy and to pursue his object; the study of Russian fresco painting and its breakaway from Byzantine influence to which, initially, it owed its inspiration. This divergence was completed by the Fall of Constantinople on the one hand and on the other by the emergence of the painter Roublev. His genius crystallized the more poetic leanings of the Russian painters into a national school. This style of ikon painting was only later formalized into those ideal representations of the Virgin and Child or saints, peering out of their carapaces of silver.

---

4 January 1932

British Embassy, Moscow

Darling Mother

I can scarcely know where to begin I want so much to describe this place to you, but I think you will have to wait till I come home. Really I think the Kremlin and the Red Square (which has *always* been called the Red Square) must be the most romantically beautiful thing in the world. It is fantasy on so huge a scale that it becomes magnificent. All a lovely soft pink brick with the golden eagles of the Tsars still glittering from the top of the towers – a church at the end of the square looks like a coconut-shy of coloured pineapples and onions – the ground all white – and Lenin's tomb in highly polished pink and black marble – rather like an austere public lavatory – but impressive as a mass. I stood in a queue to see him yesterday, next to a young Turcoman in a huge sheepskin cap, who looked an aristocrat of artistocrats among these hideous uniformed hangdog creatures. Inside, Lenin lay in a sort of glass cradle

– a dear little man with a beard and moustache the colour of dead daffodils. Then when I came out one of the great clocks began to chime – a marvellous set of deep bells, and thousands of rooks flew cawing overhead – the snow was falling and the lights coming out – and I fell in with a company of the Red Army, looking like goblins, and all carrying skis – they started to sing some song in parts, as they crossed one of the bridges, with the towers of the Kremlin standing up in a row behind them – it was more like a Russian opera than you can believe.

And then to come back here and find oneself in a marooned English household with excellent food and a surfeit of chess, makes it almost impossible to realise that Moscow is just outside the windows. The Oveys are very kind indeed – and I hope I shall be able to insinuate myself into some of the vacant staff quarters after this week and mess with the staff – which would give me more spare time – at present my bedroom leads out of the dining-room, which means I can't brush my hair if I am late for meals.

I have written to Michael [Rosse] and I hope he will come out here and join me – we may meet in Leningrad – and then return here and finally work down to the South and be in Constantinople the first week in *February*. But I don't know. If he doesn't come I may come straight home. Money is resolving itself – it was rather disconcerting having to give the porter at the station 9/–!

As for Bolshevism and the Five Year Plan and all that – it seems too uninteresting to bother with, besides its actual home – though I daresay I shall become interested. There can be no doubt but it is the most inefficient, smelly, uncomfortable, obtuse and intellectually blasted population in the world – but that, I suppose, is only a visitor's point of view, and it was probably worse before. The Ambassador takes a purely realistic point of view – and having suffered acutely from the Church and the Oil capitalists in Mexico, his last post, has no sympathy much for them here. He begs me to notice that all the population wear a bit of fur. So they do – but they scuttle about, noses to the ground, bumping into you without noticing, generally rather silent and strained – not particularly diseased or emaciated – but ignorant of what we mean by happiness. At least so it seems, it may have been always like that. The children are frisky enough though, and all look well and plump – I have frequent conversations in the street, trying to find places etc. but I never know what they mean. I tried bargaining for a second-hand book today – which wasn't at all well received!

Everything is very obstructive. I can't photograph anything I want – however I hope permission will eventually be forthcoming. It is not yet too cold so I want to get my photographing done while I may.

I spend all my time just walking about – in absolute bliss – though the pavements are glass. I daresay I shall get tired of it but I feel as if I should like to be here for months. There are two operas on and I hope to get to them soon. I must dress for dinner – so goodbye and do write, direct here until the next bag goes. I shan't be able to say anything much in my future letters as they are apparently opened. Will you please keep them all together as I may want to refer to them when I get back – as it seems a waste of time to spend daylight writing and at other times the Ambassador plays chess.

Love to everyone [. . .]

Bobs

11 January 1932   British Embassy, Moscow

Darling Mibble

I was so pleased to get your letter at last – though I must confess I have scarcely remembered that England exists during the last 10 days. The effect of this place is extraordinary – I haven't been so content since I landed in India – everything is *so* interesting. I never tire of just walking about. I have been to the opera or a concert for the last 5 nights – all tickets given free – communism has its advantages when the theatres are state run! The theatres are packed – it took us 25 minutes to get out the other night, and that was quick, as we had left our things in the car. It is pleasant, despite the almost grotesque discomfort and inconvenience of everything – after the supercilious emptiness of things in London. The smell I now don't notice.

Today we saw round the Kremlin – and actually took photographs in it though they have been snatched away by the Foreign Office, to make sure they are innocuous. It is incredible the suspicion with which one is regarded, if only they knew how little enmity I feel towards them – but there is no way of convincing them – so everything is as difficult as possible and considering how great are one's supposed potentialities for evil, they are really rather considerate. The treasures of the Kremlin are incredible – I was thrilled to find a real Byzantine vestment covered with crosses like you see in the frescoes in my book – it is the only one in the world.

A great blow is that Michael has been refused a visa – representations have been made, but I don't know how successful they will be. He only wired last night. It is an awful bore as I suppose I shall have to travel down to Odessa alone. But I don't know what I shall do. I go to Leningrad tomorrow – and thence to Novgorod to see the old churches, returning here today week. I am going to move into one of the wings and join the staff mess – so I shan't inflict myself on the Ambassador so much. They have been most awfully kind – and it means a good deal here when one has a car to go about in, as the distances are large, the pavements glass, and the trams like the Black Hole of Calcutta. There is so much I want to do that I may be here till the end of the month – that is if I can get my visa extended. I am *fascinated* by it all, by *Russia* and the Russian aesthetic.

[. . .] I have made friends with the daughter of the Norwegian Minister [Mlle Urbye] who is also a Byzantine maniac. I have seen the famous ikon – the Lady of Vladimir – which I describe in my book from reproduction – it alone would have made the journey worthwhile. I have never felt in better health, am eating little, and walk miles, also skate, the weather has been almost hot and I left off a vest today – it is odious when it thaws – and directly it begins to snow, everyone perks up and becomes cheerful. The audiences at the big theatre are very like Viennese – but last night I was really proletarian and had to bite and punch my way out. [. . .]

I am so looking forward to being at home when I come back – it is *lovely* to have no plans and nothing hanging over one to write. [. . .]

Love from Bobs

14 January 1932   British Consulate, Leningrad

Darling Mibble

This can go tomorrow by Finnish bag, so I can take the opportunity of telling you I am here, staying with Bullard, the Consul, who used to be in Athens. Tomorrow night I go off to Novgorod for 2 days with an interpreter – which will be interesting as no foreigners ever go there. How desperately uncomfortable it will be I shudder to think. There are no sleepers – but I have my flea bag. Fortunately the weather remains *comparatively* mild, though I may be glad of my absurd rubber gloves photographing today.

My last letter, you may have observed, was about nothing. But it went by post and they open them all. Even now I can't really begin to tell you what I have observed or gathered from others – it would take too long. But nothing could be more sinister than this regime based from top to bottom on a system of spying. No more shall I be deceived by English intellectuals who come on conducted tours – by our standards it is all *evil*, the sin against the Holy Ghost, the hatred of truth and denial of the spirit. If the five-year plan works, it will be the industrial barbarism come true – apes in possession of machines, violently, madly nationalistic, hating and hated by the opposing human beings. But will the five-year plan work? It may seem stupid to write like this after a fortnight here – but then there is the other side. They have cast off so much, all the futilities and extravagances that hamper us – somehow in spite of the devil worship, one breathes a fresher air, and however much their experiment may menace our civilisation, one can't wish it different or fail to wish them success up to a point. In fact one's mind is filled with a flat contradiction – apparently insoluble, and the only concrete impression is simply one of intense interest. Actually, I have almost gone out of my way to avoid the state manifestation of communism – factories, clubs, etc. – but there is a sort of frantic tension that obtrudes at every step – half fear, half sane effort – existing side by side with extreme chauvinism, fantastic incompetence, and a hideous lack of amenity. This isn't my imagination – for as you know I came expecting nothing in particular.

Anyhow I am very busy with my architecture and shall write of nothing else when I get home. I don't want to be prevented from coming here again. This town is magnificent but horribly decaying. I go back to Moscow on Tuesday to join the staff mess – If Michael can come out I shall wait for him – if not probably make my way south alone.

Don't shew this letter to people, as I loathe immature judgements mixed up with personal 'reactions', but perhaps it will interest you. I hope to catch the bag on Tuesday with another letter. Please understand that when letters come by post, there can be nothing in them.

Best love from
Bobs

19 January 1932   British Embassy, Moscow

Darling Mibble

Thank you so much for all your letters – three – which I found waiting for me here, when I arrived this morning from Leningrad. [. . .] Leningrad is a *lovely* city – mainly built in a peculiar empire style – and painted tawny yellow – the decoration, pillars, rustications, reliefs etc., in white – some of the palaces are mauve, others deep blue. The Hermitage is overwhelming – so that I did not look at it really at all. One great achievement was seeing all over the Yusupov Palace – our guide happening to be a member of the club that now occupies it, we just drove up and asked and it was arranged. Great magnificence and they are proud of it and take good care of the furniture – we saw the secret room where Rasputin ate the cakes and the cellar beneath, where he drank the wine – all very sinister. Felix Yusupov must have been far from pleasant. We also got into the old Embassy, now a school of political instruction or some nonsense.

Eventually, with guide, I went off to Novgorod – the oldest Russian town, a night's journey – it really was thrilling to be met at the station in the dark by a sledge and gallop through the sleeping town under a great arch into its local Kremlin where we put up in the former archbishop's palace, with a lovely view of the 11th century cathedral – of which I have done, or am doing a rather good sketch. There was food in plenty, though it was not cheap even with contraband roubles which I have now got at 52 to the £ instead of 6. Each day we drove out into the country to village churches to see frescoes of the same date and school as those on Athos – the earlier ones. I can't tell you how exhilarating it is to drive behind a really fast horse in a sledge – we went for miles along a frozen river in a snowstorm and biting wind – the horse, Princessa, was the pride of the proprietress who had just bought her – very fast and more at home on ice than earth – though of course there was some snow on it. When we got to the village, which just 'happened' in the middle of a field, we had to get the keys of the church – and went and sat in a peasant's house. The icon was still in the corner, the lamp burning before it. The women were making pies. There was a queer arrangement for making wool, and the usual embroidered towels. The house was wood, sheltered from the wind on one side by hay stacked up behind stakes. The church was at the end of the village – very old 12th century – 3 times as high as it was broad or long – standing by itself in a little graveyard, with wind and snow sweeping through the fir trees round the wall. I had just got inside, when there was a terrific roar – I rushed out, to see four grey aeroplanes with the red star on their underwings, boom overhead scarcely 50 feet above the tree-tops – and disappear across the desolate white landscape into the leaden sky. It really was the old Russia and the New.

We had another night in the train back, and having misjudged the time by an hour, almost missed it, and had to gallop full pelt through the streets, the driver yelling, and the luggage following on a baggage sledge with a grey who couldn't keep up with Princessa. We shared a compartment with an old man and his wife – four sleepers and no bugs. I spent next day in Leningrad, very sleepy, doing my drawing most of the time – and then caught the 'Red Arrow' express back here, arriving this morning – having had a frightful row in the train with two comrades who woke me up having a tea-party at 1.30 a.m. Now of course my luggage has been put into a room in the wing, and got locked up, and the key has gone off with the Chancery servant on some interminable errand – so I can't shave and am just going out to lunch with the Norwegian minister and feel rather embarrassed.

It is maddening about Michael, but I think I shall persist in my plans, and go south.[1] First, however, I want to go to Yaroslav and Vladimir – the other old Russian towns besides Kiev – in fact, having just come back from lunch, I have more or less arranged to go with the daughters of the Norwegian Minister, Mlles. Urbye – who are very pleasant and are interested in the same things as I am. [. . .]

I have at last got into my room and must go and shave before having tea with the Ambassador. Fortunately the Norwegians lunched by candlelight, so my beard did not show.

---

1. Michael Rosse was to change his plans and turn up after all.

My last letter from Leningrad was perhaps rather exaggerated. But it does get on one's nerves, the perpetual atmosphere of lies and spying, etc. It is curious, but I feel somehow that in Russia I have met my fate and shall come back here again and again – though it remains to be seen for the moment whether I can get my visa extended. [. . .] Will let you know my plans as soon as I know them myself.

Best love from
Bobs

6 February 1932   British Embassy, Moscow

Darling Mibble
    [. . .] We have had a fearfully busy week – doing all the things I ought to have done before, struggling with officials etc. They refused to extend my visa – this in itself took days of telephoning and rage to overcome. This morning at last I got leave to export all the books I have bought and also my diary and notes which have been placed in a package whose seal must not be broken till the frontier is passed. It has been very cold – 10 below zero Farh. – so that one's nose is always frozen within just as you described and the iron doorhandles burn one's hands. Today is a bit warmer. Michael is more cheerful, in fact quite enjoying himself. This morning we saw the Crown jewels guarded by a squadron of soldiers in the cellars of the state bank. They are seldom shown and are indeed very magnificent – nearly all 18th century and therefore lovely design – what was more they were mostly laid out on tables so that one could touch them, which I like. In the middle the light went out, which occasioned a great deal of agitation lest something should be missing when it went on again.
    We leave tomorrow (Monday) for Harkov and Kiev – and then to Odessa where we have reserved berths on a ship, Russian, leaving on the 15th for Constantinople. Possibly I may go off by myself on a boat to Batum and still get to Georgia and Tiflis as I told you I might in my last letter. [. . .] Anyhow I hope to be home by the end of the month. It will be lovely to have the spring to look forward to.

Best love from
Bobs

8 February 1932   Constantinople

Darling Mibble

Just a short line to say we are here at last after an incredibly exhausting journey from Moscow involving 5 nights out of 7 in different trains and five separate accidents in one of which 19 people were killed and 40 injured – this was the train ahead of us and we had to assist the wounded with the Ambassador's whisky. Finally our train to Odessa became ten hours late, and we had to wire to keep the boat – the port was wholly deserted, finally we found some customs officers and took them on board. Michael smuggled out a lot of roubles in the lining of his coat and I had stuck my remaining films into new boxes, which deception was successful. I got all my books – a whole suitcase full – out, diary, notes, plans, sketches etc. The boat was very small but pleasant food and a lot of Sarts from the western borders of China on their way to Mecca. Fortunately the Black Sea was calm – but no sooner had we entered the Bosporus than a blinding snowstorm descended and has made the town loathesome. We were met by a friend of Michael's from the American Embassy and also by someone from ours and a Cavass who did the necessary bribing.

I must say my nerves for the moment have more or less collapsed – but am spending most of my time in bed and shall be all right in a day or two. I go to see Whittemore,[1] the man in charge of S. Sophia tomorrow. It is curious to return to a place after 6 years, of which one has thought and written so much in the interval. I find my impression of S. Sophia fully confirmed – there is *no* building like it. Sometimes one finds one has just been building up a picture.

Now unfortunately I have to get up and dress and go to a diplomatic party – Americans – a frightful bore as I am not drinking and shall loathe everyone at it. [. . .] I shall probably stay here 10 days – or less – and then come home stopping a day or two in Paris.

                                                    Best Love from
                                                    Bobs

---

1. Professor Thomas Whittemore.

6

Persia
1933–1934

I N JUNE 1932 Robert held an exhibition at the Abdy Gallery of his
drawings and photographs of Greece, India and Russia. The year
ended by his producing a slim book, *An Appreciation of Architecture*,
published by Wisharts, a publication which he later regretted. The winter
of 1932–3 he was working at Savernake but was also brooding upon the
prospect of more travel. He was determined to push out further the horizon
of his experience and proceed with his plan for a preliminary exploration of
the major civilizations of the world before he was 30. As he wrote to his
mother: 'I am afraid I shall be permanently discontented until I am again
embarked on some *work* – not mere money making, but something calling
for a real mental effort.'

His first idea was to explore Chinese Turkestan. Penelope Chetwode,
with her contacts in India, attempted to help him: Michael Rosse offered to
come too, but final permission for the journey rested with the Foreign
Office and was refused. In retrospect, Robert thought that perhaps, in
spite of Aurel Stein's discoveries, there would hardly have been enough of
architectural interest for such a journey. Another idea was to explore the
early Armenian churches round Lake Van as described by Strzygowski and
the Marquis de Vogüé. But Sir George Clerk, Ambassador to Turkey, had
'no luck' in obtaining permission from the Turkish General Staff to allow
travellers near Lake Van, though the local authorities might have been
more lenient.

Since 1931 Robert had had in the back of his mind a journey to Persia
accompanied by Christopher Sykes, who knew the country well having
been an attaché at the Legation. From his studies of Mogul architecture in
India, and of what Islamic architecture he had come across, Robert felt he
was unable to identify the origins underlying such elaborate façades.
Photographs of early Seljuk brick towers, remotely situated in northern
Persia, had convinced Robert that this was where he must start looking for

a solution and he now began to set in motion the realization of his plan. By April 1933 he was in touch, for the first time, with Upham Pope, prospective editor of the great Persian Survey.

In May Robert was given another reason for departure. Macmillan finally turned down his application for a retainer to enable him to write his history of the Great War, but they were willing to advance him £100 for a travel book (*The Road to Oxiana*) and he felt he could command more money from periodicals like *The Times*, *Country Life* and the *Architectural Review* on his arrival in Persia. Another incentive was the proposal of a friend of his, Bosworth Goldman, to undertake an expedition through Persia and Afghanistan with cars running not on petrol, difficult to obtain in those remote regions, but on charcoal. Boz, as he was always known, had great charm, was ex-Navy, flew his own Gipsy Moth, and was rich enough to enjoy gliding and motor-racing. Speaking Russian and Turki he had travelled on his own across Siberia coming from the Kara Sea to Samarcand and then across the Caspian to Batum and Constantinople, a journey he wrote up in *Red Road through Asia*. Another Persian fanatic, Mark Dineley, joined the expedition, enthusiastically allowing his Ford van to be used for conversion and drawing up lists of spare parts needed as he volunteered to act as mechanic. But as the summer progressed Dineley foresaw trouble from Boz's light-hearted and amateur approach and withdrew his support. Another enthusiast, John Henderson, took his place, producing £500 towards expenses. Robert might have been warned by practical Dineley's withdrawal.

By the end of June 1933, Robert had got as far as asking the Persian Minister for permission for himself and Mr Goldman of Parker Producer Gas Company 'to obtain a general view of Persia's famous monuments and antiquities'.

Having delivered the manuscript of *First Russia then Tibet* to Macmillan, Robert set off late in August ahead of the expedition, from now on known as the Charcoal Burners. He was to stay with the Abdys in Venice and to gather up Christopher Sykes in Cyprus on his way to the East.

---

20 August 1933   Palazzo Barbaro, Venezia

Darling Mibble

Here I am feeling so much *rested already*, and my eyes so much better, despite not a wink of sleep in the train and great heat all yesterday. It was such a relief to have nothing to do and think of nothing. Diana and Bertie[1] had only got here two hours before me. This palace is lovely – one steps out of the boat into a very deep square courtyard, up 2 sides of which runs a very steep outside staircase to a height of 50 feet. This brings one to the state rooms which are magnificent. In the courtyard is one tree which doesn't branch till it reaches the roof about 80 feet up! We went to see the joy-hogs at the Excelsior in the Lido last night – Mark [Ogilvie-Grant] and Lord Melchett with Princess Aspasia of Greece and no one else I knew. Desmond[2] is here, also the Channons,[3] and our host Mr Odom has succeeded in introducing one friend of his own, an American called Truex, much to everyone's surprise and indignation – however he is very nice. I shall go to the Lido this morning to have another look at the Joy-hogs and then I think it won't see me again. I had rather be hot than bathe in that grey spittle. But life is very different here when one has a fast motor-launch always waiting at the door. To be quite honest, the decay of Venice and the sloth of the gondolas is more oppressive to me than poetic. I don't know why, because there is nothing in the world like it or so beautiful – and it isn't really decayed, it is an alive town. However I regard myself as not really here at all, but simply staying in a large house somewhere with some friends I want to see. I have a large room with a marble floor overlooking the Grand Canal and so can stay in it and be alone if I want to. [. . .]

I leave Cyprus on the 3rd of Sept. Till then 'Poste Restante, Nicosia, Cyprus.'

Love from Bobs

13 September 1933   Hotel St Georges, Beirut

Darling Mibble

Such a pleasure to get your two letters here this morning – we arrived from Damascus after the most fearful journey in a car with a huge fat

---

1. Lady Diana and Sir Robert Abdy.
2. Desmond Parsons, brother of Michael Rosse.
3. Henry (Chips) and Lady Honor Channon.

Arab in a black and yellow striped gown and an Arab widow who had to stop every ten minutes to be sick.

Also bitterly cold in the mountains and I was only in shorts and my stomach has gone wrong. But now I am swathed in the cummerbund and it is gradually getting right.

The cars should arrive tomorrow – but we wait till Tuesday to start from Damascus, so as to go across the desert with the Nairn convoy of motor coaches. [. . .]

The Melchetts have beds of lobelias in the form of coronets in their garden on the shores of the Lake of Galilee! How awful they are.

Christopher is growing a beard. [. . .]

I am afraid I can't write you good letters – I have had so many to answer and my diary takes all my effort. I shall probably send you the first instalment from Baghdad in case the Persians steal it. They sound the most odious race. I think you will be able to read most of it this time. But it isn't interesting so far. I have done two sketches in Jerusalem – one a black and white drawing of the town from a distant hill, which is rather good, though mad, but not madder than the landscape itself though no one will believe this. [. . .]

I must go to bed. I will try and write again before we leave Damascus. You must forgive *dull short* letters. They are all I can manage.

Love from
Bobs

18 September 1933   Damascus Palace Hotel, Damascus

Dearest Mibble

The expedition has momentarily collapsed. The cars got as far as Fontainebleau, by which time one had broken down altogether and another been substituted for it, and it was obvious, into the bargain, that the charcoal plant was useless. So Rutter[1] came on to Beirut (you can imagine my feelings when I found only him on the boat), while Boz and Henderson have returned to England in *secret*, to ensconce themselves for a month in a flat in Ealing, there to perfect the invention in order to start out with it again in the middle of October. I feel very sorry for Boz, having put so much money into it. But it now appears that he hadn't tested the cars *at all*, not even in England and I'm afraid that what I had always thought to be a vein of competence in him has proved nothing but the most irresponsible absurdity. Meanwhile, his only hope of retrieving both reputation and money is absolute secrecy – they are terrified that I should return to England to scoff and have sent Rutter to expedite me to Persia, where I shall see what I want to and wait for them. I have wired for £100 to meet me in Baghdad and Rutter says it will be forthcoming. I should hope so considering what I have already spent myself in their abortive enterprise. In which case I shall go on to Persia with Christopher, which will be very pleasant as he speaks Persian extremely well and knows a great deal about the country. I am already trying to learn a little. Also living there is unbelievably cheap – so it will be better than waiting about here. Please therefore *don't* say anything to anyone about the charcoal's having failed. They may get it going in the end. Anyhow as long as I am being financed by the expedition I must be loyal to it, even if the expedition consists of me only, I am still determined to get to Afghanistan somehow, if it is at all feasible.

We were to have left for Baghdad tomorrow in the desert bus, but yesterday at Baalbek Christopher got sunstroke, had a dreadful night during which he nearly went mad, and this morning, though better, has still a slight fever. Fortunately there is an English doctor here, who is coming – so I hope he will be all right by Friday, when the next bus goes.

Baalbek is *lovely*. We spent a night there. It is 'ruins' *in excelsis*. I have done what I think will make a frightfully good drawing, when copied out and drawn properly. I have discovered how to do these skies: 2 kinds of blue and pink.

Rutter is a most delightful companion. His Arabic is perfect (he

---

1. Frank Rutter, art critic of the *Sunday Times* and author of numerous books on art including *El Greco* (1930).

went to Mecca as an Arab) and he know far more of the Koran by heart than most Arabs.

I must now complete my diary. Goodbye. I will let you know our movements when I know them.

Please continue to write to Teheran. And remember to keep the secret! I shall tell Peter[1] the cars have been delayed by financial disputes in the charcoal company.

Love from
Bobs

24 September 1933   River Front Hotel, Baghdad

Darling Mibble

[. . .] Thank you so much for all your news – and lots of long letters. How I enjoyed them. I wish I could write back at the same length but simply haven't the energy. It is very hot (though the residents call it cold and are almost in furs) – this whole place is most depressing – rather like Edgware Road in a hot fog – a horrid surprise after the beauties of Jerusalem and Damascus. We dined with Peter [Scarlett] last night – he shares a house with a very amusing friend of Arthur's[2] called Ward. Peter seemed more than usually boring – neither interested in the country or funny about it. Etchings of Eton on the wall. But he played the 8th Symphony.

I am still half dead from the desert crossing. Can you imagine *our* car going at 40 miles an hour over a frozen ploughed field for 24 hours with only 3 stops for meals – hermetically sealed in boiling heat during the day? We travelled in a sort of trailer on two wheels. I can't really tell you how horrible it was in the daytime and I had the most awful headache. But night wasn't so bad. However there was unlimited iced water. Rutter goes back from here to meet the others. Christopher and I go on to Persia. Boz has wired £80 for the moment. I shall get a little more out of him.

---

1. Peter Scarlett, third secretary at the British Legation, Baghdad, later KCMG.
2. Arthur Byron, Robert's first cousin, first husband of Patricia Arbuthnot, her second being Claud Cockburn.

My big photos have really come out wonderfully, though the photographers here have done their best to spoil them. The small ones aren't so good. *Country Life* have wired for an article on Cyprus so they evidently liked my pictures of there. [. . .]

I can't remember if I told you about the fortune teller in Damascus. You know I *never* have had my fortune told. I found him in the street squatting over a tray of sand – a poor woman with a terribly diseased son was consulting him. When she had finished, he put a little sand in my palm and I sprinkled it on the tray. He then made three rows of hieroglyphics, dabbed about on each and gave some thought to a last diagonal. Then he said (Rutter translating) 'You have a friend whom you are fond of and he is fond of you. He will soon be sending you the expenses for your journey (it was exactly that phrase, particularly 'expenses'). Eventually he will join you and everything will be well between you and you will have a successful journey.'

Don't you call that most wonderful? I wasn't even thinking about Boz or the money at the time and Rutter was as astonished as I was. I gave him threepence.

[. . .] I have done an absolute masterpiece of a drawing in quite a different manner, very modern – the ruins of Baalbek. I do wish I could get it home, the Persians are sure to steal it.

I shall be sending the first volume of the diary before I leave here – I hope it will be some compensation for the fewness and boredom of my letters.

I am getting fearfully excited about Persia. [. . .]

Goodbye and love to everyone. I am looking forward to the next batch of letters at Teheran.

Love from
Bobs

9 October 1933   c/o British Consul, Teheran

Dearest Merge
    [. . .]I can hardly bear your description of the garden and everything – it makes me want to be back so much. Why does one ever go away?

Persia

This is really the result of Teheran stomach, which everyone gets, and I am just recovering from – one becomes quite insanely irritable, and last night I almost murdered the proprietor of the hotel, rushing into the restaurant in my pyjamas, because a dog was barking in the garden – this to replace the cinema as an instrument of keeping us awake, the latter having gone inside. However we leave tomorrow, depositing our things in a French *pension* in a large garden, and going off to Tabriz in the evening by lorry. You will see on the map that Tabriz is most remotely situated. It would cost £20 to take a car there and back. All one can do is to travel 'goods' which rather lets Christopher down as a character, as last time he was here he always travelled with a chauffeur and two servants. From Tabriz, we go to Maragha and Ardabil, if you can find them, and then back here for a bit, before going south to Isfahan and Persepolis.

We are much entertained, having this moment come from a King's birthday party at the Egyptian Legation. We stayed for a little at Gulheq, about nine miles away, at the foot of the Elburz, in the summer Legation – it was delicious, huge plane trees, and a stream running into a blue tiled pool. They gave us horses. The Anglo-Persian Oil Company is our great standby – they arrange everything everywhere. Jacks, the head of it, is a most charming man, with a lovely collection of stuffs, many of which were in the Exhibition.[1] I expect I shall end by working for them somehow. Oil is my fate. I keep on referring to them as Shell by accident. Altogether there is something oddly familiar about Teheran. Going in from Gulheq was rather like going to Reading for the day. Tonight we are dining with the most extraordinary man named Hannibal after his ancestor, a negro slave at the Russian court, whose grandson or great grandson was Pushkin, through whom Hannibal is descended. It is to be a 'Persian supper' – at nine o'clock because the moon won't be ready till then.

Yesterday we spent in the country looking at those lovely fluted brick towers and a most wonderful ruined mosque. I have never seen such lovely decoration – it makes everything European and everything else Islamic seem coarse and vulgar. As I was photographing, a man looking like a decayed railway porter suddenly walked past with a most beautiful falcon on his wrist, hooded in a little leather arrangement which he

---

1. Exhibition of Persian Art at Burlington House, 1931.

removed for its portrait. Christopher and I are determined to go hawking when we get back.

Everyone is very obliging and helpful so far, expeditious and reliable. This is a very pleasant surprise, as I had been led to believe it would be almost as bad as Russia. The Persians have the most exquisite manners; their speech is affected like that of Bloomsbury aesthetes; but they love a joke and seem to see everything as comic. So if you do too, there is no end to one's mutual laughter. They are really just a bit of Europe in Asia, with a much more civilised tradition in many ways than most of Europe. Unlike ours, their history has been continuous; there has been no Dark Ages to separate them from Antiquity; so that Darius and Alexander are remembered as names like Alfred or Elizabeth. But they have no sense of time. Any building older than the 17th century is a thousand years old, sometimes twelve hundred and generally built by Alexander.

Next morning
We dined with Hannibal. A servant met us with a gigantic lantern about three feet high and led us through the little streets of the bazaar to an old house with a wind-tower. We went down and down to a tiny sunk court with a fountain playing and shrubs by it. We sat in the most lovely old Persian room, very tiny, with elaborate plasterwork and bits of mirror let into it. We ate off the floor and discussed Omar Khayyam. It was rather theatrical – Olde Persian Hampstead – but the house was genuine. We began dinner about half past ten and got back to the hotel at two. So this morning I am nearly dead and Christopher has been sick owing to the food. However thank God we have got a servant, who has been doing the packing, I dread the journey to Tabriz – it will take three days. But it will be nice to get out of this town, which agrees with nobody's health. [. . .]

Love from
Bobs

There was a Persian princess at dinner, who was very elegant, but I thought by her speech and sentiments she must have captained lacrosse at Cheltenham – I find she learnt her English in Hongkong. I have noticed this effect of Hongkong before.

24 October 1933   Teheran

Darling Merge

I am sorry not to have written for such a long time but we were away
for a fortnight longer than we expected, in Azerbaijan, and I have only
just got back. Thank you very much for your long letter describing the
wedding. I do hope you have got your copy of the book[1] by now. They
don't generally send out the presentation copies till the day of publication – which was October 10th I think. If you never got one, it means
they have forgotten my instructions – so would you, in that case, write
and ask if they have sent one to Lady Cunard 7 Grosvenor Square W.I.
I am glad it looked nice.

Your letter is very tantalising, because at least one, or possibly two,
previous to it have been stolen or lost. [. . .] Perhaps I shall get the
letter eventually. It is so aggravating – you mention the new car, 14 h.p.
I know nothing about it – and as I said to Christopher, such an event is
only comparable to a birth or death!

A wire from Rutter in Beirut tells me that the cars would leave there
on the 21st. But I don't know if they have. I suppose they ought to be
here pretty soon. I am now so interested in Persia I don't want to go
away. Anyhow it is doubtful if we shall be able to get away. There is said
to be trouble in Afghanistan – the snow is imminent.

We had a fascinating time on our journey. You will read about it in
the diary which I shall soon be sending home. Half way to Tabriz we
travelled by lorry – a hideous experience, shut up in the back with very
smelly companions and I had awful neuralgia. At Tabriz we called on
the Governor and the Chief of Police, who were very helpful, then by
car to Maragha, where I photographed various buildings and we rode
out in a cavalcade to an extraordinary fire-worshipper's cave, which was
later used as an observatory by the Mongols. From Maragha to Mianeh
– Mianeh being half way between Tabriz and Zinfan – we did a horse
journey of 5 days – over completely unknown country, where they had
never seen a European before. We were quite unprepared for any such
journey, so lived entirely on the country, slept in the headman's house
in each village, etc. My health, which had been wrong in the town, was
completely restored. I am burnt about the face and am growing a

---

1. *First Russia then Tibet*, dedicated to Emerald, Lady Cunard.

moustache (I *had* a beard) – but now that I am back here I over-ate on caviare pancakes last night with Jacks, head of the Anglo-Persian, and am upset again. Poor Christopher was so terribly bitten by fleas he has had to go to hospital, as both legs swelled up below the knee and came up in huge water blisters, which on bursting left raw places of the most disgusting description. I never saw anything *like* the fleas – as you know, they never touch me – I hadn't one bite the whole journey, but they kept me awake by tickling. Christopher killed 8 on himself when we got back, and our last night away I disposed of 5 in my sleeping bag, besides 16 bed bugs and a louse! We lived mainly on curds, eggs, honey, milk and chicken – entirely on the floor. In one village we found a sort of squire, a boy, with steward etc., who put us up very comfortably and lit us a fire, by which we dined off a large round tray, everything in bowls, and played 2 handed bridge. Our muleteers and a young policeman who accompanied us smoked opium at every stop and used to get quite silly with it. I took a few whiffs, which had no effect and tasted like the jacket of a baked potato.

We are now living in a *pension* run by a Frenchman and his wife, in a pleasant garden – it is very nice except for the sanitary arrangements. We also have a servant Mahmud, which makes life a lot easier. He calls me with tea and the local French newspaper.

Further plans I can't tell you, till the expedition arrives. You might write once or twice on chance to the Consulate. But we may make a dash for Kabul. I will let you know as soon as I can.

[. . .] Persian *brick* buildings are what excite me – much more than the later tile work. There never was such a use of brick. They have done all the things with it that the Dutch and Germans think so modern and think they have invented – and much more besides. I shall have to come back here I think, the distances are so gigantic that travelling takes up a great deal of time. No place is less than 100 miles from another. [. . .]

Best Love to all
Bobs

Persia

24 November 1933   Herat

Dearest Mibble

I have written to you from more cheerful surroundings than an Afghan bedroom lit by one hurricane lantern, with doors that won't shut and unglazed windows opposite, so that a very cold winter wind is tearing through – the room, as you can imagine, in an appalling muddle, covered with my sketches, pencils, clothes, food, cameras, and the bedding heaped in a corner, fleabag, sheepskin, Afghan quilt etc. – the walls white with a sky blue dado and the ceiling of wooden poles. The reason for the dilapidations is not age, but newness – the hotel isn't finished. However I have a very fine carpet on the floor and two plates of different sorts of grapes, with a bottle of whisky, cheese, sausage, Ovaltine and soup cubes in reserve – in addition to which the food is rather good here, mostly pilau, with a most delicious preserve made of some mountain berry, some of which I am taking with me tomorrow to Kabul.

I wanted to go by the northern road to Mazar-i-Sherif – but nothing is going – and it is said to be blocked by snow – the others may try it, if they get here. I shall try and go up from Kabul, whence there is a regular post, which one could accompany. I leave tomorrow with an Indian doctor, who has chartered a lorry for his wife and family and possessions. He speaks English, which will make things a little easier. We go by Kandahar.

Everything is unbelievably cheap. So it has to be, as there are no notes, and if one had to carry any more silver about, the population would be hunchbacked. I cashed a bank draft for £7.10.0. in the bazaar and came away with a bag of 672 pieces as big as shillings and each worth only 3d.

I can't tell you what a magnificent race the Afghans are – so tall, superb features, piercing eyes, swinging walk, and gorgeously dressed mostly in white – great white serge cloaks hanging stiff from the shoulders with false sleeves embroidered and nearly touching the ground. I am very busy here – the buildings are immense and practically unknown – so I have tried to be thorough in my photography (pray God they come out) and have done 3 sketches, one of which threatens to be rather good when it is finished.

I arrived here in great state, *driving* a Rolls. I must say I never thought the first time I should drive a Rolls would be in Afghanistan –

or, for that matter, that I should arrive in Herat, which has been the goal of my plans for the last year, driving a Rolls with 2 Englishwomen beside me, Noel asleep in the back, and another woman crying because of the bumps. I drove very well – much better than Noel, with fewer crashes and greater speed. The road was indescribable. We were out half the night the other side of the frontier. The other Rolls, a huge dowager's limousine, got impaled on a culvert and had to be dug out with *grandpa's knife*. That knife, which I popped in at the last moment to sharpen my pencils with, has proved the mainstay of my journey – I eat with it. It is also the only thing about me which provokes any respect or admiration.

A Hungarian arrived here today from Kabul, having been unable to eat for a fortnight. I gave him Ovaltine and soup and a charcoal pill – he seemed really on the point of collapse. So I hope he will post this in Persia, as he is going on to Meshed.

I am afraid I have been very bad about writing – but it has been difficult to find time. Travelling in these parts is a positive profession. I have enjoyed a quiet stay alone here. Every day I have gone about with an old giant in uniform, who carries my sketch book and reports my movements. Being so near the Russian railhead at Kushk, the political atmosphere is tense – and one is automatically regarded as a spy.

I really can't sit in this hurricane any more, but must go down to dinner, so goodbye. I will let you know my plans from Kabul.

How is Aubrey? Give him an apple from me. I wish I was hunting. Yet it's rather the same feeling being here!

Love from
Bobs

8 December 1933   Herat

Dearest Mibble

I am afraid it is a forlorn hope sending this as a Xmas letter – the posts from here are said to be uncertain – so I don't know if it will ever reach you at all – but if it does my best love and wishes to Father, Anne and Lucy [. . .] Anyhow I will try and wire from Kandahar or Kabul to shew I am alive. [. . .]

I set off eventually for the north – Mazar-i-Sherif, just under the Oxus frontier, if you can find it on the map. My conveyance was a lorry with 7 soldiers returning from leave and a white-bearded sage in a quilted coat and large turban. We slept the first night in a shrine, a lovely place in a garden of huge pines that reminded me of Ravenna and my first trip abroad – it had also a fish pond – and I went down to the Madrasseh, the school, where boys were learning the Koran and even larger fish, in an even larger pond, fought with ducks for bread thrown them. Next morning we proceeded up an endless valley, till we reached the approach to the farmost pass. The next mile and a half took us *six* hours. The whole road had to be dug – snow having fallen and it being only earth and uphill – it was six hours like that day we went to fetch the washing and got stuck beside the Grand Avenue Gate. Fortunately there were 10 men, 3 spades, a pick, chains, ropes etc. The descent was much worse – a hairpin-bend track down precipices of snow and slush and mud – how the lorry didn't go over the edge I can't think. Eventually we got down, finally in the dark, and then the lights broke. So we slept where we were, self in the road in a howling gale, but very comfortable and warm all the same, and with whisky and *plenty* of food. Next morning we reached a *town*, about the size of Bedwyn, called Kala Nao. You may find it on a big map. There we decided to spend the day mending the lamps. That evening it rained – so we didn't start next day. Next evening it snowed and all next day. The day after that we couldn't start, nor the day after that. Then I got ill, stomach, from mere greed over raisins but it was too much and I decided to get back while I could. I was in a room whose only daylight was through an open door – so that I had to lie *in* the snow almost (I have a hot water bottle) – there was little food, and the lavatory was a dungheap down a flight of mud steps in a tunnel, down which I generally *fell*, particularly in the middle of the night. There were already forty Bokhara Jews stranded in the town out of lorries, waiting for horses. I went to the Governor, said I was ill, dying, and must get to Herat. He said there would be horses tomorrow. Tomorrow dawned – two horses were paraded, one of which *literally* could only walk on three legs, while the other wasn't much better. I went to the Governor again, before he was dressed, and seated myself with his secretary, before *he* was dressed, and said go I must and would that very morning. At last they gave me three fine horses, for which I paid £5.0.0. – a vast sum – one for me, one for the man, and one for the luggage. We set off and reached Khotal, at the foot of the pass that night, where I slept with 3 others in a mud room with a bonfire in the middle of the floor whose smoke escaped, or rather didn't escape by a hole in the roof. Next morning we crossed the pass early and rode on until after dark – 50 miles on an Afghan saddle with stomach ache – it was the worst day I have ever had. Finally we got lost in a cloud on the edge of a big ravine – the horse-man began to recriminate, 'You don't understand, you don't know any Persian.' R.B. 'It's you who don't know any Persian' (his own language). Man, 'Oh, I don't know any Persian, don't I. I don't know anything. I don't know where this road goes.' R.B. 'There isn't a road.' Man. 'No, there isn't a road. I don't know Persian. I don't know anything.'

Sits down on an aromatic tuft and groans into his hands. Luckily I had a lamp, as it was quite dark and there was no moon. So once more I went to bed, dining in bed, and covering my head with a mackintosh to keep out the cloud. At 12 I woke up, with my money bag between my feet and the knife open at my hand, to find a bright moon and a vast ravine on one side, about $\frac{1}{2}$ a mile wide, in the bottom of which the river wound away like quicksilver. The man was too cold to sleep – the horses had nothing to eat (having tried the sleeping bag already) – so I got up, and we went on having now located Kharokh, eventually reaching a big caravanserai, fortified, at 2.a.m. I had some Ovaltine and was awakened next morning by three men spreading a sheet and praying on it in a loud voice, while I perked at them over my sheepskin. That afternoon I rode into Herat, and the whole staff of the extraordinary hotel rushed out beaming to greet me. Within five minutes my room was arranged exactly as before, with a large new carpet – but in those 5 minutes the *knife*, which I had put on a ledge, was stolen by a boy loitering in the passage. Then I learned that the expedition[1] had arrived the night before, and as I was having tea in they walked, a gloomy little party, each dwelling in whispers on the shortcomings of the other two. They might well be gloomy, having spent about £1,000 and failed in everything they undertook – 3 weeks earlier and the road to the north would still have been easy. Boz particularly is depressed. I feel sorry for him, but he has only himself and that vile charcoal (which now isn't working at all) to blame. I was planning to go back to Meshed – but shall now go on to Kabul, if we can still get through, and make £50–£100 by

---

1. Boz Goldman's expedition of charcoal-burning lorries.

telegraphing the *Daily Mail*. If we can't get through, one can always get down to India by an easy road from Kandahar, whence I shall take the train to Duzdab in Persia and return to Meshed.

My ride from Kala Nao has caused some amazement here. It generally takes 4 nights – I did it in 2 – it is over 100 miles, with a bad pass. But that middle day was not an experience I shall repeat. I rode 20 miles at least standing in the stirrups, and finally changed onto a horse with only a pack, which was much more comfortable.

Since then I have stayed in bed finding myself *really* tired and having also a streaming cold. This is now better. We go on the day after tomorrow.

I grew so homesick in Kala Nao – everything came back so vividly and how *comfortable* all the discomforts one always complains of (like crossing the garden in the snow to the bath) seemed! I don't want to go on at all – and shall try to get back to Persia as quickly as possible though fearfully tempted to try and get a lift down to Delhi for a day just to see how my Delhi is getting on. I fear I shan't be home till March now – but shall try and make it the end of February. I am supposed to go on that cruise in April.

We have partridges for dinner tonight and they are ready so I must go down. Goodbye darling Mother, and best wishes for 1934 – (in which year I start my war book).

Love from
Bob

P.S. In Kala Nao I started a play. How easy it is. I must really finish it. Cheap vulgar muck, but I think it would sell.

We have certain amenities here – bridge every night and a gramophone with Jazz and Tauber records – I would give a lot for some classical music and a pint of champagne – but my cold has left me rather low.

15 December 1933   Meshed

Dearest Mibble

I wrote the enclosed letter at Herat, intending to post it there or in Kandahar. But in the end I chose not to go on with the expedition.

There were various reasons, which I won't go into – but the main one was that I did not want to be landed in India – and though it would have been interesting to have seen Kabul, it wasn't worth the expense & hardships of the journey back here by Quetta, Duzdab, etc. My interests are in Persia at the moment. And as far as Afghanistan is concerned, in northern Afghanistan. If I could, I should wait out here till June and try again then. But unless a job crops up miraculously in Teheran, this won't be possible.

It is lucky I didn't go on, as I am rather done up for the moment. An excrescence developed on my left thigh, the result of that ride I suppose, which became really awful – the whole leg swelled and I could barely put that foot to the ground and had a not very pleasant three-day journey here in a lorry – trying ineffectually to dress and poultice the thing while sleeping in ruined caravanserais, with three separate and icy draughts converging on the single teapot of hot water. In fact I became extremely irritable, and when some soldiers stole my saddle-bags I burst into their room and reclaimed them with a flow of violence and abuse which quite upset them. Anyhow I got in yesterday afternoon and am now staying with the Hambers, Major and wife – who are in charge of the consulate here, the consul having removed to Seistan. The pleasure of a bath and breakfast in bed was delirious. I went yesterday evening, and again in the morning to the American hospital to have the excrescence cupped – so that it is now *very much* better and the swelling of the leg in general has disappeared. My worry is whether it will heal or not. That is the bother of these things. After 2 months, I hear that the sores Xtopher got in Azerbaijan are still open. However I have been in such rude health, look so well, am so much thinner, and have such a rosy tongue that I think it *ought* to heal all right. Forgive all these disgusting details. For the moment I am elaborately resting – anyhow I can't walk – but hope to be up and doing in a day or two. There are various things I want to draw and photograph here, and then I must get back to Teheran before the worst weather (the road goes over 8,000 feet). I may afford the luxury of a car for the journey, as I have spent so little since leaving Teheran 5 weeks ago – in all about £15.0.0. During 3 weeks in Afghanistan, including my fare back, I spent £10.0.0., of which exactly half went on the horses from Kala Nao.

Xtopher has become *Times* correspondent for a year. De Bathe offered it to me – but a wage of £150.0.0. a year wasn't enough.

I hope you will get this letter – and have had the one posted by the

Hungarian. Anyhow I shall have wired for Xmas as I dare say you will like to know I have escaped from Afghanistan. My one thought now is to go back there – it was so tantalising being baulked of Turkestan when I was so near and I now half wish I had gone on. But I think it would have been *too* exhausting, crossing the Hindu Kush in winter without proper equipment. The journey to Gyantse was a lesson which I shan't forget, and then we had every comfort, together with properly fitted rest-houses.

I have come back with 5 drawings, of which two I think really are rather good – anyhow they are very interesting. I am longing to get the letters that must be waiting in Teheran – with possibly some news of the book – which I suppose is being a complete failure as usual.

I will let you know my plans in about a fortnight. Boz wants me to motor back with him from the Gulf through Turkey – Basrah, Baghdad, Samaria, Mosul, Aleppo, Konia, Constantinople. But I doubt whether I shall, though such a journey would more or less complete my architectural survey of the Middle East. It is maddening being so hampered – if I stayed out here another 6 months I could produce a classic – as it is, it will be only superficial. I hope to goodness my pictures will come out all right.

I think so much of you at home – half the pleasure of being away is thinking how much I shall enjoy getting back.

Incidentally I bought you a lovely Afghan waistcoat for a Xmas present, but am obliged to wear it *myself* now, as I have only my flannel suit and it is very cold – so am finding something else!

Best love
from Bobs

25 December 1933   Meshed

Darling Mibble

Xmas morning! I must write and thank you for all the letters that must be waiting in Teheran – the papers (up to Dec 15th – Hamber takes in the *Statesman* from India) say it is being very cold in England. Here the weather is of unprecedented mildness – so much that everyone fears a drought next summer. I sat out all day drawing yesterday in my flannel suit and had to take off my fur waistcoat (or rather yours, but I am afraid it will be too dirty for you by the time it gets back) – yet Meshed is notorious for its cold. I only hope I get back to Teheran before the winter does start. I leave in a day or two, and shall stop at one or two places on the way if the weather holds. If not, I shall hurry on, in case the passes get blocked. If they do, I shall be helpless, as the thing on my leg, though going along well, isn't healed and I couldn't ride.

I am involved in Xmas here, though escaped the American missionary service yesterday. Hamber gives a dinner tonight, for which I have decorated 16 parlour-games cards with holly, mistletoe and a robin each. Thus one makes oneself agreeable – by request! [. . .] We lunch with Mr and Mrs Hart – he is the consul's clerk and they have a small son called Keith. So I have bought Keith a penknife and the Harts a primula – and have done Hamber a picture of his house, with the two tame gazelles sitting on the lawn in the foreground – because Mrs Hamber, before she left, said she would particularly like a sketch. It is a contrast with Polesden[1] last year – but just as pleasant in its way. Still I would enjoy a few minutes' conversation with Sachie and Georgia.[2]

My art is very active. Yet how long each picture takes. I have done 5 of Herat, and 2 here – the latter not yet finished. The great shrine here, which one isn't allowed to enter, I drew from a roof, keeping the police officer who accompanied me up there 3 hours, till he nearly went mad – and even then I had only got the drawing done and had to do the colour in separate sketches with notes, to put in afterwards. I must say, I do advance.

After a week or two in Teheran, I shall go and spend some time in Isfahan, waiting there till I hear from Macmillan's etc. about more money. If I can get more, which I think I can, I shall stay out till the spring – if not I shall get home as cheaply as I can, joining the Hellenic Travellers cruise as a lecturer in the Mediterranean. If I can stay out till the spring, I can write a book on Persian monuments which will be of *permanent* value, if not, my book will just be a travel book, quite a good one perhaps, but not what I should like. I also intend to come home with a finished play.

---

1. Polesden Lacey, home of Mrs Ronnie Greville.
2. Sacheverell and Georgia Sitwell.

I am thankful I didn't go with the expedition. India would have interfered with everything.

The thing about Persia is that it isn't all Bulbuls and lovers under trees and pretty stuffs and all that Omar Khayyam idea. That side exists – it dates from the 16th century and still governs modern Persian taste, in so far as there is any. But it is all that came before that is so interesting and so much more worthwhile. That is what I am after and what is so little known. I only hope that this time my photographs are successful. It will be ghastly if they aren't.

There is nothing to tell you. I have read *Anna Karenina* with great pleasure. But it isn't what I call *writing*. No Russian book is – no novel either for that matter. That is what prevented me writing my novel – contempt for it. I wish I didn't feel like this [. . .]

I will go on later.

27 December

Xmas day reproduced itself even here – a dull drizzly day, too much for lunch, that sick feeling at tea, and a nightmare of a party in the evening followed by highly organised parlour games for all. I had the unforseeable misfortune to win 1st prize. It was appalling. Even now I would have preferred to spend the day by myself in a caravanserai.

I saw a picture of Nancy's wedding[1] in the *Daily Telegraph*. I thought she looked lovely, and Peter had brushed his hair.

I have started to read *The Forsyte Saga*. The badness of it accumulates by degrees.

Best wishes to all for the New Year.

Love
from
Bobs

---

1. Nancy Mitford's wedding to the Hon. Peter Rodd.

8 January 1934   Teheran

Darling Merge

A letter to wish you many happy returns, if it gets there in time, which it ought to do. I wish I could send you a present – and wish still more I could be at home. I hope you will enjoy your birthday, I can't even write you an amusing letter for it – I have no more news, having been very lazy since I last wrote and hardly left my room, tomorrow I shall start work, so to speak – articles, drawings etc. Then go to Isfahan in about 10 days or a fortnight.

My photos, taken with Jack's camera, are splendid and really make a good record of the architectural side of the journey. The other side of it has not come out of it so well, as I relied on the small camera for that and had to use the same vile English films – but fortunately I can get others now.

Our servant said to me today in Persian: 'My name is not Damnfool but Mahmud.' I said: 'If you know English, you can talk English.' He is a most loathesome man, never shaves and belches incessantly – but rather a good servant. Tonight the Jacks have a ball. The Mallets[1] are dining with *us* for a change.

I went to an old chemist, Bonati, about my sore, which is now refusing to heal. He was dressed in a cap and jacket of cat-fur and surrounded by bottles containing scorpions in spirit. He said, as soon as he saw it: 'Had you been eating dried fruits?' As I had made myself ill on them just before it first developed, this was rather clever of him. He cured Christopher and has given me some ointment which has made a great improvement in one night. I am sorry to give you so much news anent this affliction, but it is one of my central interests [. . .]

I am perpetually filling up forms for the police who demand your birthplace and I don't know it. How the Persian administration will survive without it I can't think.

Goodbye and forgive a short boring letter.

With best wishes and love from
Bobs

---

1. Victor Mallet, Counsellor at the British Legation, Teheran, and his wife Peggy, a considerable personality.

10 February 1934   As from Teheran

Darling Mibble

I prepared a letter to send to you from Isfahan. I left Teheran on Thursday morning with the Hoylands – he is Consul in Shiraz – who have two cars and very kindly offered to give me a lift. Xtopher wired he would wait in Shiraz. Ordinarily Isfahan is one day's run from Teheran. It was pouring with rain, we should have been better in a boat. So awful was the road that by the first evening we had not gone halfway – and spent it at Gum. The next morning we had just left this village when we came on 3 lorries and a Ford *embedded* in a torrent 50 yards wide – the water sweeping over their engines, wheels disappeared and their inmates huddling gloomily on the bank beneath blankets, while the rain poured down and the barren mountains all round were half hidden in cloud – patches of dirty snow everywhere. I have never seen such a gloomy wretched sight – so we came back here, and this will be our second evening in an old Persian house with wind towers, nice big rooms well carpeted. I am lying by an open fire, trying to dry my clothes which got wetted while I was testing the depth of the water this afternoon. Those who know say there will be no water tomorrow (there had been 96 hours' rain solid), so we shall set off early – but I am not very hopeful. I really am getting *sick* of my bad luck. Since January 15th I have been trying to get to Isfahan – the easiest journey in Persia ordinarily. A month utterly wasted. I shall have to hire a car and do things quicker now. I must be back in Teheran by March 20th.

My back is going on well, thank Heaven – and I am travelling with a little box of injections – so far I hope to prevent repetition, *if* I ever get anywhere to have them injected. The dressing of it is so difficult in these barbarous places. I realise, looking back, how ill and depressed I felt the last 10 days in Teheran – discharging the poison (in buckets) has made me feel a different person.

Yesterday was punctuated with crashes, day and night, as the whole village gradually fell down – being of mud it has not withstood such rain. You never saw such desolation. People pop in and out of my room to warm themselves and are always trying to take away the fire in a shovel to somewhere else. This evening I struck and shoved them all out. Yesterday the mullah (priest), an inmate of the house, read me a scripture lesson out of an old manuscript while I drew him. I have done a picture in colour of a Persian garden in February, which I hope will make you laugh – though it isn't as funny as it ought to have been. Now I must go and help with the dinner, I will finish this in Isfahan – but *when* God knows.

Isfahan

We got here yesterday (Sunday) afternoon, it rained all the night before, after I wrote the above, and we thought it was useless to try – but suddenly we got news that the torrent had subsided, but was rising again – so we bundled everything into the cars and made a dash for it. The 1st car took it slowly and sank in the mud up to the axles – but we pushed it back – and then both got across at a tremendous pace, yours truly being left marooned on an island and eventually carried across on the back of a peasant youth. We got here for tea and I had a drive round afterwards – a lovely fine evening with spring in the air. It is a very beautiful place, but I won't describe it now, as I am just going to get up and I want to post this first thing.

We go on to Shiraz in a day or two – whether Xtopher is still waiting I don't know. I shall come back here after seeing Persepolis and various Sassanian reliefs in the south.

Goodbye and love from
Bobs

15 February 1934   Shiraz

Darling Merge

A quick note to let you know I have at last arrived in Shiraz – this evening, after a worrying day with the petrol feed of the car wrong – we took 5 hours longer than we ought to have done. In addition I now have one of my eyes all swollen – there is no peace – but I have just been to the C.M.S. hospital where lady-doctor Mentz said one's eyes do do that here and she has given me some drops which she says ought to put it right by the morning. At present I am in bed with a flagon of Shiraz wine (very famous, Omar Khayyam etc.) beside me, having just dined off a partridge and tangerines. The Hoylands I left at the Consulate – a crucial moment for them, since they will be there 2 or 3 years. Xtopher is here, with his beard very neat, plus Mahmud our odious servant and

Jamshyd Taroporevala the Indian chauffeur, a Parsee, who speaks English better than you or I.

We passed Persepolis on the way, but I only had time to run up on to the platform – the stone, I must confess, is a disappointment, I had imagined something dark and shiny – actually it is light, weathered to tawny brown, and of a transparent texture. The small reliefs, on the other hand, seem to be in a hard dark grey stone. The light stone is the pillars etc., the edges are very sharp still. But all this is only a minute's impression.

No words can describe the beauties of Isfahan – they really excel their reputation – but who has ever tried to describe them, which I hope to do – there is a wonderful atmosphere about the place, airy and fresh – and then these tremendous coloured domes and minarets – and lovely old trees and superb bridges over the river – an atmosphere of amenity and urbanity – I am longing to get back there.

For the moment I have no plans – but may do a short horse journey with Xtopher to Firuzabad to see a Sassanian palace – then to Sharpur near Kazerun (between here and Bushire) and then back to Isfahan via Persepolis.

Yesterday evening, we fetched up in a small village and I went for a ride on a most wonderful horse, the best I have been on in Persia – galloping at full speed into the setting sun, so that one couldn't see the countless ditches, banks etc. – a policeman was with me and the horses were racing. [. . .]

Love from
Bobs

7 March 1934   Isfahan
6 a.m.

Darling Mibble

I suddenly discovered last night late that the airmail via Russia goes off today. For some odd reason everything in this town has to be photographed in a dawn light – so I am obliged to get up at this hour and have just been called – with tea. I am staying with Wishaw, the Reis i Napht, or captain of the oil (i.e. Manager of the A.P.O.C.), which is very comfortable and pleasant – and he says he will take me down to

Kirman next week which will save me about £20.0.0. I get back to Teheran between the 20th and 28th and leave about April 10th. [. . .]

I have a lot to tell you about my visit to Persepolis, but you will have to read it in my diary. Rather than stay with Herzfeld[1] then, I slept on a (*fresh*) dung heap outside, and eventually had the most awful row with him *backed up* by the Persian authorities – he threatened to cut short the excavations if I dared to take any photographs – but remembering that you were looking forward to them, I persisted – as a matter of fact they weren't very good – it is too much photographed and I only took one or two things for reference. The new staircase is really wonderful – of course it isn't great art, no art which makes you wonder all the time how much it cost can be that.

I am having a Persian miniature done of myself, which may amuse you – it is an experiment. There is one old genius here (he did that picture for the queen), but he is always encouraged by the Europeans to do copies of old miniatures and picturesque scenes of the past. I sat to him yesterday and he *can* draw from life – but I had great difficulty in explaining that what I wanted was a Persian picture, not a copy of a European one – now I think he understands. He says it will take six hours more – it won't be coloured but will have a little gold. It is interesting dealing with him because it is just like dealing with a house decorator – you have to *order* your picture exactly as you want it, have things taken out, put in etc. – there is no nonsense about temperament. But it is about equal chance that it will be the most awful failure – so don't look forward to it, and anyhow there is the moustache!

This is such a *lovely* place. [. . .]

Goodbye
Love from
Bobs

---

1. Ernst Herzfeld, Professor Ordinarius of Berlin University. An archaeologist, he had been excavating in Persia since 1928, especially at Persepolis which he regarded as his own preserve.

March 1934   Isfahan

Darling Mibble

[. . .] I haven't stopped since I last wrote and am nearly worn out with it, and can do nothing when I get in every evening but sink into bed with a cup of Ovaltine. Fortunately I am sleeping all right – so it only needs a day or two's rest for me to recover. [. . .]

I leave on Thursday with my host in a free car for Kirman, which is a long way away – near there is a wonderful tiled shrine which very few people have seen, but which those who have say is the most beautiful thing in Persia, as far as setting is concerned – then we go to Bamin, which is really in Baluchistan. It will be interesting to see that, and then I shall get back to Teheran about the 26th or 27th, and stay with the Hoares,[1] or if they suddenly get full up, the Mallets. Both have a profound understanding of comfort – so there I shall rest and will write properly. So don't expect a word for a fortnight at least. The Hoares are enraged about Xtopher apparently, Lady Hoare refusing all official invitations, and he threatening international scandals. Xtopher is still hanging on at Bushire, a prisoner in the Residency.[2]

This place contains a woman called Mrs Dodge Dillman who is worth £32,000,000 – travelling with a party who are worth only a million or two each. The Governor gave a tea-party for them yesterday, which I attended in my one suit – everyone else in deep black – today at lunch I am going to meet her more closely as she was the woman who got D. H. Lawrence to America and must be rather interesting. [Upham] Pope is arriving in April with a *much* richer woman, Mrs Moore – who is travelling in her own aeroplane and going on to Russia – but I think I may have left Teheran by the time they arrive.

Macmillan's say they think I should do 2 books – an amusing one and a learned one – but anyhow they think as long as I have enough money to see what I want, that is the main thing, without going into details. They are a nice firm. Goodbye angel. My tea is late this morning – have I told

---

1. Reginald Hoare, British Minister at Teheran, and his wife Katharine.
2. Christopher was at first refused Persian permission to leave Shiraz and to travel further in Persia. He was then allowed to proceed to Bushire where he was confined to the Residency in consequence of orders from Teheran. The Chief of Police blamed the General Staff, and the Foreign Office blamed the police for the order. He had finally to leave Persia but was allowed to travel in Afghanistan with Robert.

you about my servant Ali Asgar, with his non-conformist face and British habits – he was cook to a British regiment here in the war. [. . .]

Love from
Bobs

5 April 1934   Teheran

Darling Mibble

[. . .] How lovely it is to think this ought to be one of my last letters from here. You can answer it c/o the Legation, Kabul. We spent yesterday morning with the Afghan Ambassador. He promises all facilities – so we hope to leave Herat by the 1st of May.

We had a *frightful* journey from Isfahan, had to push the car through a flood up to the waist, me leading the charge, Christopher beating on such peasants as we could collect out of the landscape with a stick. We then had to take down the whole engine to dry it – 5 hours wasted – we got in here at 1.30 a.m. I drove most of the way.

I have had the last injection and am anxiously waiting to see if more boils develop. I really don't know what I shall do if they do – it will drive me to despair. I am going on with the tonic as I think it is an antidote – and rest every afternoon.

Upham Pope has most kindly sent me a present of £30, which is a great help. He arrives here with his millionairess, Mrs Moore on the 21st – and wants to take me about, lend me a camera, and come to Afghanistan. But I don't think I can wait. On the other hand as he is not well off, I think the £30 must have come from Mrs Moore – so there might be a little more if I waited for her. She is very generous apparently and gave McGovern (of Lhasa fame) 1,000 dollars to come out here, though she didn't know him and he just wrote to her. She is going to Samarcand in her aeroplane, the lucky brute.

I have been looking at all my drawings – 22 now including a very funny one of me at Persepolis which is exactly like – I did it in the looking-glass. I can't make up my mind whether they are really good or not. You shall decide that and *finish* them all, as I shall be too lazy and there is a lot of work to be done on them. I am running out of paper and people *will* steal my pencils which I can't replace – it is maddening.

It is delightful staying here – the Hoares are perfect hosts – one doesn't meet till lunch and the Minister has the most delicious 1920 champagne with which he is very generous. I am just going down to lunch – it is wonderful to think one can eat it! The only thing is I can't sleep, Teheran always has this effect – there was a ball at the English bank to welcome us back.

Forgive short letter – I have no news, but will write again before I leave to tell you my plans definitely. Till the middle of May write to Kabul – but don't send anything on, as one can never tell what may happen in those parts, and I may always have to flee owing to boils – but I trust not.

I saw a third of the photos today – they are wonderfully good. I took 4,000, on the last trip.

Best love from
Bobs

12 April 1934   British Legation, Teheran

Darling Mibble

[. . .] Tomorrow I go on a short trip to Sultaniya again – it will be interesting to revisit the first place I went to here and see it with a trained eye – also it is the finest thing in Persia, and as my photos weren't very good, it is worth another visit. We shall go off at the end of next week or beginning of the week after. I hope to get permission to go to Asterabad and Gumbad i Qabus on the way – but as the latter is in a military zone there may be difficulties – in fact there are.

The weather has been appalling – every road in the country blocked by streams – but now appears more settled and is really delicious – all the judas trees in full blossom, blue sky, the background of snow mountains, and a warm breeze – Teheran appears quite attractive, but I shall be glad to forsake it for ever.

I met my friend M. Datiev the Russian Consul, in the street yesterday and he said he had news for me from Moscow re Samarcand. This I have no doubt means a refusal – but it will be interesting to see if my writings have been quoted as a reason. I am going to see him this afternoon.

The boils I think *are* better. [. . .] I am recommended to have a milk injection before starting, it is drastic and painful, but may be worth it – also may give me an excuse to go into the nursing home for a few days' solid rest. I *can't* sleep in this place for some reason, which is such a bore.

[. . .] I have been very busy reading up information about northern Afghanistan – there isn't much – but fortunately I brought the most essential books out with me. I doubt if we shall get through in the car, in which case it can go round to Kabul and we shall continue by horse – if this happens of course it will delay things, but I hope to be home by the end of July, unless by some terrific bit of luck we can get to Russian Turkestan – you will see on the map how tantalisingly near Mazar-i-Sherif is to Samarcand and Bokhara – and there is a railway to Termez, which is only about 30 miles north of Mazar or the Oxus – so it would all be deliciously easy if only we could get the permissions.

How I long to be home – you can't imagine how much. I shall just be in time for cubbing again. A year! Goodness knows what I have been doing all the time – but I hope there will be something to shew for it. [. . .]

Best Love from
Bobs

19 April 1934   Teheran

Darling Mibble

A last letter from Teheran – unless we are driven back here by any untoward adventure – we leave tomorrow morning, motor to Shahi in Mazandaran, and thence take the new railway to Asterabad. There, since it is a 'military zone', I shall be dependent on the favour of the prevailing general for permission to go on to Gumbad i Qabus. It will be a great disappointment if I can't get there. I am looking forward to seeing a bit of Mazandaran – on the north side of the Elburz, it becomes impenetrable jungle, tropical – instead of the barren wastes of the plateau. I shall absolutely love seeing the Caspian. We finally return to Shahi again, resume the car, and go on to Meshed by the ordinary road –

Samman, Sabzevar, Nishapur. Hamber wires he is expecting me to stay again.

I made a last short trip 3 or 4 days ago up the Azerbaijan road to Sultaniya again, sleeping in the village, which wasn't too delightful and then having literally to flee for my life over a mud plain for 10 miles, which was rapidly becoming an impassible bog in a storm – I had just settled down to do a drawing, when the paper was split in half by a blast of wind. Altogether it was not a very pleasant trip – there is so much water in all innumerable watercourses now – I don't know what we shall do in Afghanistan.

You will be pleased to hear I had a long and final consultation with Davies, the doctor last night – he has given me a couple of German milk injections to be injected if there is any recurrence of boils by the time I get to Meshed. I also have elaborate written instructions against fever – he says that with quinoplasmine malaria is no longer a danger, but merely an inconvenience.

Yesterday afternoon (having as usual left everything to the last moment) I frantically had a box made, popped my drawings and films into it, rushed to the customs, kept the whole staff half an hour over time, bribed the lot of them, and finally emerged sweating and triumphant, with the whole thing laced up in a sack and addressed in the indelible pencil on a wet surface to Eric Byron, Savernake station, G.W.R. – then depositing it in Jack's office next door to whom I shall give the necessary documents this morning. [. . .]

There is one lot of films in a flat tin cigarette box. The rest are in envelopes in the portfolio. I'm afraid they won't be of much interest to you yet, as very few – and none of the best have been printed. There must be altogether nearly 1,000 I think – certainly during the last $2\frac{1}{2}$ months I have been taking very good pictures. The drawings are below the films – I hope you will like some of them – I am afraid a good many are unfinished – the sandstorm for example, which is one of the best, must have more body to it. The three diaries are on top of the portfolio. These you may be able to read in parts. They are numbered. The customs thought it a terrific joke when I declared the value at £100. I am insuring it for more.

I am really looking forward to being in Afghanistan again, despite the sufferings of my last visit – I am longing to see Herat in spring. The Ambassador here, who is a member of the royal family, is providing us with a packet of immense firmans, which proclaim our importance and will mean, I think, that we shall be guests everywhere – so long, that is, as the present royal family still obtains. We have a large package of vulgar clocks to serve as presents, and also some gaudy ties for the hotel people in Herat. It is such a comfort to think of their sponge cakes. I hope we shall be able to take the most devoted of them with us as a servant. We shall get a servant of some sort. If trouble breaks out, it will almost certainly be in the south, near the N.W. frontier – which needn't cause you to worry, as we can easily get out of the country without going to Kabul, via Badakshan and Chitral. The passes are not difficult – I think we may try and do that anyhow. The latest news from Chinese Turkestan is bad, and I have given up any hope of getting there. [. . .]

Love from
Bobs

Am laying a store of *porridge*.

2 May 1934   Meshed

Darling Mibble

[. . .] Our journey here passed all bounds of catastrophe. (Do you follow my letters by a map, because if not they must be largely unintelligible?) We left on Sunday 10 days ago. There was a snowstorm in the Elburz, and we only just got through the pass down to Mazandaran – the eastern of the two provinces between the Elburz and the Caspian. You never saw such an extraordinary change – the *whole* of Persia is desert – but on the north of the Elburz is tremendous forest – it happens in half an hour – and the coastal strip seemed just like England, fields with hedges, blackberries and nettles etc. We drove to Ashraf and ate lunch in an old garden during which I almost trod on a cinnamon-coloured snake 5 ft. long, to the alarm of our servant – it was rather alarming. At Ashraf we put the car on the train (the new Persian railway) and went to Bandar Shah, a port on the Caspian just below Asterabad. There, although I had been told by the Minister of the Interior in Teheran that it was quite impossible to go to Gumbad i Qabus, we were welcomed by the military authorities, went to Asterabad that night, and next day launched out on to the Central Asian steppe, the most lovely thing you ever saw, an endless sea of lush green, wild barley and wild oats, full of flowers, irises, poppies, etc., with larks trilling in a spring sky, droves of camels, horses, sheep and cattle grazing here and there, and always a group of kibitkas on the horizon, those black round huts made of felt and poles – *gorgeous* – and not a 10 foot rise in the ground between one's car wheels and the Arctic Ocean. After about 50 miles we saw the tower in the distance – and of course it *is*, as I thought it must be when I put it in my book, one of the most wonderful things in the world – over 300 ft. high, on a green knoll alone on the steppe, made of the finest, strongest brick, pale *café au lait*, with that exquisite kufic writing and a sort of grey green glaze on the roof. Inside circular and quite empty and devoid of the faintest trace of moulding or ornament – with a five-minute echo, which I exploited by singing the 'Arrow' in my best voice.

Now our troubles began. You will see on the map that we were more than halfway to Meshed. But the Bujnurd road proved impassible. We wondered whether to go on by horse and send the car round – but thought better not. So we drove back to Bandar Shah. Then, next morning, we had just got the car on to its truck, when the train went off without us. Rushing to the station master, we shook him – on which a squad of soldiers irrupted, knocked us about and took us to the police station, where we spent a depressing day – peace being made eventually by the old German railway superintendent, who took us to his house and gave us his best room. Simultaneously his daughter, whom he had not seen for a year, and his son-in-law whom he had never seen at all, arrived for one night only – and there were we in the parlour. We got off next morning by the train, disembarked at Shahi and started to drive up the pass on to the plateau. It was snowing again. Suddenly round the corner came a lorry. We collided – there was a fearful crash – I got out, to find the car was all right, everything all right in fact, except my suitcase which was under the wheel of the lorry. All my films destroyed – £15 worth – though fortunately not the ones I had taken of Gumbad i Qabus. This happened on the 24th of April – 10 days, I believe, after the insurance ran out. Will you ask Father to look at the insurance paper and make sure? I threw the suitcase away, rescued a few clothes and my drawing of the tower, which had miraculously escaped. That night, in a pouring deluge, we got to Samnan. Then next morning at 7.30 we broke a back axle. This took till one o'clock to replace (I had luckily insisted on a spare one). At 2.30 we were going along at 40 miles an hour when a cut in the road appeared, very neat and sharp, 3 feet wide and 2 deep. We jumped it. I almost cracked my skull on the hood strut – and the front wheels were like this [drawing] however we proceeded to Damghan. There we met Pybus, returning from Meshed, who had just left his car in a river 2 miles away with the water washing over the roof – a brand new limousine uninsured. This comforted us a little. I tried to comfort him with the tale of my films. We drank 3 bottles of wine for dinner, and had cigars. Next morning we managed to get across the river after a great deal of wading, lunched at Shahrud, and then ran into terrific storms. The road was largely soft sand – twice we had to be pulled and lifted out. I was driving – it was most exhausting, as one had to go a good pace to get through at all, yet if one did one skidded sideways all the time and one had to have one's head outside as the windscreen was quite obscured with spray. Nearly dead, we collapsed into a tea-house at Abbasabad. The next day, it had dried up a bit. We stopped the engine once in a river, but otherwise made very good pace, visited the tomb of Khajgam and Gadar Gar, and got here for dinner, to find the consulate upside down for a fancy-dress ball – I hastily dressed as a charwoman and was very pleased to see all the American missionaries again.

Yesterday we rested. Hamber, by the grace of God, has given me films amounting to 200 pictures for the small camera. So I am not absolutely baulked. It is nice to be back here again – I remember everything so vividly as it was such a haven of comfort and rest and happiness when I got back from Herat after that terrible journey. There is a schoolmaster called Swan here who is also going to Afghanistan, and one problem is how to avoid him, as he is writing a book called 'Through Afghanistan with an opera hat' and is carrying an opera hat in his luggage for the purpose.

I must say I feel really restored to health after the long rest in Teheran in the comfort of the Legation and have been sleeping wonderfully – I am having new luggage made here – suitable for horse journeying. What I am so terribly worried about is the fate of my drawings and films already sent off. I am wiring to the A.P.O.C. about them. If they went down to Mohammera on the outside of a car in the recent weather, they must be utterly ruined. I must go out now, but will go on with this later.

Later

We spent the afternoon looking for luggage to replace what has been destroyed – ineffectually – but there is a lot of old English army equipment here, which we may be able to get hold of. We ought to get off to Herat Sunday or Monday – if the road is still dry. The weather is still unsettled.

I may not have time to write another long letter before we go, so will tell you our plans – but you will only understand them with a map. First Herat, then to Mazar-i-Sherif. Beyond Mazar it is uncertain. We might
1) Make a short excursion east into Badakshan, return to Mazar, and go thence to Kabul – and so to India.
2) Go a little way further east up the Oxus valley, and then turn south to Chitral – and so down to India.
3) Go further east still and down to Gilgit and Kashmir.
4) Go to Kashgar and Yarkand and thence down to Gilgit.
5) Go straight down from Mazar to Kabul, without going any further east at all.

The fifth alternative is *far* the most probable – the others we should only attempt under very favourable 'non-adventurous' conditions. Of our doing no. 4, there is only one chance in a thousand.

But at all events I shall use every means possible to write to you from Mazar – I believe the Afghan post does work, more or less. I will also try and get a letter to the Legation in Kabul to send on to you. But, even if I also write from Herat which I shall do, there may be a very long interval before a letter from Mazar can get to you. This will depend on whether we *can* get up there by car, or whether we have to do it by horse. It will depend on the rivers, and as this has been an exceptionally wet spring, our prospects aren't bright. Then of course, there *is* the possibility that the Afghan post won't work. So you must *not* fuss if you don't hear for 6 or 8 weeks or even 12 weeks, if we go on. You must promise not to fuss when you get this letter – I shall know. It won't be fair if you do – because though not exactly formidable, it will be a fairly difficult journey and if I have the additional worry of thinking *you* are worrying, it will be more than I can bear and I probably *shall* get ill, in which case it will be all your fault. Also I mustn't be accused of not having let you know my plans. I have told you as much as I know myself. You must remember that I don't travel merely out of idle curiosity or to have adventures (which I loathe). It is a sort of *need* – a sort of grindstone to temper one's character and get free of the cloying thoughts of Europe. It is how I develop. I have become quite a different person from what I was when I went away, and the change is for the better. I must develop my life in my own way as my instinct bids and it is hideously agitating to feel that *you*, of all people, who have made me all the good I am, might become an involuntary opponent of further good, for the absurd reason that I can't let you know once a week whether I have caught cold. If you worry, it is an obstacle – I feel caught in a net. You know that I care. The thought of you, above all things, makes me a cautious traveller. If a course is proposed, involving a risk of some sort, it is at once to you that my mind springs. I ask myself if it would be fair to *you*. So you must ask yourself if it is fair to *me* to be upset because of a slight irregularity in communication. Other sons *explore*, seek danger, court disease. So you must let me for once undertake an infantile journey that may take me out of reach of the post for a few weeks. (We have six bottles of whisky. That surely shows a cautious temperament.) When you have read this, promise, promise me to be unconcerned at a silence that may last till August and be astonished at any letters that arrive before. Then I shall be able to enjoy the journey and stand up to it.

I have put the silence at its worst. In all probability, I shall be home before the end of July. Meanwhile, if the drawings and films don't arrive by the middle of June, please enquire from the Anglo-Persian Oil Company in London, and when they do arrive send postcards by airmail both to Kabul and to Cook's Bombay to reassure me.

Incidentally the last person to do the Mazar–Herat journey was an elderly French Professor,[1] curator of the Musée Guimet in Paris.

Goodbye darling – I shall write again before I leave here –

Love from
Bobs

2 June 1934   Mazar-i-Sherif

Darling Mibble

I dare say a message from some less remote spot will reach you before this – but in case it doesn't I write to tell you we are still alive and leaving for Kabul tomorrow in a lorry of our own decorated with flowers and landscapes. We had what I suppose might be called an 'adventurous' journey from Herat – were out all night on that awful pass over the

---

1. Joseph Hackin.

Paropamisus and had to borrow a gun for fear of wolves – eventually the car broke down altogether – no sooner had it done so, in a very lonely spot notorious for robbers with evening coming on, than round the corner rode a rich pistachio merchant who *bought* it for a good price and sent us on by horse to Murghab. At Murghab we found a crazy little old Ford with tyres like old stockings, whose radiator kept falling off – but it got us to Maimena. There we were at *last* in Turkestan, all the people in long flowered gowns, rich green hills, wrestling on the town meadow in the evening, partridge fighting, and abundant food. It was delightful. From Maimena we hired a lorry, and came slowly here photographing the famous Karakuli sheep whose skins produce what is called 'Persian Lamb' – also Turcomans – a Turcoman woman attacked me with a large stick when I tried to take her portrait. We stopped in Balkh, the oldest city in the world, and got here in the dark, about 15 miles away, just as the most awful storm began. Here we found a very civilised place, with a new hotel having a tiled bathroom to each bedroom, soda water, a sort of Harrods run by an Indian, and a doctor educated at Cambridge, an Indian – to my horror, boils had begun again after the terrible day we had getting down the pass – I had started the stannoxye, maximum dose, and it had begun to take them away – but *here* in the chemist's I was able to get stannoxye injections *and* another supply of tablets, and I don't think there will be any more trouble. Thank you very much for having sent them. Without, I don't know what would have happened to me. The Russian consulate have been most hospitable to us and gave a great party, which was very pleasant as there was a lot to drink and they have a very nice collection of records. They say they *may* get us a visa for Samarcand – if so we shall return from Kabul and get the train at Termez just north of here on the Oxus – but I don't think it at all likely, and expect to be home by the end of July if not before. As you can imagine it has been very strange finding all this amenity in a town which is simply *unknown* to the outside world. About 4 Europeans, not counting Russians, have been here in the last 10 years as far as I can make out.

I had hoped to buy you some lambskins, but they are desperately expensive even here – so I am afraid I can't. A good one fetches up to £2.10.0 – and it would need several for a collar and cuffs I suppose.

One drinks sherbet with snow in it – it reminds me of all I have ever read about the east in story books. We have been here a week, very restful. I have done quite a good drawing of the big mosque at Balkh.

The Russians have invited us to dinner again tonight – I must now go out and replenish our stores and get money, which takes the whole morning, as one has to count about 2,000 coins. Goodbye darling – how I long for the moment when I see you standing in the porch. How are the foxgloves? I hope there will be one apricot coloured one for me to see.

Love from
Bobs

The garden here is full of sweet williams and hollyhocks. I'm sorry this letter has got all over Ovaltine.

15 June 1934　　　　　　　　　　　　　British Legation, Kabul

Darling Mibble

[. . .] We now visit Ghazni – then go straight down to Peshawar, and thence by train to Bombay, stopping at Delhi for a day or 2. I couldn't pass through the station without going to look at it again – it really has had such an effect on my life, and there are new things to see. We hope to sail by the *Rawalpindi* on the 30th, arriving Marseilles July 13th – so I should be in London on the 14th – by the P. & O. special.

The Legation here is like a large country house in a beautiful garden – we are enjoying the Minister's hospitality immensely – too much so in fact, as I have over-eaten, and as a result am feeling very ill this morning with stomach-gripes etc. So forgive a short, dull letter. You shall read all about our journey in good time. It has been rather remarkable really – we are the first Englishmen to do it, I believe, since 1885 and the first to motor it. I enclose 2 photos – of our vehicle, chauffeur, chauffeur's assistant and 2 guards – the one with me in has been spoilt by Xtopher moving his hand, but I send it all the same. It is a comfort to think the camera is working. I shall have the rest developed in Bombay.

I don't think I have overdone it – don't feel depressed or anything, though naturally very tired. We travelled slowly – that is what saves one. But I dread the heat in India, which has already been making records this year, and is apparently up to about 127°. Also the journey will be dreadful, the sea very rough to Aden owing to the monsoon, and no way of avoiding this disgusting P. and O., as the Italian boats don't fit. So I may get home a bit of a wreck. What a moment it will be. I have never spent such a *busy* year – not a moment's respite from travelling or preparing to travel – and can truly say I have accomplished everything I set out to accomplish, provided the drawings, films and MSS all get home safe. You are quite right, I shall be at home for a long time working on them. I trust Aubrey will allow himself to be caught some time.

Goodbye darling – this will be the last letter I hope, I shan't write from India unless something unforeseen happens. What an autumn it will be – I think I should never come back to England if I hadn't a home in the country. Will you meet the train this time? I think you must – for you never have yet and it is 11 months – or will be.

Best love from
Bobs

I have just read *Brazilian Adventure*[1] – or part of it. Very disappointing – in fact I have ceased to feel jealous!

---

1. By Peter Fleming.

7

America
1935

ON RETURNING from Persia in June 1934 Robert and Christopher, eager to unwind, indulged themselves in an orgy of jokes, creating an anonymous novel, text written by both of them, illustrated by Christopher and published by Macmillan. This production, entitled *Innocence and Design* by Richard Warburton, is now something of a rarity, only 750 copies having been issued. Robert struck a more serious note with his articles on Persia for *Country Life*. These aroused admiring comment and enabled him to contemplate a lecture tour in America, arranged for him by the Institute of Persian Architecture in New York, run by a Miss Elkins. Before leaving he showed his new drawings of Persia and Afghanistan at the Walker Gallery. The staff regarded this exhibition as a modest success 'considering the poor times in which we live'.

The poor times were also Robert's concern at home. Mr Byron, who had never recovered from the financial disasters of 1931, felt he could no longer continue to live at Savernake. It was difficult to get staff; a little waiter imported from Austria complained bitterly of the loneliness; to get anywhere meant negotiating three miles of unmade-up roads through the forest, always liable to produce punctures from their flinted surfaces and often, in winter, with trees down. The great question was where to go? The family's first enthusiasm centred round Ancombe, a derelict keeper's cottage lying in the woods of the Longleat estate. But after many discussions Henry Weymouth felt that having to provide electricity, sewage and a new road rather outweighed his kind intentions to house them. Another landlord, Lord Cardigan, was not so co-operative over a house they liked at Chisbury, situated in a Celtic fort. In anticipation of a move, Robert was broken-hearted at having to sell his hunter Aubrey. Even while in New York Robert started to mull over the idea of travelling on to Peking, where Desmond Parsons had taken a house and had a suite of rooms waiting for him. In China he would avoid the arguments at home over housing, which were bound to be insoluble since his taste and his father's pocket could never be reconciled.

Early in January 1935 Robert set off for New York to stay with Mrs Otto Kahn, who, besides being a Persian enthusiast, presided over Manhattan's musical circles.

---

12 January 1935   The Shelton, New York

Darling Mibble

[. . .] I haven't written because I felt so ill and depressed *after* the crossing – it had the most awful effect – fearful headaches, no sleep etc. – but am all right now and beginning to enjoy myself and look about.

The dinner on Thursday was a complete fiasco: it began at 7.15 and not till 11 did my turn come to speak, by which time the audience of 200 were writhing in their chairs with boredom and fatigue – however I did speak all right, my jokes were laughed at, and the pictures much admired. Who should appear at the other end of the table but *Herzfeld*! We didn't speak.

I have left Mrs Kahn's and settled here – I send you a picture of the hotel shewing my room with a cross. It is a corner room, with two windows looking different ways, and the morning sun is streaking in. Though *only* 20th floor, it has lovely views and I shall hope to do you some drawings, I chose it for that really. It isn't a bad hotel, having a library and a swimming-bath – much frequented by the English, and I find to my horror that S.B. is lurking in it, again down and out – and doubtless prepared to involve one in any swindle if he can. Maurice Bridgeman, who now represents the Anglo-Persian Oil Co. here, is in terror. Odom, whom I stayed with in Venice, is also about – but otherwise I have hardly seen anyone, as I was too lazy to send out my letters till yesterday so am leading a rather lonely life, which is quite pleasant for a bit while I do my sightseeing. I went to the Metropolitan Museum and at last saw that *lovely* landscape of Toledo by Greco – and also the picture of the Cardinal – this morning I go to see a collection of pictures belonging to the Lewisohns[1] – modern French I believe and shall return to the Metropolitan. Yesterday I heard the Philharmonic orchestra – with Schnabel playing the Emperor concerto, but it made no particular impression – but perhaps I was too far off. [. . .]

I can't start and tell you what New York 'is like', as I am still rather numb. But it is much *more* like England than I expected. Everyone dresses and does their hair exactly like you – the skyscrapers look lovely in some lights, I send you a postcard of the latest one which I went up yesterday – when one sees the town from that height, hemmed in by 2 rivers, they have a sort of *raison d'être*.

The noise and the steam-heat are the worst features.

My lectures haven't been so well managed as I thought – but I can't tell for about a week how they will pan out. The last one is at the end of February so I shan't be home till the beginning of March. [. . .]

Best love darling
from
Bobs

The Shelton, New York

17 January 1935

Darling Merge

Thank you so much for your letter of Jan. 7th, which arrived yesterday – I am so worried to hear you are still bad. [. . .] I too have been a victim of what I imagine must be your trouble this year – a kind of bronchial flu, a new kind, which upsets people. Mine hasn't been bad, but I got worried about a constriction in the chest, besides being very depressed and unable to do anything, so this morning I went to a doctor, the old family practitioner type, said to be very good, who tested my lungs, examined my throat and ears, took my blood pressure and temperature, and pronounced all *perfect* – so that having imagined I was suffering from pneumonia, dysentery, apoplexy and frostbite, I came away quite cured. But I still feel rather low and without energy.

I have begun to see newspapers here and there seems to be a chance of

---

1. Collectors of the French Impressionists.

my getting a good deal to do – only it has been held up for a day or two by my debility. As for the lectures, the Institute[1] have really let me down completely, and though I have a few, I shall have to go after them myself – I shall try and what they call make 'contacts' now, with a view to a transcontinental tour this time next year, which might take me across to China. You will be glad to hear that the Persian trip in the spring has been postponed till the autumn – so I now have no time limit and shall have comfortable time to get my travel book done in the summer – and also probably to employ Anne during the period, if she is still at home. [. . .]

I am beginning to go out here a good deal now – and have succeeded, thank heaven, in attaining various quite separate environments, so that I can always get a change. I am a member too of 3 clubs, two of them the best in New York – but haven't dared use any of them yet.

What I find here – which I didn't expect, is that there is a very large stratum of purely English people who approximate in behaviour and tastes to the English university – educated professional people, to people like ourselves – their standard of manners is what ours was before the war. They strike one as the real thing, rather boring perhaps, but essentially non-vulgar. This gives a very pleasant background to life here. The rich intelligent Jews are like they are anywhere. There is, I suppose, a pseudo-aristocracy of the billionaires, but them I haven't come across, though one knows them from London. But altogether, social life strikes one as strangely pre-war – people have At Home afternoons. At a large lunch at the Lewisohns, who have very fine modern pictures, half the men were in tail coats. One sees old ladies out in their broughams – the buses are primitive to the last degree, and haven't self-starters. People here, when one says one has just arrived, look at one like a medical case and wonder how one is standing up to it. Personally, I find it rather a restful, easy place, once one has got used to the noise and the big buildings. [. . .]

Love from
Bobs

---

1. The American Institute of Persian Art and Archaeology.

I have just been to the Morgan Library, where I unearthed the manuscript of Byron's *Isles of Greece*, which they didn't know they'd got!

This is the only country in the world where *no one* asks me if I am a relation of Lord B. – such a comfort.

28 January 1935   The Shelton, New York

Darling Mibble

I am so glad to get a little more cheerful letter from you – if only filled with hate, but I can imagine how horrible it must be in a hotel at Torquay. By now I expect you are safely back and I hope better, and also Father.

I have no news – I can't remember what I do from one day to the next – except that I never seem to have a meal alone. Peter Hesketh[1] has arrived unexpectedly, on his way to California to grow peaches. He calls 5th Avenue Piccadilly, which is such a proper attitude. In fact I have had my first good laugh at everything with him. We went up the Empire State Building this afternoon (the highest, over 1,000 feet). 'This elevator', announced the lift-man 'is travelling 1,000 feet a minute.'

'Good Heavens,' we replied, 'twelve miles an hour – it's the slowest thing we've ever been in.' He was speechless with rage.

The squalor and filth of all but the centre of New York beats anything I have seen since pre-Fascist Naples. As for that snowfall it has already cost the city 2,000,000 dollars trying to get the streets clear and has become a political scandal. The roads haven't been cleared at all, and are therefore higher than the pavements – but as they are filled with extraordinary metal ventilators at intervals, out of which steam pours (presumably from the subway), the taxis fall into a series of pits and it takes about an hour to get anywhere.

It is dreadfully boring here really despite the gaiety and hospitality – boring that is, compared with one's life in England or even Persia. However don't tell people I say this, as it sounds so bad when everyone is so kind.

---

1. Trained as an architect and illustrator.

I go to Washington Thursday till Tuesday, mainly to see the *National Geographic Magazine* [. . .] its illustration editor, thanks to Kermit Roosevelt,[1] visited me the other day – and really seemed much impressed by my pictures. However, as he was returning to Washington at once, I have sent the whole lot, 1,000, down to him by post with a catalogue, to go through before I get there. I really have hopes of this. I am also writing for the *New York Times* and a magazine called *Asia* – and ought to make £100 out of articles and photos, which, with what I get from my few lectures, ought just about to cover expenses.

I am making a collection of 18th century words still in use, which are attractive in conversation –

> benefit = charity
> chimney piece
> pitcher = jug
> closet = cupboard
> pocket-book = lady's bag
> (is this 18th century?)

I went to see Lady Lindsay[2] yesterday, who is up here (she is American) – and she has arranged for me to see the Embassy besides recounting another Lutyens saga almost equal to New Delhi. She said she and the Ambassador had pored over my articles on that subject.

I am also going to see Mrs Winthrop, which is said to be a great honour – a descendant of one of the War of Independence Governors who still has his 18th century family portraits and possessions.

Such vestiges of history as one observes here are very touching, and *so* English, in such a domestic way. I was much moved too, going to that ghastly film *The Iron Duke*, when the whole audience clapped the Scottish pipers.

I have no other news I don't think. Everywhere I have ever been abroad before I have always wished: if only you were here, if only you

---

1. Son of President Theodore Roosevelt. In the First World War Kermit won the MC while serving with the British army in Mesopotamia before transferring to the American army in France. Author of *The War in the Garden of Eden*, *The Happy Hunting Grounds*, etc.
2. Elizabeth, wife of Sir Ronald Lindsay, British Ambassador in Washington.

could see this. For the first time, I don't wish anything of the sort. I think you would be bored stiff!

Goodbye darling
Love from
Bobs

6 February 1935   The Shelton, New York

Darling Mibble

[. . .] I went to Washington for a long weekend – Thursday–Tuesday mainly to see the *National Geographic Magazine* people – and with some success, I believe, though nothing is actually settled yet. They have a reputation for paying enormously. Also, I find on getting back here that I have got another lecture – in Philadelphia on the 16th – so I think my expenses should be nicely covered by the end. Meanwhile I am consumed by a desire to go on to Peking – Desmond writes perpetually offering me a *suite* in his house – but there is no chance of it really, unless I have a sudden windfall. [. . .]

Washington is a fine city – or will be in 10 years, when all the new buildings and lay-outs are completed. They have one lovely memorial there, to the Merchant Marine – a bronze *wave* with a string of sea-gulls hovering over it. I went down there with Peter Hesketh who has now gone on to California. We did the conventional sightseeing, went out to Mount Vernon, Washington's house and estate – a grubby little wooden building, but with pleasant rooms and beautiful mantelpieces – also a lot of the original furniture – a fine park, with a vista down to two lodges – and a superb view over the Potomac river at the back. It is a romantic place, and gives one a sense of the enterprise that must have been needed to set up out there to live like a gentleman in the 18th century.

We also went to hear a debate in the House of Representatives neither more nor less edifying than the House of Commons.

The White House is a charming old building, rather like Government House, Calcutta, but better and a little earlier. The President has no privacy. One is allowed to walk right up to the windows.

I made myself ill one night eating turtle for dinner, and was rewarded while being sick at 2 a.m., by a rattle of shots in the streets outside. A street-car (tram) hold-up. The bandits got away with 2 dollars!

The Ambassador very kindly took me round the Embassy – Lutyens' last big work – full of faults, but it is *architecture*, which nothing else is somehow – Queen Anne style in the grand manner. Lutyens himself has never seen it finished, so I shall enjoy telling him about it.

I also dined at the Canadian Legation – the first civilised meal, as far as drinks were concerned, I have had in this country – very imperial, portraits of the King and Queen, etc.

My most curious encounter was little Lelis, who used to be Governor of Mount Athos – do you remember Mark's drawing of him? It was funny to meet again in America.

I flew back in a howling snow-storm – being unable to face the appalling heat of the trains. They tried to make the aeroplane as hot, but luckily a few draughts got in.

I can't tell you how loathesome, how inconceivably disgusting, the landscape is here. Even from the air it almost made me feel sick. I dare say it is better in spring or summer – now everything is under snow, which adds to the squalor of the millions of little detached houses sitting by themselves, but without any gardens or hedges.

I went to a new Russian opera last night called *Lady Macbeth of Mtsensk* – a plagiarism of all the others, with 3 murders, 1 suicide and a flogging – no doubt a typical week-end party under the Czar. Stokowski and Toscanini were both in the audience, but Alas! the Philadelphia orchestra season is now over, and I shan't hear it. I am going to another Toscanini concert next week – all Wagner unfortunately – he chooses the most *ghastly* programmes. [. . .]

I am so glad to get a cheerful letter from you at last, and to hear you are really better, and also Father a little. It breaks my heart to think of Aubrey really gone – I didn't realise I should mind so much. I kept thinking of it all through the opera last night. I hope Anne's new horse suits her. [. . .]

Best love darling
Bobs

19 February 1935

Darling Mibble

A hurried line on getting back from Philadelphia – imagine my feelings on arriving there to see people in *queues* at the Museum – I had an audience of over 1,000!!!!

The lecture was really quite a success – a travel lecture – they saw my jokes and I had arranged the pictures so that they illustrated what I was

saying automatically. I have just this moment repeated the same lecture, this time in a rather more accomplished fashion, at the Colony Club, New York's most fashionable and exclusive (no Jews) ladies' club – with equal success apparently, so now I feel really a new confidence and almost wish I had more than one more lecture to give – at Princeton University today week. I was horrified to find in the audience today a Persian female spy – who was largely responsible, I believe, for Christopher's arrest in

Shiraz, and will now, I have no doubt, hurry off my various sarcasms on the subject of the Persian inferiority complex to the Shah – making it more difficult for me to go back there than before.

I saw the *Saturday Evening Post* in Philadelphia and have hopes of getting them to accept an article. [. . .]

Gabriel Herbert[1] has just arrived and I am going to take her to the Rainbow Room for a cocktail – it is on the 60th storey of Radio City, and is by way of being New York's smartest and gayest night club. I went there the other night and saw a lot of people dancing very slowly, on a floor revolving equally slowly, in the dark, to a *wurlitzer organ* – and drinking small doses of gin in the intervals – this is what they call gaiety here. In haste.

Love from Bobs

---

1. Sister of Mrs Evelyn Waugh.

23 February 1935   The Shelton, New York

Darling Mibble

[. . .] I still can't make up my mind what to do – whether to come home, go to China, or stay on here. My whole purpose in going to China would be to get those books written in a place where it costs nothing to live – I find England so much more expensive than *anywhere* else – and having now exhausted Persia and Afghanistan journalistically, I don't know how to make any money when I come back – whereas China would give me some more material. But it all depends what turns up in the next fortnight.

I feel that after seeing China, I would really settle down to my History of the War, which I am more determined than ever to do. China would almost complete my preliminary survey of the world, which I always said I would get done by the time I was 30.

I am going to lunch with Mrs Kahn, of whom I am very fond – she is the only *human being* in New York. I went to the Rockefeller Mansion the other day – incredible objects, but the horror and misery of the house made one almost ill.

The week-end in the so-called 'country' was exactly like Netherleigh, scattered with the flotsam of international antique shops, in a wood, among a thousand other woods, each containing a thousand other houses. I walked 8 miles on asphalt roads – and saw a cardinal bird – a red bird with a long tail and crest that sings in winter – which was the only feature of the hideous landscape that didn't make one want to burst out crying. However I feel much better for some air – and my hostess was really very kind and delightful. She lent me a book by Flora Annie Steel – *On the Face of the Waters* which I found fascinating.

Goodbye darling – I will let you know my plans as soon as I know them myself.

Love from
Bobs

8

Russia
1935

A FTER HIS return from America, instead of writing his travel book
commissioned by Macmillan, Robert spent months working on his
chapter for the prospective Persian Survey now being fathered by
Arthur Upham Pope who had moved to Oxford to encourage its production by the Oxford University Press. Endlessly garrulous on paper, Pope,
whose charm did not compensate for his editorial irresponsibility, only
realized after Robert had produced his chapter on the Timurid Renascence
that its 30,000 words would greatly exceed the maximum allowed to
contributors. Pope tried to assuage Robert by offering him a place in the
second part of the Survey. This Robert turned down, convinced that it
would never materialize and pointing out with some bitterness that he had
taken more time over his chapter, though quite unremunerative, than it
would have taken him to write a book. To conclude the unhappy progress
of the Survey, delayed until 1937: Robert supplied a short chapter on the
Timurids. Pope could not resist rewriting even that, to achieve what he
called a corporate style from all his contributors. Finally Robert had to take
refuge under the protection of Cumberlege, Vice-President of the Press,
who held his proofs inviolate until they were actually in the hands of the
printers. Thus Robert's most scholarly work on architecture, on which he
expended much effort and spirit, has never been published. The Survey,
however, has never been superseded as a monument of erudition, production and printing.

From June 1935 onwards excitement was being created among Persian
scholars by the setting up of an International Congress and Exhibition of
Persian Art and Archaeology, starting on 10 September at the Hermitage in
Leningrad. Robert wrote, 'The exhibition aims primarily at shewing
objects of all dates in relation to objects of similar dates produced by
adjacent cultures.' As *Times* correspondent for the exhibition, he added in
an article referring to Russian policy: 'For now that life in Russia is easier,

that bread and boots no longer absorb the ambitions of a whole population, the State is concerned to promote a new interest in culture. And culture in the true sense of the word – which the Russians understand, for all their ideology – postulates an international exchange of ideas.' This venture took shape under the auspices of Upham Pope (with David Talbot Rice as treasurer) in collaboration with the Russian Professor Orbeli, who had struggled almost single-handed to keep archaeological exploration alive in the dark days. Scholars from all over Europe and America gathered to enjoy the exhibits mainly supplied by Russia, many of which had never been shown before or had been borrowed from remote museums such as those of Alma Ata, Kazan, Bakhtcheserai and Askabad. To be seen were such treasures as the gold foundation plaque from Persepolis, Timur's great cauldron which stood as high as a man, silver from the Jacks' collection and many such riches filling eighty rooms. As a lecturer, Robert was classed as an 'active member' and received Intourist concessions for his journey. Christopher Sykes went along as a tourist.

Robert and Christopher were becoming anxious over the possibility of British involvement in the increasingly belligerent attitude of Mussolini towards Abyssinia; but the Italian invasion on 3 October incurred only cautious sanctions from the League of Nations, under British and especially French influence. Robert was still able, after the Byzantine conference, to contemplate a trip from Leningrad to Central Asia with the ultimate goal of Samarcand, there to complete, possibly in collaboration with Eric Schroeder, his study of the Timurid Renascence, of 'the Oriental Medici'.

The Russian authorities, however, refused to grant Robert a permit to visit such a sensitive area, but extended for two months his visa for Russia. This was not to be wasted, inspite of his disappointment, and the same impetus which took Robert over fences too big for him while out hunting, impelled him to set off for Siberia with one flannel suit, a skimpy coat and plenty of black roubles. It was not until he reached Novo Sibirsk that he decided to push on to China. The chance to finish his Persian travel book in Desmond Parsons's house, away from the upheavals at home, lured him on. With Vladivostok as his exit he decided in transit to explore Lake Baikal and its surrounding tribes, which meant popping in and out of the Trans-Siberian Express, much to the surprise of the passengers. To shorten distances, he flew when he could. Out of sheer necessity his Russian improved, but he maintained: 'Travelling in Russia might rank as a learned profession'.

It is only by looking at a map of Asia that one can grasp the sheer size of the land-mass of Siberia. India looks small in comparison, the Himalayas mere hatching. Lake Baikal is so far east that it shares the same longitude as Peking; it was another three days' journey for Robert from Baikal on to

Khabarovsk, then there was the triangle of Harbin, Mukden and Tientsin to unravel. To be in Korea was a relief. Robert arrived in Peking delighted to see Desmond and the Rosse family, but exhausted.

---

6 September 1935   Leningrad

Darling Mibble

[. . .] It was a great pleasure to see this town again – it is even more beautiful than I remembered, and looks better without snow – Christopher was quite entranced – they have been repainting things a good deal – the Winter Palace is now tomato coloured with white pillars supporting black capitals. Yesterday we went out to Tsarsky Selo, where the big palace beats any palace I have ever seen. In the other palace we saw the Tsar and Tsarina's rooms just as they left them – with all their thousands of photographs and knickknacks – most pathetic – quite *large* rooms, done up at the height of *art nouveau*. Only of course what was lacking in *her* rooms were the flowers, ferns, etc. that there must have been – which made them look bare and gives everyone a wrong impression.

Russia is now becoming rather a bore, to my thinking, the novelty of Bolshevism is wearing off (there are far more shops and food now, and clothes are a little better) – and its attendant inconveniences remain. I was right to have come originally in winter – there is a sort of grimness then which excites one, and is lacking now in the few fine intervals when one can go out. The people look *uglier than ever* – one couldn't believe ugliness on such a scale was possible unless one had seen it. There is the same total ignorance and disregard of standards in other countries – for example, now that there is an Underground in Moscow (for which the plans were prepared before the War) no one can believe that anywhere else has had such a thing for years. All the modernist buildings have grown shoddy and horrible in three years' wear and weather. The persecution continues – since the murder of Stalin's friend Kirov here, between 20,000 and 80,000 people have been 'liquidated' – i.e. sent away, heaven knows where, after being given a few days to sell all they possessed.

And how they all smell.

Lady Muriel[1] is really a most remarkable person – her career in the Revolution here is an epic – she finally got across Siberia, after being in Kiev when it was taken by the Reds, dragging with her 20 governesses and President Masaryk. The British subjects she looks after here are very pathetic – she gets support from our government for them – about £1,200 a year – and the Russians are pretty good. She has built them a little house in the suburbs with a large garden, filled with English flowers, phloxes, gladioli etc. – and lots of fruit. Here she has a large flat and lives *properly*, with properly trained servants – we are paying here 4 gns a week, which goes to the home – this is ⅕th as cheap as a hotel and five times as nice. She gave a party for them all the other day, I talked to an old Mrs Ambrose, widow of a jockey, who is 84 and thinks she's lucky if she gets a seat in a tram. She talked a lot about the Revolution – and once told Lady Muriel that when there was only horseflesh to eat she couldn't touch it, being a jockey's wife!

Our future plans are still uncertain, but the possibilities of an official trip to Central Asia are improving. The chances of this are about even now, I think. If we don't get permission, I don't know what we shall do – as black roubles are very difficult to get at the moment, and without them of course one can't move a yard – we have got a few for pocket money but this won't help a journey.

Now we are just going to lunch with the Consul – so goodbye darling – I will write again soon.

Love from
Bobs

13 September 1935   Leningrad

Darling Mibble

[. . .] I'm sorry not to have written again sooner, but now that things have begun we haven't a moment. The lack of organization is truly Russian – and the bother I have had sending my meagre telegrams to

---

1. Lady Muriel Paget had nursed with the Russian army in the First World War, and returned to Leningrad in 1924 to organize relief for British subjects stranded there after the Revolution.

The Times is unbelievable. I hope they will have published one or two of them.

The first day there was a party in the palace of the Grand Duchess Marie Pavlovna which went on till one – the night before last a banquet which began at midnight and lasted till three – last night a visit to Peterhof.[1] This was the most lovely thing I have ever seen – a low pink and white baroque palace on a hill *all* lit with candles, down the hill a series of cascades and jets of water among which *gold* statues – at the bottom a gigantic fountain about forty feet high with a gold Hercules in the middle of it – and then, cut through a wood, a long waterway lined with fountains, leading to the sea where floated an old three masted sailing ship. It was the most romantic and beautiful scene I have ever seen outside a picture – but very cold – a band was playing and when it got dark there were fireworks. Then back to supper.

Tonight is a concert and reception by the Leningrad Soviet.

Miss Clare Luce (Loos?) the film star has joined the Congress in order to enjoy the festivities. So has Lord Warwick,[2] who followed her to Russia without a visa and when the Embassy in Moscow complained of the trouble this caused them, said he didn't see why the Government shouldn't do something for him for once, since he was always having to entertain *their* guests (i.e. distinguished foreigners) in England. It is all great fun – Mrs Kahn is here, and Mrs Markoe aged 74, and the Kenneth Clarks[3] – I went round the Hermitage with the latter yesterday, which I enjoyed very much. He has got his eye on some of the pictures for the National Gallery.

Unfortunately Lady Muriel is going to Finland tonight – so we shall be all alone here with her curious staff – and I don't know if we shall see her again, as we go to Moscow on Monday and she won't be back. I can't tell you any more about plans yet – and probably shan't know anything till we get to Moscow – I have been able to get some roubles (on *no* account mention these through the post) – and may be able to get more – in which case I shall be tempted to go somewhere. But to tell you the truth I suddenly feel rather tired of travelling, which makes me wonder whether I ought not to go on to China and be done with it before I

---

1. Country palace of the Russian Imperial family.
2. Charles, 7th Earl of Warwick.
3. Kenneth Clark, Director of the National Gallery since 1934, and his wife Jane.

become too inert. *If only* something were settled about the house, I think I would come back, but it really is difficult to work in the state of uncertainty which we have been in all the year – particularly as we all disagree about everything. [. . .]

I am afraid this is rather a dull letter – but I haven't time to start writing about Russia, as I have to be at the Hermitage by ten and it is a long walk. It has turned cold, and I must get out my little coat – I wish I had a bigger.

Goodbye darling – how I wish I was at home\
Love from\
Bobs

20 September 1935   Hotel Metropole, Moscow

Darling Mibble

Don't you admire this writing paper? I am so sorry not to have written for so long – but you have no idea what a rush the end of the Congress has been, getting off my telegrams, saying goodbyes etc. – I don't know if anything I sent has been published – it will be amusing to see if my one or two feeble jokes came out.

Fond as I am of Leningrad, it is lovely to be in Moscow again and to find that everything I wrote about is just as I described it, without exaggeration – particularly *Our Lady of Vladimir* and Roublev's *Trinity* – it confirms one's judgements to find that one's youthful rhapsodies had some real foundation, and I am glad to say that Kenneth Clark agreed with me. It was a remarkable experience going round the Hermitage with him – I have come to the conclusion that I am a very bad judge of pictures when they are presented *en masse* – but I do appreciate the knowledge of others.

As for the Kremlin, you can't imagine how strange it looks to me with all the snow replaced by brilliant apple green grass from which the red walls rise. Unfortunately the Red Square has been *completely ruined* – they have whitewashed the wall behind Lenin's tomb – with the object of showing up the tomb – but as the whole point of the tomb was that its colour harmonised so beautifully with the old brick, the result is heartrending. We went to the Kremlin yesterday – a greater privilege now than it was – and to my horror I found that the staircase of the Granovitaya Palace illustrated in my book has been demolished to make way for a low modern annexe – quite harmless in itself – but that staircase was one of the most historic things in Moscow.

Mrs Kahn, Irene Ravensdale, etc., all leave for Persia tonight[1] and I am very depressed at not going with them, as our original project now has no chance of success – and I am wondering what to do with myself. I will explain the situation more clearly when I write again, but the chances are that I shall be home fairly soon. The only thing that worries me is the news from Europe – Duranty and Fischer, the two most experienced correspondents here, talk as if war was inevitable – and though if it were a question of national life and death, as in the last war, one would have to come home and do what one could, I don't see much point in getting embroiled in a temporary and localised affair. Christopher, who is in the Yorkshire Yeomanry, is still more perturbed. But I expect this sounds to you a gross exaggeration – as it probably is.

We went to *Prince Igor* last night – it bored me so much and was so badly done that I only sat through two acts out of four. They have a new ballet called *The Flames of Revolution* about the French Revolution – this was so *awful* I only sat through one act – like a children's charade [. . .]

Love to all from
Bobs

I can hardly bear your description of hounds in the forest – and I *can't* bear the thought of Mr Scarlett on Aubrey.

23 September 1935   Moscow

Darling Mibble
   [. . .] We have failed to get permission for Turkestan. It is a disappointment I expected. At the same time the Foreign Office have

---

1. Upham Pope was conducting an expedition to Persia consisting of American millionairesses like Mrs Kahn and in addition Irene, Baroness Ravensdale, and the Earl of Warwick. Such socialites turned the expedition into an unhappy failure.

been unexpectedly obliging in other ways, have given me a correspondent's pass for 2 months and also extended my visa. If the rouble problem can be solved, as I hope it can be, it seems silly to come home quite yet – as there is so much of such interest to observe here – and I have a sort of feeling that I might benefit myself considerably by some articles in *The Times* on Russia – though by the time I get back, probably the only subject will be Abyssinia. The news grows worse and worse. We are thinking of going off to Siberia therefore and just seeing where we may get to – Christopher is appalled by the language difficulty, but this doesn't worry me so much as I am so used to it – besides which I can now speak a certain amount, and can even do my own telephoning – which would be an achievement even in English on this system.

I have just finished a final article for *The Times* and have sent them what are really rather good photos of things in the exhibition, considering I had to take most of them through glass. I hope they will publish some of them.

I spent yesterday afternoon in the country with a party of Americans. We drove out along an arterial road, guarded every 100 yards by police, because Stalin's villa is out there (despite the fact that he is in the Caucasus). I went for a long walk – very beautiful country, not unlike England – rolling valleys, half wooded – sun setting, smell of earth and *threat of approaching winter* – desolate – though not desolate to look at. A small village, and a village church – all shut up, grass growing on the steps, a rather vulgar church like St Catherine's or Cadley, with the same kind of railings round it – vulgar tombstones inside, black marble – sad as it could be from the very fact that it had no artistic or other interest.

I took Christopher and Joan Eyes Monsell[1] to the Dragomilovsky Cathedral the other night – it wasn't quite so full as when I went before – but there were far more young people, children etc. [. . .]

We dine with the Urbyes tonight.

No letter – so goodbye darling.

Love to Anne and Father

Bobs

---

1. Married first John Rayner and then Patrick Leigh Fermor.

30 September 1935   Sverdlovsk (Ekaterinberg)

Darling Mibble

Here I am in the Bolshoi Ural Hotel with a private sitting-room and a bath – though the latter is unconnected with any water supply. At the last moment those mysterious authorities in Moscow refused to extend Christopher's visa – so I am now alone – and I must say, was slightly depressed when I got here yesterday morning and could communicate with no one. However at last, by dint of telephoning, two of my travelling companions found a lady who spoke French. I said, 'You speak French like a Frenchwoman'. She said 'I am French, born in Paris' – so she now goes about with me. I also made friends with the Hotel barber, who speaks German, having been born in the old Austrian Empire at Cernovitz (now Rumania) and taken prisoner in the war and remained here ever since.

We went to the house where the murder[1] took place and could go inside, but not see the cellar in which it happened – this being now filled with archives. Dalton saw it several years ago.

This is a most remarkable town – that is, if all accounts of what it was like before are true – broad boulevards well planted, with tall blocks of flats in the modern style, up-to-date shops and public gardens everywhere. A big theatre, built just before the war, where I saw *Aida* last night – by a company sent from Moscow for a season – good voices, at least the men's, grouping good but décor frightful – rather like Susan Robinson's drawings if you know what I mean. *They* think it terrifically modern, and rather pathetically ask if we have anything like that in England, or like 'their' new architecture!

I thought I should have to look at factories here, but thank God they don't seem at all anxious for me to do so. Did your beryl come from here? I am going to look at an Ural stone shop this morning. In fact I must go now, to meet Madame – She isn't here yet – there is a desk in my room on which stands a marble ink apparatus that would take a strong man to lift – quite new – the Russians still have their taste for size. This hotel, also quite new, has passages 15 feet wide, and of course two or three miles long. I like that.

I am going to take some photos this morning – being assured by the

---

1. Of Tsar Nicholas II and his family.

highest possible authorities there is no objection – but I am quite sure the first policeman who sees me will stop me.

I also have a telephone in my room, which helpfully started ringing at 12.45 a.m. just as I was going to sleep. There was a ball in the hotel last night – the usual village whist-drive atmosphere – with a brass band to complete the effect.

I go from here to Novo Sibirsk (formerly known I believe as Novo Nikolaievsk).

Goodbye darling – I will let you know plans soon – as I shan't be dawdling – the winter is too close.

Love from
Bobs

All Russians have their hair cut *straight* across the nape of the neck and very high up – so that they all look as if they wore wigs.

4 October 1935   Novo Sibirsk

Darling Mibble

This is the capital of Western Siberia. You may find it in my atlas as Novo Nikolaievsk at the junction of the Trans-Siberian railway with the river Ob. Anyhow that is where it is. They call it 'the second Chicago'. Why, is not apparent. There is no particular vulgarity or ostentation about it – but lots of good modern buildings. And I was interested, on going to register with the police today, to find myself in the actual building – 'Dom Sovietov' – whose plan and elevation I published in the *Architectural Review* 3 years ago, before it was built.

I arrived late last night – there wasn't a bed to be had, owing to a conference of provincial executives – but fortunately there is a German Consul here who, with his wife, treated me like a father and mother, gave me a huge dinner (though they had had theirs), opened a bottle of German hock and poured brandy down my throat to stave off a cold – which I am afraid it has not done. Herr Consul then telephoned to the Foreign Office representative here, and in a short time a room was produced in the new Soviet Hotel, exquisitely clean, and having even a pot of one of those curious variegated plants which the Russians dote on. So the misery I am now suffering from my cold is not so bad as it might have been. Some unfortunate comrade, I suppose, was turned out to make room for me – at any rate, I was lying in bed this morning when in walked a tall, very serious comrade bearing a portfolio and in search of somebody he did not know but whom he took to be me. He was very disconcerted when I began to gurgle with laughter – but it was quite a long time before he *would* go.

I enjoyed myself at Sverdlovsk after I wrote and saw a lot that was very interesting including parties of two or three sluicing earth for gold in the way one used to read of in books about the Klondyke. I also one afternoon went for a ten-mile walk *alone* in the neighbouring forests – that really was delicious. All fir trees, but the needles don't destroy the ground vegetation as with us, it was full of little intimacies, different kinds of mushrooms and ferns, small juniper bushes etc. In a meadow in a valley I came to a stream with a bridge over it, which a peasant woman (with a kerchief on her head) had just crossed, while her husband (in tall boots) was so overcome with drink that he could not leave go of the railings; whereat the peasant woman turned round and scolded him till the hills rang. It was inconceivably Russian. At last I came to a big village on the high road – the children were just coming out of school, whooping and screaming, each with his little satchel. All the windows of the loghouses were draped with lace curtains and filled with geraniums, begonias, fuchsias and those variegated plants. An old woman was filling buckets at a well – one or two young men were bicycling home from their work in the town – and I thought how [much the] same villages are all over the world. The sun was nearly down – on the other side of a lake the white trunks and bright gold leaves of a line of birches were reflected in the still water – behind them stretched 'the dark forest'. It was a beautiful scene, but quite unpaintable. I had noticed that in the galleries of Moscow and Leningrad, Russian landscape-pictures aren't really paintings at all, they are just a collection of associations to try and make one cry.

Herr Consul tells me war began on the second – the papers in Moscow before I left seemed to think things would be arranged. I don't know what I shall do if I hear that we and Italy are at war. But whatever it is, I really *will* let you know my plans very soon now.

Siberia thank goodness is having the most lovely weather (whereas in Moscow there was nothing but rain and cold) – cold mornings and evenings, but *hot* at midday, blue sky, etc. – a spell of south wind has set in, which is prophesied to last a month – if it doesn't, I shall have to buy myself an overcoat as my little short one gives too little protection to the knees.

I wonder if *The Times* have published my long article on the Congress yet and have used any of the photographs. It really was a tribute to my new camera being able to take those pictures, some of quite small objects in glass cases. [. . .]

Goodbye darling [. . .]

Love from
Bobs

9 October 1935   Novo Sibirsk

Darling Mibble

I have decided to go on to China – such an opportunity as I now have will not recur, as I will explain to you when I can write at greater length. I go on by train from here, and hope to stop at Irkutsk (on Lake Baikal) and Birobijan, the Jewish republic, on the way. I did not tell you I had flown here, as I intended flying further and I thought you might be worried – but the service from here is too uncertain – and as by great good luck I can get a wagon lit from here, I am taking it instead. I feel rather disinclined towards adventure at the moment – travelling in Russia without a secretary or guide is *too* difficult, particularly at this time of year when the cold is just beginning. In addition to which I feel rather low after my cold, and have a slight neuralgia. In fact I should have been rather unhappy here, but for the infinite kindness of the German consul and his wife, with whom I had all my meals, and who have doctored me. I am purchasing a winter outfit.

The flights were really wonderful – one saw the great Russian rivers unfolding as though on a map. We stopped the first night at Kazan – then Sverdlovsk – from Sverdlovsk we flew here in a day, lunching at Omsk on the way. Siberia is different from European Russia – fewer forests and those mainly birch (at least in this latitude) – endless lakes – and then the enormous rivers winding across from one horizon to another. The aeroplanes were very comfortable – I wish to goodness I could go on that way. I was very busy *mending my clothes* on the last flight!!!

Every morning at breakfast the Consul and I scan the local newspaper – it appears that the Italians are not having things all their own way. But there is no news at all of what is happening at Geneva, and what part England will play – so I don't know whether I *am* running away from a war or not.

I shall hope to be in Peking (Peiping) by the end of the month. I hope the manuscripts will have gone off all right. I explained to Father about Cook's sending them. In two months or less I ought to get the book[1] finished, and then I shall probably come home, unless some miraculous job turns up there. I have got to go to Japan anyway on the way from Vladivostok – there appears to be no direct boat service to Tientsin. [. . .]

Goodbye darling – I am so longing to hear from you again.

Love from
Bobs

13 October 1935   Irkutsk

Darling Mibble

I arrived here yesterday midday after a journey of two nights and two days – and was thankful to be met by a representative of the local authorities and an interpreter, which made things easier than they have been on arrival elsewhere. I have a huge room in the hotel and am now waiting for breakfast. As I left the German Consulate at Novo Sibirsk, Frau Grosskopf said she was sending me a packet of sandwiches for the train. A *crate* arrived, which, now that I have unpacked it, contains food for an army, medicines, cigarettes, knives, forks, plates and a bottle of brandy. So I shan't starve in these wastes. Winter began the night before last – and personally I find the snow much more cheerful than the threat of it – which generally takes the form of rain. There is a sharp cold. We went to the theatre last night – a revolutionary drama

---

1. *The Road to Oxiana.*

shewing the destruction of the Black Sea fleet. The usual Athanasian contrasts – the white officers all painted clowns, the red sailors all noble heroes. Today I shall see the town.

I hope it is all right about the manuscripts to Peking. I left all I wanted in a little heap, which I shewed to Father – also Cook's correspondence on the subject.

Siberia isn't as flat as people generally say, in fact the old story about the Tsar drawing a straight line with a ruler to mark out the course of the railway must be all nonsense – neither as a whole nor in small sections is it straight. The country round the Yenissei at Krasnoyarsk is quite mountainous.

Later

All good furs here are snapped up for export, the Siberians disport themselves in shaggy garments of calf and dog – though one sees fine furs made up at an earlier date. I myself have a long white coat, sheepskin inside with a rich collar of brown dog. I spent three hours last night sewing 2 buttons on to it and making two fasteners for them, breaking two needles in the process. [. . .]

I only wish I had come here a bit earlier as now the winter is really beginning, sledges are coming out and the hotel is filled with women pasting newspapers over the cracks in the windows so that one cannot go off into the forest and sleep anywhere as I should like to do.

I spend most of my time here waiting for people to keep appointments, *they* think it perfectly natural to be 3 hours late, but are furious if *you* are 5 minutes. My whole energies are devoted to trying to find some warm boots – pointing out that a political scandal will ensue if the distinguished English writer is allowed to freeze to death. So far there have been none forthcoming – but this morning the very highest officials are being approached. When I have got them I shall move further east, and propose to reach Peking in about a fortnight.

I grow daily thinner.

Goodbye darling – love to all [. . .]

Bobs

31 October 1935   Irkutsk

Darling Mibble

We (the interpreter, the official representative and myself) got back from our trip yesterday morning. I was both disappointed and relieved not to find any telegram from you – the first, because I longed to hear, the second because it means there is nothing urgent or agitating – in which case I am glad you did not go to the expense.

I really enjoyed Baikal. We were 9 days on the steamer – went right up to the north and rode off through the snow-covered forest to a village in search of the Tienguses and their tents. We only found *one* – though many living in *houses* – with one of whom we spent the night – perfectly clean – but our Buriat guide (Mongolian) made a noise like a lion in travail when asleep – so that I didn't sleep very much. The boat was fascinating – very old, and sailing at an angle of 45° – about the size of a cross-Channel steamer – everyone very friendly – many hunters on board, with stories of bears, wolves, sables etc. People wearing what one always imagined people in Siberia did wear – high boots, baggy trousers, embroidered blouse, enormous fur caps tied on top with ribbon (generally grey squirrel) and huge shaggy overcoats of dog or calf. The last night they all sang and danced – one most beautiful song about Baikal composed at the time of the political exiles – the most beautiful of *all* Russian songs I have ever heard – it is famous in Russia but I have never heard it sung abroad. I am getting the words written down.

I tried in the north to buy you a pair of reindeer fur boots all done in pattern. But it was the one moment of the year when they were unobtainable as all available had been bought up at the beginning of the winter, and new ones had not been made by the tribes who were up in the mountains. I bought a little mit instead which is a great comfort to my feet.

When we got back to Baikal station, instead of coming back here we went off to Vlan Udé (on map Verchné Udinsk) round the other side of the lake. In my geographical fecklessness I thought it would be a 2-hour journey – it was *14*, hard class, that is confined to shelf 2 feet wide with 2½ feet of headroom – people in three tiers and such a smell, such an awful atmosphere that every hour I had to go and stand in the snow between the carriages to breathe. We arrived in this unknown town at 3 a.m. – found a wooden cart, and got to a small hotel where I slept on the floor in the corridor. The town is the capital of the Buriat republic, Buriat being Mongols who have settled in Russia and adopted Russian habits. We saw enough of it, and them, in a morning – and by great good luck and a lot of fighting managed to get places on the Manchurian express that night, back here. The exquisite comfort of a wagon lit made me long to go straight on to China – but I want to see a bit more of Siberia first – and am now waiting to arrange about going on probably to Khabarovsk.

There was an Englishman in the next compartment of the train, travelling through from China. He regarded all Russians as fiends, felt himself in peril even in the train, and was rather surprised at my popping in one evening and popping out next morning.

I have a lot of shopping to do – having *no* clothes at all except that old flannel coat and a pair of flannel trousers – and winter is here, it is rather awkward. I hope to buy a pair of quilted trousers. [. . .]

Love from
Bobs

We had a tremendous storm on Baikal – you wouldn't think a lake could be as rough as the Channel – waves over the deck, dashing against the windows – and as nothing was fixed, and every door banged at every wave, you can imagine the noise.

10 November 1935   Khabarovsk

Darling Mibble

There seems *hope* of an envelope in this town.

I find at last, I can speak enough Russian to cope with situations. No one met me here at the station. I trundled into the town seated on a peasant cart. There was no room at the hotel – there never is. I begged to know if I should sleep in the street. On which *two* rooms, each containing *four* beds, were produced for my exclusive use. In them I was devoured by bugs and had to sleep on the floor. The next day another vast apartment, furnished in a style of such horror you might think it was a sophisticated joke, yet comfortable (with 5 electric lights and a nude female statue coloured) was put at my disposal.

This town has a wonderful situation, on a series of hills overlooking the Amur, which is about ¾ of a mile wide – with all their town planning, they make nothing of the situation – the river is carefully fenced out of sight whenever possible. A lot of new buildings – and all very gay, with banners, loudspeakers on the lamp-posts, and then endless portraits of the Bolshevik Trinity and Apostles, for the 18th anniversary of the Revolution – we even had a gala supper on the train.

Having got almost to America, as you see on the map, it now appears quite impossible to get from here to Peking without an enormous detour. I had naturally intended to go on to Vladivostok and thence by rail to Harbin. But Harbin is in Manchuquo – and the Japanese Consul here informs me without a smile that since he has nothing to do with Manchuquo authorities, he can't give me a visa to go that way. The nearest Manchuquo consul is at Blagoveschensk, further west – I telegraphed to him yesterday to ask if I could cross the frontier there and get on to the new railway which the Japanese, I mean the Manchuquoans, have made from Harbin northward. He wired back this morning to say that he has telegraphed to his headquarters to know if he can, and will then telegraph again. You can imagine what all this is like in Russian, particularly his *name* – Mr Ti-Cho-Kui-Khui-Chi – However he addresses me as '*Gospodin*', a genteel title extinct since the Revolution. Even if I do go back to Blagoveschensk, it is then doubtful if I can get across the Amur, as it will be full of ice floes, and not yet frozen. There is no bridge. If on the other hand I go on to Vladivostok, I can then get a boat on the 20th which will deposit me on the coast of Korea, whence boats to Tientsin go only *once a month*, or else take me to Japan, to Tsuruga, whence I must take a train to Kobe, and then another boat to Tientsin. Meanwhile my money is running rather short – I can only have one meal a day in the restaurant here, which is pretentious and expensive (by Russian standards) and bad – otherwise I have pathetic little dormitory feasts in my room – and have to go out shopping to get my bread and butter fresh.

Today an interpreter arrived – skating champion of the Far East, and teacher of English – but had never *spoken* any before so it is I who am teaching him.

The museum here is very interesting. I have always had a great curiosity about Kamchatka, Sakhalin and the curious yellow tribes, with Shamans and their own primitive art, which lurk in this part of the world – also about the long-haired Amur tiger. They are all on show – and I spent most of today photographing various objects.

It is much warmer here than at Irkutsk – my quilted trousers and felt boots have proved unnecessary so far. I should very much like to come back to Siberia in the summer – travelling off the beaten track is so difficult now – one can't afford to be caught by the cold unawares, but one could spend months here studying obscure people – and it is fascinating to be in a country where wild animals are still a menace and an adventure – as one used to read of. Where small boys tell stories of packs of wolves pulling the roof off papa's cowhouse and women picking raspberries suddenly see bears looking at them through the canes, the bears being similarly engaged. I should like to come out here with some people who shoot.

I have just done – completed that is – a sketch of a boatload of people on Baikal – the general *scene* is so unsketchable here that I am reduced to people, and am reverting to my old Eton style, like the Fourth of June. (Incidentally among the many useful words in my Anglo-Russian *pocket* dictionary, compiled in *Moscow*, I find 'oppidan').

I have really spent most of my time in Siberia playing patience. In the train I racked my brains to try and remember that enormous game that Punch plays, but couldn't, then tried to invent one, but again failed.

Everything is running out. Books (I have only one volume of Gibbon left to read), clothes in tatters – I have only one coat and a pair of trousers, besides the German coat. I broke three needles putting buttons on to my sheepskin coat – ink and paper are both practically finished. If it hadn't been for those angelic Germans in Novo Sibirsk I don't know what I should have done, they equipped me with *plate* even – not to mention a fringed napkin – so that I have the most elegant meals. [. . .]

Goodbye darling, I do hope I shall get to Peking to find a letter from you.

Love from Bobs

21 November 1935   Off the coast of Korea

Darling Mibble

At last, at last I can write you a *letter* – instead of a few selected anecdotes.

You may have been surprised at my telegraphing so often. Each telegram cost me about 6d. or less – and my entire journey about £11.0.0. – which would have been less if I had not flown the first part of the way. Food, lodging of course was extra – but very cheap considering the length of time.

On the very morning I left Vladivostok – yesterday – news came through that new currency regulations will come into force on Jan. 1st – making the rouble equal to 3 francs – so that I was only just in time. I foresaw this from what I heard in Moscow, and that is why I made no great effort in Novo Sibirsk to return via Central Asia – as I thought that if I did I should lose my last chance of ever getting to China on the cheap. Had it seemed easy I would have tried for Samarcand – but it would have been very difficult, I might have been turned back and then turned out – so I thought I had better go on and see Siberia; which I have done fairly thoroughly. The only thing I did not do which I meant to do was to visit Birobijan the Jewish republic, just west of Khabarovsk. By good luck I got wind of a typhus epidemic there which the authorities are trying to hush up – and as one has to share a room there with about 6 other people, I thought I would be cowardly and avoid the place.

I rather regret having taken the boat. I got permission at last to go by rail direct to Harbin – there is great tension on the frontier, one is searched and risks being kidnapped – in fact trains only travel by day – all of which I should have enjoyed. But my Russian money was running out and I didn't want to spend real money staying another 2 days in Vladivostok till the next train went. And also I thought Korea might really be more interesting. As it is, I have been able to get no visa for Manchuquo which I have to cross via Mukden – so I am still uncertain how I shall go.

I was very successful with my now practised technique in the customs yesterday. *Some* photos I had developed in Irkutsk – very badly, but not ruined. Of these I put the most suspicious, including two excellent views of the house where the Tsar was murdered (which I had to take secretly), in those secret pockets you made me – with all my political notes. The undeveloped films I had to re-seal. I bought some brilliant yellow paper in York for the purpose – cut out with great labour about 20 round tabs – and stuck them on to the new and old alike – they were passed without a murmur, while the G.P.O. man was laboriously looking through all the most innocuous of the developed negatives. The only thing that really aroused their suspicion was a bit of Baikal sponge, the only freshwater sponge in the world, which was discovered by a Polish scientist in exile and named *Lubomirskaia* – so I thought I would send a bit to Henryk.[1] My drawings of Russian drunkenness were also neatly concealed in a page of the *Times Literary Supplement* at the bottom of the suitcase.

I can't write about Russia in general yet – as I am in a state of relaxation prior to arranging my ideas and notes etc. – I hope *The Times* will publish some articles – though not for one to say, they will be *extremely* interesting if I write them – indeed almost definitive, for several years to come.

This boat is charming – chrysanthemums and dwarf trees – it seems a miracle of cleanliness and comfort after Russia: and it is nice to get some beer one can drink. But I would willingly go back to Russia for another 3 months tomorrow – or shall we say next week.

The Japanese preface every remark with a noise like wheezing wood – it is most disconcerting and sometimes lasts about half a minute, so that one wonders if they have throat trouble.

I can't think of plans yet – but will write fully when I get to Peking, and get some letters from you. How I am longing for them. I have been very much out of touch. I didn't even know there had been a general election till yesterday – and still don't know the result.

Goodbye darling – I shall post this on the boat so it will go from Japan.

Best Love
Bobs

I disembark in 2 hours – after only one night. It is entering a new world, I feel rather alarmed. I am afraid this is rather a dull letter – but I am dazed still. It is an *escape* to leave Russia and in Vladivostok I had great trouble with my exit visa, was followed when I went out etc.

---

1. Prince Henryk Lubomirski, a close friend of Robert's at Oxford. They kept up a correspondence until the war which the Prince, who had become a Jesuit, managed to survive in Poland.

9

China
1935–1936

ROBERT'S DELIGHT in seeing the Rosse family and Desmond Parsons in Peking was soon overshadowed by the discovery that Desmond, who for the last three months had been suffering from swollen glands, had developed Hodgkin's disease, not then known to be fatal. It was decided by the family that he must go back to England at once for treatment, they must use the Trans-Siberian as being the fastest route. Hoping to return to Peking, Desmond begged Robert to stay on and look after his house and servants. Robert agreed. It was not till after Christmas that the shock of Desmond's illness and the exhaustion of his journey, with his struggles to make himself understood, really hit Robert. A bout of 'flu brought on a breakdown. For a month he was in a collapsed state but by February he began to spend half days writing his book (*The Road to Oxiana*), his precious Persian diaries and notebooks having been sent out from England by his father. Though recovering Robert was unable to cope with other people; a sober walk with Harold Acton, his neighbour, was all he could bear. Whilst the Chinese way of life began to endear itself to him, he found only a vacuum as far as architecture was concerned. He lacked all stimulus to combat his mental depression. He did struggle to photograph some buildings, thinking he must have something to offer in the way of articles on returning home. A suggestion to *The Times* that he might become their Far Eastern roving correspondent resulted in silence until May, when Deakin, the Foreign Editor, indicated by telegram there was no job at present for him.

Upon hearing this, Robert decided not to linger. Partially recovered, after what he described as the worst winter of his life, he finished his book at the end of May. He decided to go home across the Pacific, making for Washington but stopping off in Japan on the way. He was sad to leave Peking but summed up: 'This is a place for cowards who have given up the struggle with the world, and I haven't quite done that yet.'

30 November 1935   c/o British Consulate, Peiping

Darling Mibble

I have been very remiss about writing since I arrived – for 3 or 4 days I felt quite incapable of action of any sort – and then yesterday we had to take an opportunity of an armed guard to go to the Great Wall – but I am sorry to have been so long.

I hardly know where to begin. I wrote to you from the Japanese boat. Next day I landed in Korea – at Seisin. I had no visa – I could change no money – no one would speak one word of English, for 3 hours I struggled with them in Russian. At last I got on to the train to Hsinking, the new capital of Manchuquo – and hurried into my pyjamas and to sleep, as I thought it would be more difficult to turn me out of the train if I were in bed. However there was no difficulty at the frontier – I bought a visa for 2/– and that was that. They were in a fearful hurry to get the train through, and I learnt afterwards that this route is the most bandit-ridden of *all* – much worse than the Pogranichnaye one from Vladivostok to Harbin, every train has a pilot engine, armed guards etc.

However there were no mishaps, and I forgave the Japanese a lot for the dwarf trees on every table in the dining-car.

It was entrancing in Korea really to see a Korean hat – with all white clothes and curious ivory 'chatelaines' from the waist – the whole thing of transparent black, with the hair sticking up inside like a bird in a cage.

Hsinking was a bore, I stayed one night and then caught an early morning train to Mukden, where the vice-consul's wife Alice Morland was a vague acquaintance of mine. I stayed the weekend with them, which was very pleasant – a social evening at the club – and a long ride next morning with the Consul. The Far East is not so stiff as India. But English cooking has conquered.

Desmond finally met me at the station here. He has a most charming old house, a series of courtyards, with trees, bamboos etc. in them. Lady de Vesci[1] is staying with him at the moment. When she goes, I shall have the whole of one pavilion, with a bathroom.

I have arrived with no clothes at all, and so am now indulging in an orgy of clothes. A tweed suit costs 25/–, an evening suit 30/–, silk shirts about 4/– each. I bought a huge desk like Father's only bigger, with

---

1. Mother of Desmond Parsons and Michael Rosse.

green leather top for 15/–. One pays a servant 16/– a month, and a head servant 30/–, they feed themselves. When Harold Acton lost all his income (it has come back a bit now) he lived here with a large establishment of servants etc. in a lovely house on 300 dollars a month, which is what he earned as a university teacher – the dollar is 1/2 – that is to say on £200 a year, and had a little over for collecting. You and Father could live like princes – plus about £60 each each way for the journey. So if ever you feel you can't bear England any more, there is always Peiping!

My plans for the moment are to settle here for 2 or 3 months, till my book is done – in which time I shall be able to see if money is to be earned journalistically out here, or in any other way. Till I have seen this, I can make no further plans.

I had a wire from Deakin here asking for Siberian articles, so hope to send something really good in a week or two.

Michael and Anne are here – Anne really charming again, though a little too gushing and slightly inclined to be gracious (not to *me*! God forbid). A special party was arranged yesterday for Sir F. Leith Ross[1] to visit the wall – guards out, special coach on train etc. – he never turned up, as it was snowing – but we had the benefit. It was a *wonderful* sight, but we had too little time there – and walking up the wall was so slippery that I had to be dragged up by two men so I shall go back again by myself and try and do some drawings when it is finer. I loathe visiting things like that in a big party.

I start Chinese lessons tomorrow – it is most inconvenient knowing none – Desmond and Harold are very fluent. Harold enquired after you with great affection, before I gave him your message. He sends you many in return. Michael and Anne are going to New York – and I hope they will see Lucy. Michael is very pleased with the seeds I have collected for him in Siberia. He was much touched by your book.

As for Chinese art and the beauty of Peking – I must wait for it to grow on me, or not to do so. But of architecture in the real sense of the word, there is nothing. That I can see straight off. They can build a wall, and make it very big – they have an exquisite capacity for space and layout, both large and small – but cubically and intellectually it is all a vacuum. The colours one must see in different lights – at present they

1. Chief Economic Adviser to the British Government.

are by no means up to expectation. Perhaps with a *blue* sky and *green* trees the effect is different.

Otherwise – apart from the temples and palaces – all is *grey*, the most positive and emphatic grey you ever saw – all the brick is grey – the landscape is as grey as an engraving – the tiles are grey, so is the air.

However in time I shall probably write you a very different description with different feelings. The first impression has left my curiosity curiously dormant – which is just as well perhaps, as I have now to write about Russia and then about Persia. [. . .]

Thank you so much for getting the manuscripts[1] off. They ought to arrive about Dec. 15th, just when I am ready for them. I hope you put in the *whole pile*, which I left ready. I only mention this as you say Father didn't know which they were – and as it was he to whom I explained which they were, it makes me a bit nervous. They were 5 or 6 diaries and a few odd notes etc. – also a batch of typescript.

While I remember: will you please send me out by Trans-Siberian that copy you made of our arms and crest. Something may always take me to Japan – and if I go, I shall not lose the opportunity of having a dinner service made – which would cost about £2.0.0. as far as I can make out. I would design the arms myself but could not be certain of getting the crest right. [. . .]

My Siberian clothes cause quite a sensation here – but I shan't be sorry to get some new ones.

In this house, 3 sides of every pavilion are made of brick, the rest of paper. It is curious how warm they keep. Desmond has only Chinese food – we are all very pretty with our chopsticks – it is delicious I must say.

Goodbye, darling – I will write again soon, when I feel a bit more settled, and try and tell you what Peking is like. I can't absorb anything at the moment [. . .] It must be nice having a new dog though I don't take to setters – I wish I had one here.

Love from
Bobs

---

1. Robert's notes and diaries of his travels in Persia.

China

7 December 1935   c/o British Consulate, Peiping

Darling Mibble

[. . .] I am now beginning to settle down a bit, after a day or two of fearful depression, during which I nearly arranged to come home at once. It is tantalising having no money here, owing to the very cheapness of things. A perfectly good, rather smart tweed suit has cost 30/– to have made. New evening clothes will cost £3.15.0. Both would be £15.15.0. in London. Everything is the same. I am engaging a servant at 15/– a month. One can get such lovely furniture, fixtures etc. for practically nothing. Only *tea* is expensive but I will manage to send you a *little* when I can find a way.

We have done a certain amount of sightseeing, and I have been altogether too bewildered to get on with my Russian articles – though am now in the middle of them and hope they will be good. After the first disappointment at the emptiness of it all, the *charm* of Chinese art is beginning to grow. They have such delightful habits. Every day at dawn and sunset thousands of pigeons fly over the city with whistles attached to their legs – the sky is full of sound – a deep note. During the rest of the day we are treated to demonstrations of Japanese aeroplanes. One is perpetually meeting people going for walks with their little birds – each bird attached to the end of a stick by a string. Then the birds are let off – they fly off and come back again.

The climate is lovely, crisp and cold – it suits me to a T – a pale blue sky, and the golden roofs of the temples of the Forbidden City, when I say gold, I mean imperial yellow. I hope gradually to learn something about China. I have lessons every evening for an hour in the language – which is easy to begin with as there is no grammar at all – but becomes very difficult at a certain point, because all meaning depends partly on the order of the words and partly on those horrible inflections of tone which my ear can't grasp.

Harold gave a dinner, inviting various Chinese, among them a Manchu prince and his wife, both of them painters and poets – and fascinating to look at. We go to see their house tomorrow afternoon. Michael and Anne and Lady de Vesci all leave in about 4 days' time which will be very sad – but will enable me to work properly. The MSS should arrive any day now.

[. . .] The Ambassador and -ress[1] came to lunch the other day – very dull. I suppose I must go and write my name on them, in case I want anything out of them later. She, I found, was one of my public – and displayed proper excitement at hearing that I was me.

I will try and send you some photographs in a day or two, but have not taken anything very interesting – and the buildings here depend so much on colour that they are hardly worth photographing. However, I think they will lend themselves to chalk, but they are very small beer after Persia.

Goodbye darling, best wishes for Xmas and the New Year – it is a comfort to think we are at least connected by *train* – and I am also relieved to find I can get home on a freighter for £57.0.0.

Best Love
from
Bobs

25 December 1935   Tsui Hua Hutung 8, East City, Peiping

Darling Mibble

[. . .] As for Xmas: My teacher Mr Jo, sent me a bottle of liqueur and a student acquaintance, Mr Chang, a card with Lake Lucerne on it, the servants gave me some dried persimmons for my cold, and Harold a picture. I dined with the Cadogans last night, which was pleasant. He is very nice and talked of Constantinople when he was an attaché there with Gerald Berners.[2] Tonight I am dining with Harold and some students.

No one knows how I detest going about in a rickshaw. Harold feels the same – everyone else adores it. I think it is humiliating to feel one is humiliating someone else every time one goes out. But there is no other way of getting about. I am half thinking of getting a pony and governess cart! You never saw anything like the cabs here – very elegant and all glass, looking like Louis XIV *calèches* – and drawn by minute ponies which are quite lost in the shafts.

---

1. Sir Alexander Cadogan and his wife Lady Theodosia.
2. Gerald, 14th Baron Berners, rich and talented eccentric, composer and author of *First Childhood*, *Far from the Madding War*, etc.

I have been obliged to get a decent overcoat – very dark grey, almost black, with a pseudo-sable collar and lined with spotted cat – extremely smart I imagine myself to look – it all cost £4.10.0.

I don't know what has come over me. I *cannot* write. I work all day at the articles – they are still only ⅔rds done. What there is of them is excellent I believe, and ought to cause something of a sensation in *The Times*. But by the time I do get them off, they may not want them. I really can't think what is happening to me – softening of the brain perhaps – I hope it won't continue when I start the book again. But really, I realise now that when I got here I was utterly exhausted – not physically at all, but mentally. My mind wasn't functioning – I can't *remember* anything I saw or did my first fortnight – and then on top of that, this terrible business of Desmond, packing them off, taking over the household, paying all their bills etc., etc. has been been enough to account for some degree of mental atrophy.

I wish you could see my cook – I must do you a portrait of him. Which reminds me that I have sent you two pictures for your birthday and Xmas – though I am afraid they won't arrive till the middle of February. They aren't what you would most like – but nothing good of the type I wanted turned up before Michael's chest went. They are *portraits*, of ancestors. The old woman has a great panel of writing on top of her, which spoils the whole picture. If you have her framed, I thought it would be a good idea to have this writing inserted in the back, as it says who she is – the wife of a Ming emperor. The other one is really rather a fine bit of painting I think, in a minor way. However at Easton I don't suppose you'll want them – so I should just keep them rolled up. In fact it would probably be better *not* to frame them at the moment, as I may get some better ones later.

I must go to dinner. Goodbye darling – I hope you aren't having too melancholy a Xmas with all the moving etc. – I think of you all.

Love from
Bobs

1 January 1936   Tsui Hua Hutung 8, East City, Peiping

Darling Mibble

Only a scrawl – I am in hospital, recovering from 'flu – the doctor found me shivering in my paper rooms with a temperature of 101° and packed me off – unluckily it has left me with bad bouts of neuralgia – so bad that I have to have narcotic injections when they come on.

In fact it is the collapse that ought to have happened when I first got here, so I've no doubt I shall profit from the rest.

I think of you all the time, moving – it is horrid not to have any *home* in one's mind any more, only a nettle patch! When I have been lonely and hopeless before – as in Afghanistan – I have always been comforted by thinking of the Ruins and everything going on there just the same – However I daresay Easton is already very nice only I can't imagine it. Horses keep going past the window, and each time they do I wish I was out hunting – I began to cry the other day on opening a book at a picture of a Sussex village – so you can imgine I am almost cracked for the moment and a week or ten days in bed won't have done me any harm.

Thank you very much for your letter about my things – I'm afraid they will add to the general nuisance of everything.

The hospital is German – I have lots of books – the food is excellent – and the place is run like a hotel instead of a prison.

Gerald Reitlinger says he may be out here in February.

Goodbye darling – I can't write more as any effort brings on my head. [. . .]

Love from
Bobs

16 January 1936   Tsui Hua Hutung 8, East City, Peiping

Darling Mibble

[. . .] My ill health is flourishing – despite the most old maidish precautions, I caught another cold, the 3rd in a month, on leaving the hospital – but was able to console myself on finding that practically everyone in the place is suffering in the same way. Today there is a roaring gale – the lamps are swinging about all over the room, pictures flapping, walls bulging. I sit huddled in my sheepskin between two stoves lamenting my muse, who is now finally extinct. Harold's giving a lecture this afternoon – I daren't go out to attend it. Last night we ventured into the extravagance of a taxi to go to dinner with an American woman who heard me speak in New York – she insisted on going to the cinema afterwards – at which we ran away and hid. But she *found* us and without bothering to conceal her anger dragged us off just the same. I didn't bother to conceal what I thought of the film.

My latest Chinese sentence: *ping ping chö ping* which means 'the sick soldiers are eating ice'. In another month I ought to be able to speak a little Chinese, I think – enough to get about with. [. . .]

Love from
Bobs

18 January 1936   Tsui Hua Hutung 8, East City, Peiping

Darling Mibble

[. . .] I had a letter from Moscow from Michael – they arrived there 36 hours late. Desmond appears to have stood the journey well – he and Lady de Vesci had gone on to Berlin, Michael and Anne were staying in Moscow 3 days.

It is *such* a relief to me that you haven't minded leaving Savernake – my heart is broken now that the moment has come – in fact I can't write about it.

Please don't ask me about my plans yet. You needn't think I *want* to stay here – I detest it. But I *do* want to discover first if the Far East offers any opportunities to my waning talents, and I must regain some kind of health and energy before I can do this so it may be a month or two before I know anything. I am feeling a bit better today for the first time – but am still quite incapable of any sustained effort. The articles are done at last, thank God – though they need revising. When they have gone off, I shall take a fortnight's holiday before beginning the book – though what I shall do, Heaven knows. One can't go out. I believe the articles are good – and I think one of the reasons they have taken so long is that I seem to be developing a new and more concise way of writing. However you will see – that is, if *The Times* publish the beastly things.

The Chinese New Year is beginning. Everyone takes a week's holiday. Everyone expects presents. Already everyone is letting off fireworks, day *and* night – as though Woolwich arsenal exploded in one's ear every five minutes.

A letter from Upham Pope tells me that Mrs Kahn's Persian party ended in 'high words' and congratulates me on having escaped it. How right one's instincts can be.

[. . .] I never leave this house. Harold and I tried to go for a walk today, but were driven back by the eddies of frozen dust. Half the pipes are frozen and one boiler has burst, despite my most elaborate pre-

cautions. However the *hot* water is still all right, which is the main thing.

I have got some deliciously vulgar evening shirts made of old Chinese silk, with a kind of shining crisscross pattern on it. I thought they would look very artistic, but they give me the appearance of a bookie.

I now discover that Byron (Bai Run) in Chinese means White *Fat* Beauty. However my figure is stationary at the moment.

Goodbye angel, I do hope and pray I shall hear you are happy in the new house.

Love from Bobs

24 January 1936   Tsui Hua Hutung 8, East City, Peiping

Darling Mibble

Your birthday – and such an orgy here too, being New Year's Day and their *only* holiday in 12 months – so that though I hardly slept a wink last night for the fireworks, and my rickshaw boy was so drunk he couldn't get up this morning to take me out to lunch, I can't help hoping they are all enjoying themselves. I went for a seven-mile walk yesterday, through the town and out of it – and everyone, down to the smallest infant, was carrying a little parcel, from which the head of a frozen fish was generally protruding, and a bunch of artificial flowers, and one or two lanterns, and some prints and fireworks, all ending in a sort of trail of oddments on a string. It snowed in the night, which pleases the Chinese, as they think it clears the air.

Your first letter from the new house has arrived – it has cheered me up such a lot, as you seem to be really enjoying it. I do hope you are having a happy birthday today – though imagine it there I can't.

I saw two deceased naked pigs sitting on one another's knee in a rickshaw yesterday. It had a very romantic effect.

I have *at last* begun to feel better: and *at last*, yesterday, sent off the articles and photographs. Not since I first began to write has anything taken me so long. I wish to goodness you were here to correct them. They ought to be good – and if they are good, ought to cause a stir. But how can I tell? And it will be so long before I hear. However I shall have forgotten all about them in a day or two. I am going to have a week's idleness, and then start on the book! It is a relief at last, to find oneself coming to life again – I feel as if I were emerging from a nightmare.

What an upheaval the King's death must mean – I am rather sorry to miss it all. I knew nothing about it till I arrived at the legation to lunch and found the flag at half-mast; by which time it was too late to go and change my bright green tie! However things in Europe really do seem remote here – it is the only place I have ever been where they have – and the reason is that the Chinese are so like us in so many ways; with the result that since one didn't suspect anyone else of being like us, this really does seem like another world. And then the Pacific question is so different – and the Japanese so very imminent. I am slowly beginning to sit up and take notice.

What makes this town almost more uninhabitable than anything else are the unemployed American women with large incomes. They sail into one's life like bats into one's hair. I told you about the one that Harold and I hid from. Today she writes again quite undeterred, saying 'I am a very informed person', and that she would like me to dine with her alone 'to talk about your Persian work'. What is one to *do*?

I drink a lot of stout, and am taking a German tonic. But am still nice and thin.

With regard to future plans, I shall now do nothing till I hear from *The Times*. I made some suggestions to them, which I don't suppose for a moment they will even consider – but I thought it was worthwhile striking while the iron was hot – (always supposing that my articles heat it) . . .

I have got *Haig* by D. Cooper out of the club library here. It seems very dull. But then I suppose he was a very dull man. A pretentious snob, people always say who knew him.

It makes me chuckle to think of people like Gavin polishing up their coronets for the coronation. [. . .]

Julian Bell, son of Clive B., is here – a pleasant half fledged person with a most ridiculous Bloomsbury voice, which reminds one of 1920. He is a professor of poetry somewhere in the south of China and is up here on leave. He told Harold I was just like his uncle the colonel. But really Peking, with its taste of dusty, frozen lotuses, is enough to turn me into a Field Marshal.

I am just going to dine with *another* American Lady Bateman, who is rather nice – crazily vague, but hits the nail on the head underneath it.

She said it made her feel uncomfortable leading such an idle life with so much money. I said: 'Well you can't start charity at your age.' She said she'd tried it long ago, and it was no use.

Goodbye darling
Love from Bobs

6 February 1936   Tsui Hua Hutung 8, East City, Peiping

Darling Mibble

[. . .] I have got back to my book at last, and am really feeling quite restored by it. It was Russia I found such an effort to write about. I think it is mostly funny – there is very little else, in fact, except an occasional landscape – but I am noticing a few buildings, as I don't like the Peter Fleming kind of thing, which deliberately avoids anything of interest. At least that is how it strikes me, though this may be sour grapes really.

I have nothing to tell you, as I never go out or see anyone. I have begun to make plans about photographing and drawing the buildings here – studying the light etc. Not that they are worth it – at least architecturally: but being here, one may as well have some record.

Yesterday, according to the Chinese, was the first day of spring. The result was the heaviest snowfall of the winter. My minions have been sweeping the courtyard all the morning. And it looks as if more is coming. But it isn't so cold.

I think it very likely I shall come straight home after all, in about 2 months. I have been reading lots of war books and the conviction is growing on me that I *must* write that History of the War and do it *soon*. Either that – or give up writing and get some small job. But I don't feel inclined to give up writing without a last try. All this time, in spite of a certain output of literature (?), I have really been educating myself. Now the moment has come to use the knowledge I have gained – and that is the subject with the scope. If it was successful, I should be established. I am also developing a new and more concise style, which you will see, I hope, in the Russian articles. It will be a pity if *The Times* don't publish them,[1] as apart from all the effort involved, they will have their maximum effect in *The Times* and were written for that purpose.

However before making any definite plans, I shall wait and see what *The Times* say, and whether I can do anything for them in the Far East. Funnily enough, I have no particular desire to travel in China – though of course it would be nice to see it. On the other hand, I do want to go to Japan very much. I wish I could come back via New York.

If one lived in a less fashionable part of the town, one could get a great big house with garden, trees, lakes etc., for about £25.0.0. a year. Harold is thinking of doing this. The idea doesn't attract me – I don't like the place. But it certainly would be lovely in the summer.

My Chinese came to a full stop a little time ago – but it is now getting on again. The difficulty is the arrangement of the words. Every sentence is a sort of jigsaw puzzle. Every word almost, except the most rudimentary. Thus, for 'poor', you take the words 'no', 'have', 'money', and make an adjective *'mei-yo-chen-di'* which becomes *'meiyochendy'* in speech.

I am just going to lunch with Lady Bateman. She used to be a beauty and was painted 11 times by Lenbach, who did one picture of the Kaiser.

I have just found this in *The World Crisis*. Churchill writes to Sir John French: 'Above all, my dear friend, do not be vexed or discouraged. We are on the stage of history. Let us keep our anger for the common foe.' It suddenly struck me that 'foe' is the most ridiculous word in the language. Have you got a foe living next door? The cat is the foe of the bird. A foe has got into my bed (a mouse). It has made me and Harold quite ill with laughing, and as the servants hear everything they think we have gone mad.

Goodbye darling. A dull letter I'm afraid.

Love to Anne and Father
Love from
Bobs

The London Library writes frantically on Nov 9th. wanting: Bolton: *Arch. of R & J. Adam.* 2 vols.

---

1. The articles were published in *The Times* on 16, 17 and 18 March 1936.

Tipping: *English Homes*, parts 3ii, 4i, 5i, 6i. It is *my* turn to reproach for once!!

20 February 1936   Tsui Hua Hutung 8, East City, Peiping

Darling Mibble

I have no thoughts of getting Hodgkin's disease. All my water is religiously boiled. Hundreds of foreigners live as I do in Peking, merely for pleasure, not because they are here on business. I can't make any arrangements about coming home for another month. I don't want to come home till my book is more or less finished and till I myself am better. I lead a very quiet life here, have given up all drink except 2 bottles of beer a day, rest after lunch and go for regular walks. Having had this breakdown has upset all my financial plans, and before I leave I must collect some photographs and material here to sell when I get home. If, in a month's time, I find I am still incapable of any sustained effort, then I will come back. I'm sure the little house is very nice and I should be perfectly happy there, if you say so. At the same time, I should feel much happier about coming back if you had settled something – not because I mind in the least a temporary residence, but because it will lead again to those unendurable arguments which made last year a misery. Also, there is one other difficulty. If I really do settle down to my history of the war, as I think will probably be the best thing for me to do, I shall have to have a big room like an office, owing to the enormous number of large-scale maps and date charts that will be necessary. The mere *physical* organisation necessary to begin such a book will be portentous. [. . .]

I dined last evening with a charming Chinese called Mr Soltan King. He had just had a grandson, and the walls of his room were hung with long scrolls of poetry, written in the 16th century, which celebrate the arrival of a grandson and which he had got out for the occasion. Several years ago he grew in his garden over 200 different varieties of chrysanthemums. He then employed an artist for a year and a half to make pictures of the 60 best – exquisite paintings, very meticulous, but full of life, instead of rigid like Mary North – almost like looking at a series of portraits. He is also a photographic maniac, and being very rich buys a camera costing about £100.0.0. once a month, with which he takes the most wretched photographs. His food, I was interested to see, wasn't nearly as good as mine.

It is now snowing again so hard that the courtyard can't be kept swept.

Have you still got the pigeons? I am thinking of getting some pigeon-whistles here. One fixes them on to the wings or tail, and whenever the pigeons fly, the air is filled with a sort of melodious boom.

I have a camellia tree in full flower, a large pot of white irises, an orange which is in fruit and flower at the same time, and several little plum trees which, after flowering are now bursting into green. [. . .]

I am going to shut myself up entirely for the next month, and not go out at all. The parties here drive me nearly mad, except with Chinese – and even those are very tiring. Harold will be furious – he has a great sense of social duty. But I can't help it. [. . .]

Love from
Bobs

29 February 1936   Tsui Hua Hutung 8, East City, Peiping

Darling Mibble

I suppose I never have told you what this house is like. The street, like all '*hutungs*' is about 12–15 feet wide – just grey walls of one storey, with trees perking over the top. The front door is scarlet – and there are large inscriptions over it. No. 8 inside is a little court for the rickshaw and the servants' bicycle. Turn left, through a door, into a little vestibule, which is the spirit gateway – it prevents the spirits getting in, as they can only go in a straight line – so you turn to the right again, then to the left once more and you are in the main court. Behind is another whole row of rooms and two more courtyards – in one of which, in a main line with the first spirit gate and the axis of the big room is a tall wooden screen, covered with ducks and lotuses, again to impede the spirits from reaching the concubine's quarters. The back court has a big tree in it, and the small court beside it where I first lived a clump of bamboos. Round the walls are various beds which have tree-peonies in them now done up in straw. The great pot in the middle of the main court is filled with lotuses in summer. The whole is of grey brick, bright grey, but the fronts of every pavilion consist of wooden lattices covered with paper. The courts are brick-paved. It all looked very pretty on my birthday with deep snow on the ground and roofs, all the pavilions lighted up *inside* and lanterns in the trees – also big round lanterns with red characters on them hanging in the tripods beside the front door. If only there had been someone to see it who thought it pretty! I had to enjoy it by myself. But of course the servants loved it. They love anything of that sort. The Chinese get more pleasure for less money than any people. [. . .]

I am thinking of getting some pigeons, in order to have that whistling going on overhead. You tie whistles round the neck. And you have to put some brilliantly coloured porcelain object on the roof of the house so that they can recognise it. The cook's son is a great pigeon fancier. Today in the street I met a boy carrying a magnificent falcon. I asked if it were for sale. He said yes for a dollar (1/4d.). But it looked so fierce I dared not take it, for which the servants are thankful – it would eat them alive they say. I did buy a Sung bowl off a street vendor for 9d., which Gerald Reitlinger who is a great authority says is quite genuine and would cost about £5.0.0. in London. I have been looking about for bowls for you, but can't see any the right shape – and anyhow it is very expensive getting that sort of thing home. [. . .]

I have just finished my first visit to Herat in my book, getting in a lot of culture about the Timurids – it has been difficult to reformulate all that information in my rather staccato style, interspersed with personal experiences. But I think I have done it all right, and I've no doubt it is all the better for it. It will really be an amusing book I think, and have a unity like *The Station*, only much better.

I am keeping my new regime very strictly – sleep after lunch, herb tea at 6 and 10, an hour's walk in the afternoon, and no goings out. It is quite impossible to explain one's troubles to people – they won't believe – so one just has to seem offensive. Harold hates Reitlinger – so that my one hour a day when I can see people has to be divided between the two.

It is colder than it has been the whole winter – temperature down to 8°, and a vile electric blast which upsets me just like the east wind.

I go on reading war books and am taking voluminous notes – am in the middle of Lord Riddell's diaries. There's no doubt Lloyd George must be the most attractive man.

I must go to bed. It is half past ten. My little servant Lî is playing a Beethoven quintet tonight.

Goodbye darling
Love
from
Bobs

1 April 1936   Tsui Hua Hutung 8, East City, Peiping

Darling Mibble

My Chinese painting turned out to be a *hideous* failure – partly I think because I was told to get a thin, non-absorbent paper and tried to use a lot of water on it – but the trick is lightness of touch really, and you know how I *scrub*. However I shall try again on a vast scale.

The trees have begun to bud – the peonies and persimmons are out of their straw – and I am thinking of buying a couple of oleander if they aren't too expensive – they are already in bud in the shops – today is vile, a roaring wind and the sky yellow with dust, but that must be expected in the early spring.

I dined with Harold last night, and even drank a glass of absinth, without feeling a wreck this morning – which shews (to me at least) how much better I am getting.

The white cat is ill – foaming yellow at the mouth. Of course the cook at once produced the appropriate Chinese cat medicine, with which we have been dosing it. The brown cat scalped one of its kittens the night before last – I believe it was a mad kitten and had thought of drowning it myself. The floor is covered with blood which won't wash out.

Harold has been burgled and has lost 800 dollars' of objects. The burglar came again two nights later but by that time he had got a dog. They have caught the burglar and got back some of the objects. There is nothing much to steal here, but I have padlocked all my doors and secreted my MSS and camera under my bed. Harold is looking for a new house and has found one, but it already has a tenant in the shape of a fox-fairy. They drop things on one. My Chinese tutor has a brother who was thus plagued in his house. First a vast stone almost crushed him, then one of his own books fell from the ceiling on to his bed. So he left his house for another.

Liner-loads of tourists are arriving and sending the prices up though they buy such muck that it doesn't matter (cranes chiefly, bronze or painted). Lady Bateman is coming back. She travels with a maid and a lugubrious slightly mystic companion named Miss Vallet. She said she had to leave here in order to get back to Paris to get her clothes for the summer. In order to annoy the companion she decided to go to Shanghai via Mukden in Manchuria, Korea and Japan, *not stopping anywhere* on the way. I've no doubt she is coming back here in order to go home by Russia, of which the companion has a terror. An extraordinary woman – she travels with great trunks of books and spends most of her time reading.

The Chinese genius for platitudes makes me laugh out loud. They have thousands of proverbs and I have already a collection of them. I nearly fell out of bed when I found that Mencius, one of their great sages, uttered the following profound thought, which has been preserved like a jewel: 'This time is one time, that is another'. Another gem: 'He who begins well may not end well'. They have no power of *thought* at all. It is all aesthetic perception. They are the aesthetes of the world.

As usual this is a dull letter. The book goes slowly. I have my ups and downs of work, but do a regular six hours a day at least.

Goodbye darling
Love from
Bobs

18 April 1936   Tsui Hua Hutung 8, East City, Peiping

Darling Mibble

The thought of going away made me feel so well, and my brain so prolific that I have decided not to go away after all. The strange thing is that I have no desire to travel in China. I expect this is only a temporary feeling, and is really the result of being absorbed in my book – which I am beginning to think will be . . . well never mind, but the thing is that it has developed a form – and I feel about it now like a sculptor who has been hewing away at a bit of marble and suddenly sees it come to life. It is the first thing I have written since *The Birth of Western Painting* which gives me this feeling – I thought – indeed I intended – when I started it that it should be just a little bit of patter – but it is being born with real labour, and the greater part of that labour is keeping it all light and very economical. I dare say you won't agree – but you will be getting your claws into it soon now, and it is so long that anything the least heavy can well be shortened or taken out.

I'm afraid my letters must be very egotistical – but as I never go anywhere or see anyone I can't very well help it.

My court now is a mass of pink blossoms growing exactly as it does on the worst kind of Chinese screens and the lilac tree will soon be out. The parks are getting very pretty – all weeping willows lettuce-green, above the lakes and canals – dwarf trees put out on the rockeries – and the goldfish out in tubs. You never saw such creatures – I like the black ones best, with eyes like headlights and fins and tails like widows' veils trailing behind them. I am tempted to get some for my lotus pot, but one is tempted to get so many things. [. . .]

It is amusing to see children sketching in the parks, dabbing down every leaf of every tree with their brushes at right angles to the page. Harold teased an infant today, saying he was painting 'Wai-gwo fadza – European fashion'. He was furious. Reeves paints work havoc – but the real painters don't use them.

I must write to Upham Pope who appears to be lying half dead in New York and has been deserted by all his friends and supporters. I seem to have had a lucky escape from Mrs Kahn's party in Persia.

It just occurs to me that my Perso-Afghan journey is taking almost as long to write as to do.

Best Love from Bobs

17 May 1936   Tsui Hua Hutung 8, East City, Peiping

Darling Mibble

I am so sorry my letter was cross – was it? I do get very irritable here – perhaps this is a sign of returning vigour. But I still think all the same, that your cruelty over the articles has hardly been paralleled since Abraham.

I can't get enough sleep – that's the reason really – never more than 5 hours, generally not as much. What is one to do? However the book has been going like a house on fire and ought to be finished by the end of the month. I must say this has been an ideal place to write in. If I were a novelist, I should stay here. It is people I dread in England, don't expect me to see anyone ever when I come home. I tried dining with Harold the other night – it almost killed me. Another exhaustion, though a very pleasant one, has been the Morlands[1] who were so kind to me in Mukden when I arrived from Russia and whom I had to entertain and go about with a bit. However they have gone now.

A plague of celebrities has descended – Vicki Baum,[2] Anna May Wong,[3] and a woman called Lady FitzHerbert, friend of Violet's [Wyndham]. Baum has one of those sweet faces [. . .] in which the corners of the mouth are wider than the middle – do you know what I mean? – combined with auburn hair done like a parakeet, and clothes for a Hollywood cocktail party. Wong I used to meet at the Sutros' – she wants this house, but I have choked her off and refused to allow her to come and see it. Lady FitzHerbert is a friend of the King. She addresses one as dear Robert Byron, dear Harold Acton in letters, and I wonder if she addresses him as dear Edward England. She is amusing on the surface, but really one of those crypto-egoists who think no one has anything to do but amuse them.

The Morlands and I had a sort of vicarage tea yesterday under the big tree in the back court – looking very pretty with huge pots of nasturtiums all round it. I have also got two foxgloves in pots – which remind me almost too much of England. The roses are beginning to come out. One wisteria has already flowered, while the other refuses to come out at all. The blot is a persimmon tree, which hasn't yet produced a leaf.

I still haven't made definite arrangements to leave. I can get a 1st class berth in the *President Hoover*, which sails from Kobe in Japan on June 18th and goes to S. Francisco – but I am trying to find a ship which can give me a tourist class berth – there is no *point* in paying 1st class, as none of the boats in the Pacific have single cabins 1st class – so if one has to travel like a rat, one might as well do it cheap. [. . .]

The wind has stopped, 3 days' sunshine intervened, and now the rain

---

1. Oscar Morland, Consul at Mukden, and his wife Alice.
2. Austrian novelist and playwright, best known for her novel *Grand Hotel*.
3. A film star.

has begun. I rather like the rain – it makes everything smell so fresh, and brightens up the green.

Yes, Desmond is keeping this house on – and has sent me a lot of money for the rent and servants' wages in advance for the next 3 or 4 months. But he still doesn't know if he can come back or not. [. . .]

Goodbye darling – I shall decide this week definitely about a ship – Reitlinger, who was going to accompany me to Japan, has disappeared into the interior and will probably never be heard of again.

Love from
Bobs

5 June 1936   Approaching Japan

Darling Mibble

[. . .]This nightmare of a journey is already getting me down – the boat is nice enough, though very small – but how I *loathe* being at sea, the boredom is like a sort of disease. I become crippled physically and mentally and hardly have the strength to even read. I really don't know how I shall survive the Pacific, I know I shan't be able to work. I have a lot of books, as when Michael left Peking, he gave me a Xmas present of a deposit at the bookshop there, and I have saved it up for this – have been re-reading White's *Selborne* as an antidote to all this horrible East.

Yesterday afternoon and evening we passed through the Korean islands (I caught this boat at Tangku near Tientsin and am going to Kobe, so you can see the route) – they were very beautiful, hundreds and hundreds of them, many only little rocks crowned with trees, rising out of a pearly sea – and the moon like a Japanese lantern casting a long ripple of gold – and sailing boats like this [drawing]. It might have been Greece, but it wasn't, there was a sort of vacuous prettiness lurking somewhere, though as I say it *was* very beautiful. Tomorrow we sail up the Inland Sea, and I hope to get to Tokyo tomorrow night or the next morning. Reitlinger will be there and I have one or two letters – but am beginning to wonder what on earth I shall do for ten days. I feel so incurious about this part of the world. Perhaps it is the death of my travel lust – all the better.

It was sad leaving Peking, the house and all my charming servants.

I am now wondering and worrying if my book is as good as I think –

and can't get it out of my mind, which means probably I want a holiday from it, though I want so much to get the last part typed – it is such a danger having only one copy. However I think I had better leave it altogether for the next fortnight and try and start again on the Pacific, though I *know* it will be impossible there.

Goodbye darling – I will write again from Tokyo.

Love from
Bobs

7 June 1936   Imperial Hotel, Tokyo

Darling Mibble

This place is simply *Ealing*, inhabited partly by the Chicago under-world, partly by people tottering and fluttering about in kimonos with foot-gloves on, to which are attached little wooden tables instead of shoes. The genius of Marks and Spencer's and Lyons Corner House presides. The Mikado lives in a wood formed of trees whose tops are lower than their roots and overhang a moat. Everyone is charming and gay, but as stupid as the Eton eight. Old Japanese paintings are magnificent – the people in them all have faces like du Maurier's mashers. There is also a type of 19th century print which is just like the drawings in the *New Yorker*. The country as seen from the train (I had nine hours between Kobe and here) is very rich and lush and so neat that the corn must literally be reaped with scissors, they grow it in rows 3 feet long and 6 inches wide, alternating with potatoes or some other vegetable – so that the effect of the fields is like that of a detailed wallpaper or stuff – the fields are very small and irregular. Even the tea-bushes are clipped like pincushions. Fujiyama rose straight from the railway – a beautiful sight – it is slightly unsymmetrical. The Japanese have no roads in our sense but railways go everywhere and have the most extraordinary tittuping gradients even in quite flat country. The passport officials knew the date of Lord Byron's death, and were rather disconcerted – as though caught out in an examination – when I said I can't be his grandson as he only had a daughter. Reitlinger has an old friend here who is 78, and was the first Japanese to come to England to import dwarf trees, prints etc., a great friend of Sargent and so on. He arranged the flowers for the late King's wedding. He is 4 feet 6 high, has only gold teeth, and still keeps a mistress. He was born under the feudal system, has seen the whole process of westernization, and having been the first to adopt it, has now had a revulsion and clops in and out of the hotel on his wooden tables wrapped in a series of severe silk dressing gowns, over wh. he wears a coat with a cape as if he was at the opera in 1870 and a Homburg hat.

There is an exhibition of azaleas, wh. is enough to make one cry. Many of them resemble huge forest oaks about 2 or 2½ feet high; only what I have drawn as foliage is really a mass of blossom. They are sold off very cheap at the end of the exhibition, and I am much tempted to bring some home – but it is so difficult to look after them – Louise, it appears, must be a genius to have preserved maples all this time. [. . .]

I am just going to lunch at the Embassy, it will be interesting as Clive[1] was in Persia and was Xtopher's *bête noire* when he was attaché there – I shall be amused to see if he corresponds with Xtopher's portrait of him. I will go on afterwards.

Very interesting conversation with the Ambassador – I have a certain amount to *give* as regards the state of things in the Russian Far East – which makes people talk in return – as my information is not to be had from anyone else, and it is what they are all longing for. All my interest in things, which died in the mortal atmosphere of Peking, has revived now – but I *bitterly* resent the loss of solitude, and can hardly bear having to eat in a restaurant with other people – I'm afraid you really will find me a little peculiar when I come home – I am thinking of going to live in Dulwich. The Embassy is planned like an up-to-date orphanage – a lot of little concrete houses round a garden – but the Ambassador's house is quite nice.

1. Sir Robert Clive, British Ambassador in Tokyo.

It was raining as I walked back to the hotel, and everyone had put on taller tables – thus: you can imagine what they look like dodging among the traffic in a hurry.

I am going off to the country in a day or two to try and walk about and look at the farmers – also to bathe – but will write via Siberia before I leave. I'm afraid I never put Siberia on my last letter posted at Moji at the entrance to the Inland Sea (which was really unbelievably beautiful, *alive* with sailing ships) – so you will get this first.

Goodbye darling – it is lovely to feel I am on my way home at last.

Love from
Bobs

15 June 1936   Marunuma

Darling

Mibble to

Here I am in the middle of the local Salzkammergut, in the Nikko district somewhere between Lake Chunzenji and Numata – if you can find either of them on the map. This place is called Marunuma – it has a lake and a new hotel. I got hold of a student in Tokyo anxious to practise his English, picked up Reitlinger in Nikko (where the temples are frightful and the famous cryptomerias magnificent – they were planted in 1648, and apart from the ones round the shrines there is a 'Grand Avenue' of them 22 miles long) and drove to a place – or rather a series of 3 half-built White Horse Inns and some souvenir shops – called Yumoyo, where there is a lake to bathe in and the whole air smelt of rotten eggs owing to the sulphur springs. We fished in the lake at 3 yen a head and lived on various kinds of pink-fleshed trout. The hotel was filled with Tokyo business men, who spent their time bathing in the sulphur, playing baseball in kimonos, and being photographed in the sort of Japanese garden you see at the Ideal Home exhibition. Last night 200 schoolboys aged 15 arrived equipped for a retreat from Moscow and each grasping an umbrella larger than himself. They left at six and we at eight, to

b
e
g
i
n

J
a
p
a
n
e
s
e

f
a
s
h
i
o
n

cross the Konsei pass – a pathetic attempt on my part to get off the beaten track. It was quite difficult in places, as the snowdrifts are still lying in the woods and often came up to one's waist – but a friendly beer bottle was always glinting in the bamboo undergrowth to shew the path. The pass itself was like the Bath Road after Bank Holiday. The whole district is a National Park (this phrase and 'national treasure' (i.e. any cracked tea-cup over 100 years old) are part of the language) – and has the same nightmarish atmosphere as Wolfgang. But it is interesting living entirely Japanese – their rooms are really the prototype of the 'modernist' ultra-convenient pseudo-elegant one-room flat. One leaves one's shoes at the entrance – totters about on polished boards and padded straw mats – eats and sleeps on the floor – and is provided with every necessity from a toothbrush in a cellophane package up – so that one could easily travel with no luggage at all. The food is all sweet and tastes mauve like cachets. The carpentry is wonderful – everything slides – there are no hinges – the household objects, tables, fire-boxes, writing outfits with brushes and ink grinders etc. are really beautiful and quite unpretentious or fussy. The decoration of the rooms is all in panels and all depends on *textures* – they have a mania for antique mottled patinas and queer rough materials. Every room has one picture and one vase with $2\frac{1}{2}$ twigs in it. The vase is apt to stand on a slice of tree-trunk exquisitely polished (with the bark on of course).

The thing that is really beautiful is the trees. They are extraordinary – each kind in a forest or a clump, is absolutely different from its neighbours – so that instead of forming just a mass of green, they are like a lot of different people – their shapes and the patterns of their leaves and branches and their green are all so distinct. Up in the mountain here it is only just spring. All the maples are just coming out and I have even seen the cherries, two months late really. There are endless lakes and waterfalls, each one with a café and a photographer at the bottom. The undergrowth, at least in the higher parts, is all bamboo with green and white leaves about 2–3 feet high – it is very pretty and is in proportion to the trees as the bracken is in Savernake.

I had two men to carry my things over the pass this morning, and they had a dog. My student is interesting – he has the face of a warrior in a Japanese painting, which is not at all how one imagines the Japanese to look. He is 23, studying economics at the University, and will graduate in three years' time – having started his education at 7. He will have two years in the army. So that he won't begin his career till 28. It is interesting to find the whole education of the country based on Victorian England. America has left its mark in less important matters, such as baseball and business methods. But the 200 schoolgirls, also on an excursion, who travelled in the train from Tokyo, each sat down and opened a lesson book at a page containing a picture of Landseer (not *by* him but of him) as one of the heroes to be learned about. The bookshops in Tokyo are really extraordinary in this way – one finds almost any book one wants, and most of them are about ¼ of the price they are in England. I am getting one or two on Central Asia which I have been trying to acquire for years.

Reitlinger has gone back to Tokyo,[1] on his way to Mukden and Harbin to catch the Trans-Siberian. I have two more days in the 'country' and shall spend one night in Tokyo before catching the boat at Yokohama – such is the oppression of the Japanese Salzkammergut that I am quite looking forward to it. I have managed to get one really fine Japanese painting – which I hope will give you some idea of how fine they can be on a big scale.

Goodbye darling – I am longing to get a letter from you again in Washington.

Love from
Bobs

P.S. The wildest forests of course are full of signposts – and one is apt to come on 'double suicides' hanging from the branches of the trees. There is a great vogue for them – when marriages are arranged by the parents, instead of by the heart. My student was telling me about them on the way from Tokyo. One of the most popular

---

1. Gerald Reitlinger, before leaving Japan, wrote to Robert: 'You missed a great deal by not coming here. Nara and Kyoto are two sweet little places of about twenty million inhabitants each, nineteen million being school children. The temperature is that prevailing in the large glasshouse at Kew which gives the inhabitants their peculiarly rosy complexions. "The glare of the sun at noonday on the tin roofs of Nara" was a favourite subject of landscape painters in the Sung period. The temples were all rebuilt in honour of the accession of his present majesty and those containing works of art are closed permanently.'

suicide resorts is the crater of a certain volcano. Sure enough a couple of bodies were found on a tree just behind the hotel at Yumoto the first night we were there.

19 June 1936   Imperial Hotel, Tokyo

Darling Mibble

A last letter by Siberia. I sail today from Yokohama and embark in the middle of a total eclipse! – which people have come from all over the world to see – but as it is very cloudy, their pains will have been wasted.

I had such an interesting journey back from Marunuma where I last wrote from – by the sort of bus that goes from Marlborough to Hungerford via Ramsbury (only it was much longer) and full of exactly the same kind of people – farmers' daughters in their best kimonos with shiny faces and stray hairs stuck to the sweat of their foreheads, the village schoolmaster, the soldier returning from leave, the village shopkeeper, and lots of farmers in breeches and straw hats like this [drawing].

We eventually arrived at a place called Numata, where I spent the night as a Japanese might spend the night at Newbury – a delightful inn – and so back here for one day, trailing a huge bundle of their village straw hats, which the American customs will probably take away from me – but if not I hope they may complete Anne's *plage* costume.

It is a quarter to seven – I must get up and pack, as I want to get to Yokohama early (it is ½ an hour in the tube) in order to prosecute an intrigue for getting a cabin to myself – I went down a week ago and tried to blackmail the shipping agents by saying I generally typed all night and doubting – for their sake – of course – if my cabin mate would enjoy it.

I find that for £15.0.0., including carriage, packing and English duty, I could get a dinner set of 50 plates, veg. dishes, meat dishes, sauceboats etc., made with the arms big in the middle of each plate and in full colour – hand-painted each one – also a lot of gold. I haven't *got* the money, but shall bring full details in case Arthur would like to order it.

Best love darling – I shall write from America next.

Bobs

6 July 1936   2608, 36th Place, Washington DC

Darling Mibble

The journey was not as bad as it might have been. By dint of intrigues I got my cabin to myself – it was very large and properly furnished, and I did a great deal of work, typing out about 40,000 words of the book, revising various parts and getting it all ready for a final read-through when I return to England, by which time I hope to have forgotten it sufficiently to see which parts are boring and which not. I didn't speak to a single person except my table-mate (who was French) for 13 days. The boat was large and American, the crew mutinous – they refused to sail the boat out of Honolulu while a massed choir of Hawaiians on the pier kept wailing goodbye till they had no breath left. The barman was so ill-mannered that I couldn't have a drink for a fortnight, which was economical and healthy – and the food of course was just chlorinated offal, so that I generally dined off bread and butter. I visited Harold's cousins in Honolulu – they were one of the 12 original missionary families and are now, therefore, in the 3rd generation, millionaires and the aristocracy – inhabiting a Tuscan villa overlooking the bay of Waikiki (where I dutifully bathed), with breadfruits all over the drive like fir cones, and the hay just cut on the front terrace. I came back by tram about eleven, got lost in the town and thought I was going to miss the boat till I fell in with some of the crew, who took me on board with them thus involving me in their mutiny to the annoyance of the officers who thought I was a paid agitator – I had on that red tie.

It turned cold 2 days before reaching San Francisco. The harbour there is extraordinary – enormous – but approached by a bottle-neck gate between two cliffs, from which now swings the curve of the biggest suspension bridge I have ever seen – one cannot conceive how it was ever constructed or how it stands. The Oakland Bridge about which there has been so much fuss, is inside the harbour, but it is not nearly such a wonderful sight.

I disembarked at one thirty and it was twenty-to-four before I was out of those vile American customs, having had to pay duty on all my wretched little presents, although I shewed them my through ticket to England. A wire from Lucy met me at the boat. I rushed to Cook's to get her letter and her address inside it [. . .] and then to my shipping line to reclaim some money on my ticket – then to buy a canvas zip bag into which I popped a couple of shirts and a white suit – and laden with a large bundle of Japanese hats, a picture 4 feet long, my cameras, despatch case with the book in it and this bag, dashed into a car, caught the 6 p.m. aeroplane to Los Angeles on which a 'hostess' served what she called 'luncheon' sitting heavily on one's knee and thrusting a poof of scented curls into one's mouth while eating, and arrived there at 8. I waited an hour drinking 'old fashioneds' and then caught a 14-seater Douglas. Los Angeles looked lovely from above, all lit up, stretching for miles and miles along the coast, with a moon over the sea. I slept four hours and we saw the sun rise over Texas. It grew sweltering hot. I breakfasted at Kansas – or it may have been St Louis – and another hostess served another and more elegant luncheon somewhere over the Middle West. We caught up three hours on the journey, and kept on getting new morning papers at each town. Luckily we flew so high that it was impossible to see anything – that is why I did fly – to avoid the view, and also because it cost no more than the train with meals and sleepers. I changed aeroplanes at Pittsburgh and arrived at Washington at 5.30, furious that Lucy was not at the aerodrome to meet me, drove to her house where I found a friend of theirs, a journalist – then she and Ewan[1] came in from a drive, and of course had never got the wire I sent from San Francisco the night before, a typical instance of American efficiency.

She looks very well, but it is just like visiting someone in Holloway to be with her in this country. The barbarity, hideousness, discomfort and uncouthness of it all strike me more forcibly after China. One just has to close one's senses to the external world altogether. [. . .] Ewan is obviously doing his job very well, takes to it like a duck to water – and is of course extraordinarily lucky to have got such a start in life so early – I have no doubt Lucy realises this and she will have to console herself with thoughts of the future. Anywhere else of course they would be comfortably off. Here they might have five times the income they have and it wouldn't make the smallest difference. So that is another consoling factor. Money here doesn't have any value, beyond just keeping the breath in one's body.

I am arranging in my mind to take a series of architectural views while I am in Washington. The whole city is being remodelled, and has got on

---

1. Ewan Butler, a correspondent of *The Times* in America.

a lot since I was here before. I shall also take some of the Embassy if I can get leave – it is more *eccentric* than I remembered. [. . .]

Goodbye darling. I must go down to breakfast, and then we are going into the town to ask when my luggage will arrive.

Best love
Bobs

13 July 1936   Washington DC

Darling Mibble

[. . .] I can't stand this country much longer – *unless* any work turns up, and *if* I can get a passage which is problematical at this time of year, I ought to be home the 1st or 2nd week in August. We all go to New York tomorrow. [. . .] on the 17th I go down to Boston where Eric Schroeder[1] will meet me and take me to his in-law's island for a little riding and bathing – I shall then spend about a week or ten days devising the outline of our joint work on Persian architecture – and then I hope to escape. The flavour of boredom over everything here is asphyxiating. The last straw came when Lucy and I were arrested the other day for taking photographs of the Supreme Court building here. I had planned to make a complete photographic record of the new Government buildings and the main lay-out of the city – had occupied the time of the various departments responsible for several days getting 'information' – bought film – hired a driver – and then was accused of injuring a marble terrace with a tripod, though actually I was standing in the middle of the road being run over by taxis. The departments concerned which had been flattered by my interest, were almost in tears when I refused to keep any further appointments with them and said I had abandoned the idea. They rang up with apologies, said it was all a mistake, that permission could easily be got etc. – But I pointed out that whereas one gets a certain amusement out of doing down a Bolshevik Commissar or the Shah of Persia, the American cop lacks glamour as an adversary and

---

1. Eric Schroeder, Fogg Art Museum, University of Harvard. Robert and Eric were proposing to write a book on Persian architecture in collaboration.

the struggle becomes nauseating. I flatly refused to have anything more to do with their town and shall sell my camera as soon as I can – it is the end of architectural photography as far as I am concerned.

We motored down to Charlottesville for the weekend to see the University of Virginia, a set of charming old buildings rather like Marlborough College only much better, bigger and prettier. The heat was very oppressive – but is less this morning. I will write again from New York or Boston, directly I have found out about boats. [. . .]

Love from
Bobs

10

Last Letters
1939–1941

I N FEBRUARY and March 1937 Robert went on a tour for the British
Council in Eastern Europe, lecturing on English civilization and
domestic architecture. His jokes received a mixed reception. At the
University of Tartu in Estonia he hardly raised a smile nor in Riga where he
was welcomed by Peter Scarlett and his wife. A British consul, who 'looked
as if he wore a platinum satin wig and wrote ballet music', took Robert in at
Kovno, where the Lithuanians dissolved into laughter in all the right
places.

Robert described Zoppot as a sort of decaying Eastbourne, but Danzig as
a lovely town, 'one of the most beautiful I have ever seen; why I undertook
this trip was to see it'. He found that a letter from Unity Mitford unlocked
all doors, and 'the Germans are certainly more affable than the G.P.U. in
Russia, but I hardly know how to contain myself when they say Heil Hitler
to one another down the telephone.' From Warsaw he returned to Berlin,
finding 'Germany much altered – lots of blonde babies in lots of different
uniforms'. Harold Acton wrote to him: 'I'm sure you are galvanizing the
Baltic with your trenchant periods and abrupt delivery.' Robert ended up
in Brussels staying with the Ambassador, his friend Sir Esmond Ovey, and
summed up: 'All the Foreign ministers came to see how we do our
propaganda and were astonished to find it was by laughing at ourselves.'

Living temporarily in a flat in Brick Court, the Temple, Robert took on a
well-paid propaganda job for Shell under Colonel H. Medlicott. The job
was not such a sinecure as he liked to make out to his friends. Trying to pick
up old threads, writing articles and seeing his friends meant, he confessed
to his mother, working ten hours a day, either getting up at half past six or
coping with his correspondence until half past seven at night. He was
unable to throw off completely the effects of his breakdown in China and
had found on his tour that the hardest to bear was coping with throngs of
people anxious to talk to him after his lectures. His home life was also in

chaos, his parents having moved to Overton House, a comfortable, unexciting vicarage overlooking the source of the Kennet four miles from Marlborough, on the Bath Road.

Even though coping with people was such a strain, it was typical of Robert to plunge into the concerns of two sensitive souls because he believed in the cause for which they were fighting. Douglas Goldring, journalist and secretary of the Society for the Preservation of Ancient Buildings, had long thought that special attention should be directed to the preservation of Georgian buildings, especially in London where developers were causing widespread mayhem to houses designed by Nash and Adam; and the Church commissioners were wantonly offering to sell off Wren churches in order to destroy them, their sites being worth money. When Goldring met Lord Derwent, a writer and dilettante, he found at last a champion, and with Robert's support a Georgian Group began to materialize. Having already produced a small guide for London Transport entitled *Imperial Pilgrimage*, price 1/–, Robert now launched into a piece of invective called *How we Celebrate the Coronation*, printed in the May number of the *Architectural Review* and reissued as a pamphlet. Robert had hardly lost the polemic style of his Cherwell days. He weighed into such tycoons as Sir John Ellerman, anxious to demolish the loveliest Adam house in London, and Lord Ellesmere, who had already allowed the destruction of part of the Adelphi where Dr Johnson had stumped around and Dickens had played as a boy. Robert attacked the 'leeches of Whitehall and the spiders of the church [. . .] the long-nosed vampires of high finance and the desperate avarice of the hereditary landlord'. With this fanfare of accusation war was declared. A committee of the Georgian Group was formed with Derwent as Chairman and Robert as Vice-Chairman. Michael Rosse became an early and hard-working member and blessings were received from such architects as Lord Gerald Wellesly, Guy Dawber and A. E. Richardson.

Lack of cash was one of the main problems of the early days, that and the clash of personalities; at one time Derwent and Goldring could only communicate through Robert. Billa Cresswell took on the job of working secretary at £2 a week but was snatched away to marry Roy Harrod. The next lady, a more professional type, resigned, protesting: 'I have had to work under circumstances of extraordinary difficulty. But in so far as one can organize an office without equipment, keep a Petty Cash book without cash: deal with correspondence from subscribers and have no knowledge of how their subscriptions are recorded: for a committee I have never seen, I have done my best to support Mr Goldring in his still more difficult task.' The Group was better served by its next appointee, very devoted, though slightly hysterical Margery.

After eight months Robert laid down the objectives: 'The purpose of the Georgian Group is to preserve English classical architecture from destruction or maltreatment. Its work therefore is of two kinds: first the consideration of individual buildings as they are threatened; secondly, the education of the public in English classical architecture, with a view to averting such threats in the future.'

1937 was a busy year. At the beginning of April the publication by Macmillan of *The Road to Oxiana* produced a flourish of reviews expressing varying degrees of approval. It was left to his great friends Christopher Sykes and Gerald Reitlinger to accuse Robert of being too full of angry invective in his writing. The *Listener* commented: 'After the first page one settles down comfortably assured that here the cliché has ceased from troubling, and that the author's views, whether one accepts them or not, will at any rate be his own and expressed with complete disregard of anything but the facts as he sees them.' Graham Greene viewed the book from the point of view of the craftmanship of the writer; he concluded: 'We are left with three books, one a little gossipy and knowing with private jokes, the second almost too dryly instructive, the third among the best books of Eastern travel since Kinglake.' For the *Spectator* Evelyn Waugh weighed in, crossgrained as usual: 'Mr Byron suffers from insularity run amok; he sees his home as a narrowly circumscribed, blessed plot beyond which lie vast tracts of alien territory, full of things for which he has no responsibility, to which he acknowledges no traditional tie: things to be visited and described and confidently judged. So he admits no limits to his insatiable aesthetic curiosity and no standards of judgement but his personal reactions. It is a grave handicap, but Mr Byron's gusto is so powerful that the reader can only applaud.' *John O'London's Weekly*, which boasted a readership every Saturday of at least a quarter of a million people, took a more simplistic line: 'This is a glorious book, full of humour, humanity and the joy of living.'

The success of *The Road to Oxiana* was crowned on 14 November by the award of the *Sunday Times* Gold Medal for 'the most outstanding travel book of the year' presented by Lady Kemsley at the bookfair at Dorland House. The award had been decided, in conjunction with the members of the Library Association, by the staff of the *Sunday Times* including G. M. Young, who wrote to Robert: 'For my own part, I can only wonder that four thousand people should be found to agree with me in a literary judgement. After this I should think that H. V. Morton will write a book "In Your Steps".'

In 1938, despite the success of his book, Robert was enveloped in depression. Though quite cheerful among his friends he felt he was leading a life without purpose. Overton House, the home upon which the family had expended so much effort, was becoming a nightmare to Robert, 'An unanalysable gloom comes over me as soon as I get inside the gate. In a way, I suppose the house is a symbol of what is over, or rather the fact of its being over: travelling, hunting, Anne and Lucy, the forest, even writing, in fact youth and independence. It was unfortunate that the change of house coincided with the change in so much else.' In London, however, Robert's surroundings improved. He found a delightful slice of a large house at the beginning of Swan Walk owned by a Mrs Clarke who, though in residence, only communicated with her tenants by unreadable notes. His small sitting-room opened out into a long green garden, the planting of which became very much a hobby with Robert. There he was joined by Sarah, one of Nancy Mitford's French bulldogs.

After Hitler's entry into Austria, it became only too clear to Robert that Europe was heading for war. With his usual energy he began to explore the possibilities of countering Nazi propaganda in an unofficial capacity. He was put in touch with Sir Stephen Tallents, Controller of Public Relations at the BBC, and already a Minister Designate of the Ministry of Information, which was coming into being. Encouraged by Tallents, Robert went out to Berlin in June to collect propaganda material, assisted by his brother-in-law who had been moved to Berlin from New York as *Times* correspondent. So efficient was this embryonic attempt at counter-propaganda that at the time of Munich, over two million leaflets were ready to be printed and the RAF were lined up to drop them over Germany on the first night of the war, if it started.

Before the Munich crisis, Robert had persuaded Unity Mitford, of whom he was very fond despite his distaste for her politics, to get him an invitation to the Nuremberg Parteitag, taking the place of her brother Tom. Robert was determined to study the Nazis in their full panoply: marching masses, blood-red flags streaming, intersecting searchlights heightening the arena. With Unity he attended meeting after meeting, sitting so close to the front that he could meet the eyes of the Führer and his henchmen. After this experience he noted in his diary:[1] 'This morning's ceremony has left me with the impression of a people doomed on earth and in heaven. I never got that feeling in Russia. I expected to get the impression of a vigorous evil which must be destroyed at all costs – and perhaps I do. But that is subordinated to the negativeness and vacuity of it all. It is not so much intellectual poison as intellectual death, a greater death than physical death – the death of Byron's darkness.' Finally, when even Unity admitted for the first time the possibility of war, Robert got 'the jitters' and ordered a taxi at

---

1. This diary was printed in *Articles of War* (Grafton Books, 1989).

eleven o'clock at night to take him to Frankfurt. He wanted to be home.

To continue his study of the Nazis Robert returned to Berlin for Christmas, just escaping arrest since the German customs were convinced that his present for his new niece Georgia, a plush football that played a tune when bounced, actually contained a bomb. Besides covering the night-life of Berlin, he visited an impressive exhibition of anti-Jewish propaganda, where the brilliantly clever faces of expelled Jews, exposed on black-draped walls of tunnel-like construction, only demonstrated the loss to Germany of world-famous names in medicine and science, led by Einstein. Robert wrote to his mother of the Nazis: 'I went to a Jewish exhibition today and came away feeling there can be no compromise with such people – there is no room in the world for them and me, and one has got to go. I trust it may be them.'

Robert's preoccupation in seeking to counteract the Nazi menace absorbed so much of his time that he reluctantly gave up his vice-chairmanship of the Georgian Group while remaining on the committee. He also postponed writing, in collaboration with Eric Schroeder, the projected book on Persian architecture which Macmillan had agreed to publish in much the same format as *The Birth of Western Painting*.

Robert, however, still needed to earn his living. On 19 October 1938 he set out for America on behalf of the Petroleum Information Bureau to study oil installations in the Middle West. On his return he spent the following January producing a memorandum on American opinion, which, through G. M. Young, was passed to King George VI's private secretary as being of possible use for Their Majesties' coming visit to America. G.M. commented to Robert: 'Wherever the K**g turns someone respectfully tenders him a copy of your memorandum. I shall search the K.C.V.O.s for your name next birthday. But I wish someone would make the Q***n read it.'

Robert's letters to his parents, who were wintering in Neuilly, became increasingly more cheerful with a lifting of the spirit as his writing took shape. At the time of Eden's resignation in March 1938 Robert had written an article for the *New Statesman* called 'The Clerk's Apology'. By clerk he was referring to the mediaeval clerk or writer and in it he set out his confession of faith as a 'keeper of the truth'. He tried to assess the value of English civilization and what it had given to the world and what was worth fighting for.

An expansion of this theme, never published, was absorbing Robert in all his spare moments. Happy to be creating again, he was too busy to go home. At this time, Adrian Daintrey, a neighbour, painted his portrait complete with dark overcoat and bowler, a bowler which his mother proceeded to improve, remarking that it hardly looked as if it had come from Lock's.

The most magical moment of that last summer before the war was the fancy-dress ball given by the Georgian Group at Osterley Park. There was scarcely a friend of Robert's who did not appear in some sort of costume, he himself being dressed as a Greek god with a green plaster breastplate. August found him blissful still, writing his book and fishing in Ireland at Glenarm, reluctant to leave even when Hitler had invaded Poland. He had seen the inevitable war approaching for so long.

Robert's hopes of being useful in the propaganda field had been frustrated earlier by interdepartmental jealousies. Tallents had been deprived of the prospect of the Ministry of Information; the likes of Sir Campbell Stuart had taken over propaganda. From the Admiralty downwards there was no service or ministry that Robert did not attack in applying for work, bombarding them with his impressive curriculum vitae. Increasing frustration and disappointment drove him into accepting a humble job in the BBC Foreign Department which was chiefly concerned with broadcasting to Greece, Hungary and Rumania. He continued to search for better work and more than once resigned from the BBC in an attempt to jolt them into greater efficiency. He believed profoundly in the importance of broadcasting propaganda towards winning the war: 'I am determined to get propaganda going properly even if it means resorting to personal blackmail.' But even with this threat Robert was appalled at the apathy which prevailed. His personal affairs were in difficulty, his income being halved. He found little time to make it up by writing articles and he was soon in a financial mess. His time was also limited by commitments which he had taken on in inaugurating the Federal Union Club, an idea based on *Union Now* by Clarence Streit: an attempt to create a super-authority which would override the selfish policies of individual states, as the League of Nations had so notably failed to do. Because of Robert, his friends loyally joined this new venture. Michael Rosse, Ran Antrim and John Sutro were all enthusiastic; busy women like Lady Rhondda, Mrs Madge Garland of *Vogue* and Dame Una Pope Hennessy came along. Started with such an upsurge of goodwill, it was found increasingly difficult to keep the Union going and in 1941 it was reluctantly suspended until the end of the war.

Robert's life was not improved by his house in Swan Walk being burgled twice. He felt compelled to move and, after having parked himself with Patrick Balfour until he went to Egypt, Robert ended up in the Great Western Hotel while his beloved house was denuded of furniture after having been flooded by enemy action. His landlady declined to come back from Tunisia. Meanwhile at Overton, to avoid having evacuees, Mrs Byron had gathered all the family to live with her, producing little peace for

Robert at weekends. In one letter he begged her to manage a space for him free from brothers-in-law so that he could relax.

Also, 1940 meant for Robert attempts to keep in fleeting contact with his friends, now all joined up, Michael Rosse in the Irish Guards, Christopher in the Green Howards, Ran Antrim in the RNVR, Henry Yorke in the London Fire Brigade, and to everyone's amazement Mark Ogilvie-Grant in the Scots Guards. Harold Acton came home from China and lectured to the RAF, in which he served.

At last, at the end of 1940, Robert's contacts with intelligence began to come to life. He engaged himself to travel to Meshed, there to keep an eye on the behaviour of the Russians in that region. A meeting with Sir Percy Loraine, last pro-consul in Persia, suggests a briefing. His cover was to proceed first to Cairo as war correspondent of the *Sunday Times* with the blessing of Lord Kemsley. On 19 February 1941 Robert boarded a small merchant ship at Liverpool, the *Jonathan Holt* of the Holt line.

---

15 January 1939   1 Swan Walk, sw3

Darling Mib

I have been very bad about writing I am afraid – but have been working myself almost silly every night this week and the whole weekend trying to finish a report on American opinion at this moment. God knows what use it will be – except that it is to go to the King's private secretary[1] – but I feel so *frantic* about everything that it seems the least one can do, if one has any information of value, to make it available. When I was in America, I made it an absolute rule (very much against the grain as you can imagine) to get into conversation with every single person I could – and I kept full notes of all conversations – so that I have a really remarkable amount of evidence on American opinion since Munich. However the damned thing isn't done yet and I suppose I shall have to give next weekend to it as well.

I believe there is something in what *The Week* says about finance.

---

1. King George VI and Queen Elizabeth left to visit the United States and Canada on 5 May 1939.

Where are Father's remaining investments? I can't help wondering if they mightn't be safer in real estate of some sort.

I have nothing to tell you. I dined with Henry and Dig last night. Henry has finished another novel – it has taken him 7 years and now he can't get it published.

One spends all one's life trying to save things – Jews, buildings, not to mention the world as a whole. I enclose my latest effort which the paper asked for.

I'm just going to dine with Lady Cunard whom I haven't seen for ages. A pro-German stronghold – I shan't be able to meet the rich much longer. Please don't expect many letters for the next 2 or 3 weeks. [. . .]

Love from
Bobs

20 January 1939   1 Swan Walk, sw3

Darling Mib

Many happy returns. I can't send you a present, so enclose something for taxis. Will you use it for that purpose only? I hate to think of you struggling about on the Metro.

I really don't know what to advise. Of course it's perfectly safe to go to Berlin. Hitler always gives plenty of notice. I should certainly go if I were you – and I really think you would be comfortable there and not oppressed by too much domesticity. [. . .]

I gave a dinner party at my club for Ewan and Lucy last night – Yorkes, Lady Colefax,[1] Unity – we drank to the doom of the upper classes, but Henry wouldn't.

Now the Oxford Press want me to do a tiny book on the King and Queen to be sold in Canada and the U.S.A. during their visit. I believe I ought to do it, as it will be bungled if I don't – but the financial inducement will have to be large – £200 clear at least, my agent says. As

---

1. Sibyl, Lady Colefax, interior decorator and society hostess. Her invitations being illegible it was only by the figures 1.30 or 6.30 and an occasional date that her guests could guess to what they were bidden.

it is I have so much on hand that I have quite altered my way of life, scarcely go out in the evenings at all and always walk to my office – and sometimes back – this with the walk to my club and back for lunch gives me about 5 miles a day. It is terrible to feel oneself developing habits – but they produce a kind of bestial contentment.

I was hoping to come over to Paris at the beginning of February, but it looks as if I shan't have time – however I shall know in a few days about the book. If I do it I shall have to engage a secretary and turn my upstairs room into an office.

Goodbye darling – I do hope you will have a nice birthday. [. . .]

> Best love
> from
> Bobs

Robert adds in his next letter of 4 February: '*At last*, after four months of intensive thought I have reduced what I have been trying to write all this time – all during my American journey – to a coherent form and can actually start on it. It has made me feel more cheerful than I have for a long time. It is so frustrating to have thoughts and feel that one hasn't the mental capacity to put them into logical form. My American memorandum which I told you about has almost turned into a book, so that no one will ever read it. You can certainly see it when you get back.'

7 March 1939   1 Swan Walk, SW3

Darling Mib

Don't worry about me. You gave me so much happiness in our early lives that you can't expect that level to continue. I should be very stupid if I grumbled at any present situation, considering how fortunate it is. I don't call it happiness in one sense, because it isn't the kind of life I like leading. At the same time I certainly get a great deal of enjoyment out of moving among a circle of very various acquaintances who enjoy, and represent, the best that this world can offer. In fact I make the best of life in a town. But my happiness doesn't consist simply of enjoyment. I have always had a certain purpose – ambition if you like – in what I do.

At times I have felt that I have not been fulfilling that purpose and have been really unhappy. I don't feel that now. How exactly I am fulfilling it through my absurd oil would take too long to tell you – even if I could find words to do so. But I am convinced that one day there will be a result that we can both be proud of.

What I appear like at Overton I can't help. I have never felt anything but miserable in that house and never shall – except during the [? Munich] crisis when there wasn't time to be conscious of one's environment.

It does give me great pleasure if you tell me you like anything I write – more pleasure than anything else in the world. But don't bother about things like that memorandum. I don't mean that sort of thing – I mean the poetic bits, when there are any. I don't mean to snub – in fact I don't know what you mean. All critics, even complimentary ones, are potential enemies and one has to treat them as though they had drawn a gun first – if they aren't worth that much, they aren't worth asking to be critics.

I don't know what I want as regards a house, except to see you and Father happy and comfortable. I can't think about it now – I am too deep in my writing to think about anything else in the short period I have to think each day. If only you could find somewhere you like, which would allow itself to be *developed* in time into something I like. But I dread our immediate neighbourhood. To me it represents the past, which I have always hated. As I say, we were *too* happy. [. . .] I think I must detach my heart from the country for the moment – and merely look on whatever we do get as a preparation. I find too many unrequited longings when I leave the town. But I should be really happy at Farley or somewhere like that for weekends because I should then know that those longings might be requited some time. It doesn't matter about room space for me for the moment. It is the possibilities of the place – the *genius loci* – that I care about. Overton has a bad *genius*.

I live in my thoughts at present. If I can get them onto paper I shall relax and look about again – but not until. What I am trying to write is a logical enlargement of that *New Statesman* article, 'The Clerk's Apology'. It is very difficult. But I *will* do it somehow. So don't mind if I don't come home for a bit – I can only really get anything done by staying here for weekends. Anyhow I shall see you tomorrow week. [. . .]

I'm glad you liked the letter in *The Times*.[1] I forgot I had written it and got a shock when I saw it there this morning – as though one had been found in the street with one's trousers off. I would never have written it but for your books.

Three people I met this morning said they couldn't understand it.

Goodbye darling – let me lead my own life for a month or two – then I shall come out of a trance and not do a stroke and arrange things if they aren't arranged already by then.

Best Love
from
Bobs

18 March 1939   1 Swan Walk, sw3

Darling Mib

Thank you so much for sending the busts. They are exactly the right size – and though as you say they hardly fall into the category of works of art, at that height they merge into the 'architecture' of the room and will probably look as well as the most exquisite marbles. In course of time, if I find a pair which have some real artistic value, I shall probably be tempted to buy them. But meanwhile these will save me a great deal of money and have exactly the effect I want. It was kind of you to order them.

The news this evening is atrocious and will probably be worse by the time you get this. Did you listen to Mein Gamp [Neville Chamberlain] speaking last night? I could not help feeling that it was the most complete justification of my attitude during the last 3 years that could possibly have been uttered. Not that this is any satisfaction. I find that the average conservative has begun to realise that the blood of millions

---

1. Robert's letter to *The Times* begins 'Sir, The Dürer drawings from the Albertina – the hare, the grasses, and the bunch of violets – would make one love any nation. But I fear some pictures might prove a double-edged weapon. There was an exhibition of Altdorfers in Munich last September which prompted some uncomfortable reflections on the duality of the German character and were just as circumstantial in their way as Hegel, Gerhardi, or Herr Hitler'.

will probably be on his head in the next few months if not the next few days. Damn their stupid souls. I am going to a party of Mrs Margesson's, wife of the chief whip, on Monday and ought to hear a little of what is going on then. I must say I am very glad to have my dug-out. [. . .]

The Ministry of Labour asked me to join a panel of speakers who would go about the country on behalf of National Service. I wrote back: 'It seems to me that if you ask people to serve their country, you must be able to tell them what this country means. This I cannot do, because under the present government England has ceased to mean what I thought it meant. I regret therefore . . .' They have returned the charge, with a long manifesto from the Trade Unions in favour of National Service. I must explain that I am not a socialist – but I suppose one ought to do it.

My portrait was finished this afternoon. I am longing for you to see it. Adrian Daintrey thinks it is the kind of picture a mother wouldn't like. I might make an effort to buy it if you did – but it is rather expensive, though he is asking much less than the price he gets for a commissioned portrait. [. . .]

Love
Bobs

25 August 1939   Deerpark Cottage, Glenarm, N. Ireland

Darling Mib

The crisis has supervened rather sooner than I calculated. I tried to telephone to you last night, but after the call had been in three hours, they still reported 'indefinite delay' between London and Lockeridge. Do you want me for anything? I will come if you wire. Otherwise I should do better to stay here, I think, as my writing is getting on so well and I have no news yet of the job I am supposed to have in the war – though I took the precaution of letting the dispenser of it know where I should be.

I still think it possible that there will be a last-minute wriggle on someone's part that will provide an escape. But I dare say by the time you get this, it will be too late – in which case I shall come home as soon as I can.

I get no newspapers here and everyone has gone away from the [Glenarm] Castle on a 4 day's motor trip – so am very much alone. The fish won't rise to anyone, even experts – there is too little water in the river.

It is very beautiful as I sit here looking out across the valley, with a terraced lawn and roses in front and the sound of the river. But I must confess I feel depressed. I think I shall bicycle into the village and post this and get a newspaper.

I hope Lucy is all right and Georgia. The gardener tells me British subjects have been warned to leave Germany.

Best love darling – let me know if you want me back for any special reason – otherwise it is best for me to stay here for the moment, as my book might be valuable in wartime.

Love
Bobs

Robert wrote a letter to his sister Anne on 22 October with instructions to show it to his mother. It begins: 'The War Office has made tentative enquiries if I would like to take on a job for them – though "I don't know that we can very well have *another* Old Etonian in this room – I was at Harrow meself yer know. Is it true you once went on parade with an umbrella?" The squalor is Crimean – in each room one gets the impression of people camping in the Arctic regions, while the passages are filled with old beds and mattresses. I'm afraid it can't please Mr Hore Belisha's aesthetic sense (he collects Wedgwood). I don't suppose anything will come of the offer. Meanwhile I have had a contract from the B.B.C. which reads like a scout manifesto and am desperately trying to stave off signing it by questioning certain clauses – I send you a bit of news I wrote late last night – it sounded rather well in French – "*Cette homérique machination*" private schoolish as it may read, it is much less so than the things other people write, particularly the enemy propaganda dept. which consists of sixth form essayists of the most feeble kind'.

---

28 October 1939   1 Swan Walk, sw3

Darling Mib

I am so sorry to have been so long in writing.

There is nothing to tell you. I went down to Brighton for a night to dine with Ed Stanley of Alderly in the mess of H.M.S. *Alfred* which consists of a vast *garage* where the Royal Naval Supplementary Reserve are being trained – they most of them go to the Scapa patrol, which means tossing about in trawlers all the winter between Iceland and the Orkneys, with leave only once in six months – so they are making the best of life now.

Louise Loraine is back from Rome and very interesting. They packed everything in August and spent a whole night burning the archives. I have been trying to get her to give me some hints about what we broadcast to Italy.

The Federal Union idea is to form a League of Nations which will work – the members would delegate their armed forces and various other matters to a central Assembly, which would be sovereign over them and could make certain laws. There is no other alternative that I or anyone else can see to living in dug-outs for the rest of our lives. The Club, of which I am the president, is having a party on Thursday, at which I have to speak.

There is a general feeling that the Germans won't bomb open towns here – but I expect they will.

It is very nice having Sarah back.

I will write a more sensible letter later – there is nothing to say at the moment.

Isn't it *cold*?

Best Love darling
Bobs

4 November 1939   1 Swan Walk, sw3

Darling Mib

[. . .] I enclose a leaflet – about the Federal Union Club and a copy of the speech I made at the party – which was a wild success as far as the *party* went, but struck some guests such as the Bishop of Lichfield who had come up specially from the country as a little frivolous. We had 3 Foreign Ministers!

But the whole thing is such a labour – I spend all my mornings writing letters, etc. Also I have a suppressed cold, which won't come or go – the result of the filthy atmosphere in the B.B.C. Half the rest of the European news staff has gone down with asthma, pneumonia, etc.

I don't know what else I have been doing. I spent an extraordinary evening at the Beefsteak alone with the Duke of Devonshire – he has 90 fighting cocks in training. [. . .]

Goodbye darling – there is really nothing to say.

Love
from
Bobs

4 February 1940   1 Swan Walk, sw3

Darling Mib

I'm so sorry not to have written for such ages. The trouble now is that I have taken to a secretary permanently about 3 mornings a week (she comes after being up all night at the B.B.C. because she is in love with Sarah, having always had 'flat-nosed dogs' herself till a few years ago) and I scarcely write anything now with my own hand – at the same time I feel you wouldn't like a dictated letter – so yours always gets left over.

I don't know that I have anything special to tell you, except that I have resigned from the B.B.C. – as a protest against their inefficiency as a war instrument – my object being not so much to get out of it myself, as to effect reforms – of which, judging by the fuss that has resulted, I am not unhopeful. Today I was lured secretly to a bar and offered another job in another department of the beastly place – but I have more ambitious plans in view, of which I dare say something will come eventually. If you knew how many dossiers about myself I had sent to how many departments after the War Office, you would be surprised. Tomorrow morning I have been sent for by the Admiralty again.

I have at last had a letter from Princess Lubomirska in Rome to tell me that Henri[1] got back to Cracow just before she left (she escaped with her daughter who is married to a Spanish Bourbon). I will enclose the letter in fact, as it is really a tribute to the way these unfortunate people are keeping their spirits up. I'm glad to think *Oxiana* has played its little part in the war – I sent it to Henri when he emerged from the solitary first period of his novitiate, and he wrote back appreciating the jokes more than anyone. The river San, which she mentions, is the boundary between Russia and German-occupied Poland – the last news I had had of Henri before this letter was that he had been seen working in a field in disguise in the Russian territory. May I have the letter back?

[. . .] Michael is miserable in the Irish Guards – he has suddenly discovered he can't kill people on principle and begins to wonder therefore why he joined up. I had a letter this morning from Ran Antrim,[2] who has been in the far north in a destroyer for the past month and says Captain Scott didn't know what suffering was. He has only been ashore once in that time, when he went to a Scottish fishing village and bought a box of dates.

Anne has just arrived for the night in a smart red top-hat. She and Charles dined here last night with the Campbells[3] and James Lees-Milne. We had a very gay evening off salt beef. Violet came up today – she has been having an awful time in Ramsbury, absolutely without fuel and having to keep Guy in bed with hot-water bottles as the only means of keeping him warm. Incidentally Lexel Hochberg[4] has escaped from Poland and has joined a Polish army in France. Now that the thaw has come, I begin to look hopefully for daffodil sprouts in the garden – but they were put in so late they probably won't come up till July.

Ran says that Sandy Macpherson at the Wurlitzer organ on the B.B.C. is definitely lowering the morale of the fleet.

Miss Greenhalgh (my secretary) asked if she could take Sarah for a walk this afternoon as a great favour – if I let her do so often enough, she will come without being paid.

I have just read an extremely interesting secret report on conditions in Germany which so bears out all that Ewan and I prophesied in the

---

1. Prince Henryk Lubomirski.
2. Randal McDonnell, 8th Earl of Antrim.
3. Robin and Mary Campbell.
4. The youngest son of the Prince and Princess of Pless.

document we produced for the Committee of Imperial Defence at the end of 1938, that I am quite astonished at our prescience – and convinced that the war will last much longer than most people imagine.

Best love darling

Bobs

19 February 1941   Liverpool

Darling Mib

The last boat to Takoradi took 25 days – so it may be quite a month before you hear anything.

Don't worry. We are all in this war together, and think what *I* should feel if the wireless says the Germans have captured Marlborough with gas.

I regard this as a glorious war and am glad to be taking a more active part in it. My boat is small but quite new, and they say very comfortable. They have never taken passengers before, so don't really know how to deal with them. The only fellow traveller I have seen so far is a Polish officer. All Poles are in my opinion seriously mad. The Captain is a splendid old tough. I have got some gloves and look more like a chauffeur than ever. Thank you so much for all your efforts yesterday, I should never have got off without you. I hope you got back to the hotel all right.

On board

A most delightful surprise awaited me on the boat in the person of an old friend of mine, Joseph Hackin, and his wife. He was curator of the Musée Guimet in Paris and head of the French archaeological mission in Afghanistan. We were at that fantastic congress in Russia together. It is rather extraordinary that one should find a friend out of only 12 passengers. The boat is minute, but comfortable, and there are lots of books aboard. They aren't altogether what one wants to read, but still it is comforting.

Well goodbye darling – and very best love – and think of the times we shall have when it's all over.

Bobs

On 24 February Robert's ship was torpedoed by the *Scharnhorst* off the north of Scotland above Stornoway. It was not until May that hope for Robert was given up. The family had relied on rumours that three survivors had been picked up by another boat without a wireless. But repeated appeals to the Holt Line and to the Red Cross produced no news. Robert was lost at sea by enemy action. Perhaps, like his last letter, his last thoughts were for his mother, that and fury at all the things he had to leave undone.

Index

Abbasabad, 220
Abberly, 3
Abdy, Lady Diana, 189–90
Abdy, Sir Robert, 189–90
Abelson, Tamara (later Mrs David
    Talbot Rice), 83
Abercorn, Mary, Dowager Duchess of,
    3, 107
Abingdon, 20, 21
Abingdon, Bettine, Countess of, 111
Abyssinia, 237, 243
Acton, Harold, 16, 19, 24, 26, 32, 41,
    54, 100, 113, 169, 256, 258, 260–1,
    264–73 passim, 275–6, 284, 288, 294
Acton, Hortense, 58
Acton, William, 43, 113
Adrianos, Pater, 78
Afghanistan, 189, 192, 197, 199, 204–5,
    214, 216–17, 220, 226, 235, 263, 304
Africa, 122
Agra, 146, 168, 170–1, 173
Ahmedabad, 168
Aldeburgh, 56
Alexandria, 66, 70, 122–3, 174–5
Ali Pasha, 178
Alington, Revd Cyril, 3, 8, 9, 14
Alington, Hester, 14
Allahabad, 159
Allenby, Edmund, 1st Viscount, 160
Allenby, Mabel, Viscountess, 160
America, 29, 31, 53–4, 110, 113,
    116–17, 138, 213, 226, 233, 236, 252,
    282, 292, 294
Anatolia, 75
Andréas of Kerasia, Father, 89
Anglesey, 2

Antrim, Randal McDonnell, 8th Earl of,
    293–4
Ardabil, 195
Ashraf, 218
Asia Minor, 45, 67, 74, 149
Asquith, Margot, Countess of Oxford
    and Asquith, 7, 31, 97
Asterabad, 215–16, 218
Aston Clinton, 39
Atchley, Clifford, 59, 66, 82, 178
Athens, 44, 48, 58–9, 64–5, 80, 83–8,
    91, 94, 121, 149, 154, 168, 172, 179,
    183
Athens, Metropolitan of, 82
Athos, Mount, 6, 57–9, 72, 75–7,
    79–80, 82–4, 95–6, 126–7, 140, 184,
    233
Austria, 105
Azerbaijan, 197, 204, 217

Baalbek, 192, 194
Badakshan, 218, 221
Baddeley, Hermione (Mrs David
    Tennant), 5, 115
Baghdad, 123–4, 191–2
Baikal, Lake, 237, 247, 250–1, 253, 255
Baker, Gertrude (Aunsssy), 108
Baker, Sir Herbert, 152, 163, 177
Baldwin, Betty, 40, 59
Baldwin, Lucy, 40
Baldwin, Oliver (later 2nd Earl), 30–3,
    37
Baldwin, Stanley (later 1st Earl), 33, 40
Balfour, Patrick, see Kinross
Balham, 130
Balkh, 223

Balston, Thomas, 83, 98
Baluchistan, 159, 213
Bamin, 213
Bandar Shah, 218–19
Barker, Granville, *see* Granville-Barker, Harley
Bateman, Lady, 268–9, 274
Batum, 189
Baum, Vicki, 276
Bavaria, 45–6
Baxter, Beverly, 39
Beauchamp, Lettice, Countess, 31
Beauchamp, William Lygon, 7th Earl, 17, 25–6, 29, 32, 45, 53, 65, 165
Beaverbrook, William Maxwell Aitken, 1st Baron, 39, 118
Beddington, Jack, 177
Beirut, 190–1, 197
Bell, Sir Charles, 120, 135
Bell, E. A., 8
Bell, Julian, 267
Bengal, 147
Bennett, Arnold, 96, 104
Berlin, 264, 288, 291–2, 295
Berners, Gerald Tyrwhitt-Wilson, 14th Baron, 5, 261
Bethlehem, 124
Bevan, G. L., 12
Biddulph, Adelaide Mary ('Dig'; later Mrs Henry Yorke), 5, 119, 295
Birkenhead, F. E. Smith, 1st Earl of, 29, 53
Birmingham, 27, 53
Birobijan, 247, 254
Blackheath, 3
Bokhara, 216
Bologna, 48
Bolton, 2
Bombay, 145, 154–5, 165, 170–1, 222, 224
Boniface, Father, 79
Boothby, Robert, 101–3, 178
Borough, Revd, 65
Boston, 286–7
Boubalis, Governor of Macedonia, 79
Bournemouth, 75
Bower, Leonard, 49, 50–2, 58, 60–1, 63, 66–7, 70, 72–4, 77, 122, 175
Bracken, Brendan, 117
Bragg, Professor and Mrs, 69
Brett, Oliver (later 3rd Viscount Esher), 99

Breughel, Pieter, the Younger, 17, 21
Bridgeman, Maurice, 227
Brindisi, 50, 58
Brownlow, Lady, 4
Brussels, 29, 95, 288
Buddha Gaya, 145–6
Bullard, Reader, 182
Burmah, 140, 147
Bury St Edmunds, 56
Bushire, 213
Butler, Ewan, 285, 295
Butler, Georgia, 292, 300
Butt, (Dame) Clara, 35
Byron, Anne, 3, 5, 40, 58, 59, 100, 147, 200, 229, 233, 283, 291
Byron, Arthur, 193, 283
Byron, Edmund, of Rochdale, 1
Byron, Edmund, Prebend, 1
Byron, Edmund, of Coulsdon Court, 2, 4, 7, 112
Byron, Edmund, of Soho, 1
Byron, Eric (Punch), 2, 4, 16, 30, 39, 56, 95, 106–8, 112, 124, 141, 146, 153, 158, 162, 200, 217, 219, 226, 230, 248–9, 256–9, 295
Byron, George Gordon, 6th Baron, 1, 20, 70, 178, 230, 278, 291
Byron, Julia, 2
Byron, Lucy, 3, 5, 40, 111, 143, 147, 156, 164–5, 167, 200, 258, 284–6, 291, 295, 300
Byron, Margaret, 2, 3, 4, 5, 26, 95–6, 293, 305
Byron, Robert, 2–6, 16, 17, 26–7, 45, 57, 82–4, 95, 120–1, 177–9, 188–9, 226, 233, 236–8, 256, 276, 288–94, 296, 305
Byron, Thomas, 1, 2
Byzantium, 57

Cadogan, Sir Alexander, 261
Cadogan, Lady Theodosia, 261
Caftazoglu, Monsieur, 70
Cairo, 107, 121, 131, 170, 172–3
Calcutta, 121, 127, 130–1, 135, 140, 144, 148–9, 151–4, 159, 162, 163, 166, 168, 171, 173, 232
California, 230, 232
Cambridge, 12
Campbell, Robin and Mary, 303
Canada, 295

Canterbury, Archbishop of, *see* Lang, Cosmo Gordon
Cardigan, Cedric Brudenell-Bruce, Earl of, 226
Cartaliss, Sotiri, 52, 54, 55
Cartland, Barbara, 39
Caryes, 78, 83, 89, 90–1
Caspian, 216, 218
Casselli, Monsieur, 123, 174
Ceylon, 125, 147
Chamberlain, Neville, 298
Chanak, 64
Channon, Sir Henry ('Chips') and Lady Honor, 190
Chapman, Miss, 71
Charlottesville, 287
Charlton, 2, 3
Cheetham, Sir Milne, 70
Cheltenham, 196
Chesterfield, 2, 3, 4, 30
Chetwode, Penelope (later Mrs John Betjeman), 188
Chicago, 116, 245, 278
China, 140, 142, 187, 226, 229, 235, 237, 240, 247, 251, 254, 260, 269, 274, 285, 288
Chitral, 218, 221
Churchill, John, 5
Churchill, Randolph, 107
Churchill, Winston, 102, 269
Clark, Kenneth, 240–1
Clarke, Dorothy, 291, 293
Clerk, Sir George, 188
Clements, Sarah, 96, 100, 108, 117, 167
Clifton Hamden, 20
Clive, Sir Robert, 279
Clonmore, William Cecil Forward-Howard, Baron, 3, 8, 16, 19, 20–1, 23–4, 26–7, 29, 32, 35, 107, 165
Cobham, Alan, 114
Colefax, Sibyl, Lady, 295
Coleman, Mrs, 25
Columbo, 125–7
Constantinides, Dragoman, 65
Constantinople, 48, 59, 65, 81–3, 86, 114, 149, 180, 186, 189, 261
Constantinople, Patriarch of, 75, 77, 82, 88
Cooch Behar, Indira, Maharanee of, 132, 148
Cooper, Alfred Duff, 267

Corfu, 50, 121
Coulsdon, 2–4, 10, 91, 134
Cracow, 303
Cresswell, Billa (later Mrs Roy Harrod), 289
Crete, 91–4, 121–2
Croydon, 2
Culham, 20, 21, 146
Cumberlegge, G., 236
Cunard, Emerald, Lady, 197, 295
Curtis Brown, 106
Curzon of Kedleston, George Nathaniel, Marquess of, 18
Curzon of Kedleston, Grace, Marchioness, 16, 22–3, 44, 48
Curzon, Robert, 178
Cyprus, 189–90, 194

Daintrey, Adrian, 292, 299
Dalai Lama, 135
Dalton, Ormonde Maddock, 244
Damascus, 149, 190–4
Damghan, 220
Danzig, 288
Daphni, 78, 83, 90
Dardanelles, 81
Darjeeling, 131, 133, 138
Darrell, Richard, 19
Datiev, Russian Consul, 215
Dawber, Sir Guy, 289
Dawkins, R. M., 107
Dawson, Beatrice, 59
Deakin, Ralph, 256, 258
Delhi, 131, 135, 149, 155–7, 159, 203, 224
Delphi, 67, 69, 175
Derwent, George, 3rd Baron, 289
Devonshire, Edward William Spencer Cavendish, 10th Duke of, 302
Dharbanga, Maharajah of, 149
'Dig', *see* Biddulph
Dineley, Mark, 139
Dixon, Oliver, 159
Dodecanese Islands, 44, 52, 63, 66, 70
Douglas, Tom, 41
Duggan, Alfred, 16, 18, 19, 21, 23, 44, 46, 48, 51, 86, 91–2, 116
Duggan, Hubert, 22, 32–3
Duggan, Marcella, 22
Dunsany, Edward, 18th Baron, 8, 148
Duzdab, 203–4

Index

Ealing, 193, 278
Eastbourne, 130, 288
Edward, Prince of Wales (later Edward VIII), 112, 170, 174, 276
Effingham, Henry Howard, 4th Earl of, 25, 27
Egypt, 154, 160, 172, 293
Einstein, Albert, 292
Elizabeth, Duchess of York (later Queen of George VI), 22, 292, 295
Elizabeth, Princess (later Queen Elizabeth II), 170
Elkins, Ethel, 226
Elmley, William, Viscount, 26, 28, 29, 30, 32, 39
Elwes, Gloria (Golly), 122
Elwes, Simon, 97, 105, 111, 122
England, 23, 38, 88, 94, 127, 131, 153–4, 157–8, 162–3
Ephesus, 67, 73–4, 77
Epirus, 178
Erskine, Hamish St Clair, 5, 165
Estergom, 26
Estonia, 288
Eton, 3, 19, 23, 30, 35, 107, 125, 150, 193
Evans, W. S. K., 9

Fatehpur Sikri, 173
Finland, 240
Firuzabad, 211
Fleming, Peter, 268
Florence, 46–8, 77
Fontainebleau, 190
Forster, E. M., 156
Fothergill, John, 30
France, 3, 31, 303
Frankfurt, 95, 292
Fyfe, David, 121, 125, 131–2, 159

Gallipoli, 64, 81
Gallop, 122
Gandhi, Mahatma, 162, 168
Gangtok, 142
Gardner, Evelyn (later Mrs Evelyn Waugh), 103, 169
Gaselee, Stephen, 179
Gaza, 123–4
Geneva, 247
George V, King, 12, 112, 267, 278
George VI, King, 292, 294–5
Germany, 45–6, 288, 292, 300

Ghazni, 224
Gibson, Leonora, 31
Gilgit, 221
Glenarm, 293
Glastonbury, 1
Goa, 121
Goldman, Bosworth (Boz), 189, 191, 202, 205
Goldring, Douglas, 289
Graham, Alistair, 62, 67, 88, 91–2
Granville-Barker, Harley, 95
Greco, El (Domenicos Theotocopoulos), 91–2, 118, 165, 227
Greece, 1, 44, 49, 50, 57, 67, 69, 82–5, 121, 154, 188, 277, 293
Green, Elizabeth, 1
Greene, Graham, 290
Greene, Babe Plunket, 59, 97, 111
Greene, David Plunket, 41, 59, 109
Greene, Gwendolen Plunket, 40, 55, 100
Greene, Olivia Plunket, 5, 40, 56
Greene, Richard Plunket, 37, 39, 55
Greenhalgh, Miss, 302–3
Grosskopf, German Consul, 245–6, 248, 253
Grosskopf, Frau, 245, 247–8, 253
Guedalla, Philip, 28
Guinness, Bryan, (later 2nd Baron Moyne), 5, 41, 43, 54, 55, 56, 75–80, 82, 84, 89, 92, 98, 100–1, 109, 115–17
Guinness, Diana (later Lady Mosley), 5, 106, 115, 165
Guinness, (Arthur) Ernest, 36
Guinness, Lady Evelyn, 40–1, 43, 56, 117
Guinness, Marie Clotilde, 36
Guinness, Oonagh, 36
Guinness, Walter (later 1st Baron Moyne), 56, 78
Guernsey, Gladys, Baroness, 171–2
Gulheq, 195
Gumbad-i-Qabus, 215–16, 218–19
Gyantse, 131, 135–6, 139, 141, 143–4, 172, 205
Gytheuri, 62

Hackin, Joseph, 222, 304
Hamber, Major and Mrs, 204–6, 217, 220
Hamilton, Charles Baillie, 103

Index

Hamilton, Lord Frederick, 32
Hannibal, 195–6
Harbin, 252, 254, 257, 282
Harkov (Kharkov), 186
Harrod, Roy, 107, 289
Hay, John Stuart, 59, 72–3, 75, 78–81, 88, 91–2, 122
Henderson, Gavin (later 2nd Baron Faringdon), 19, 44, 47–8, 51, 54, 55, 73, 77, 85–7, 104, 120–1, 127, 135, 137, 139–40, 142–3, 159–60, 167, 170
Henderson, John, 189, 191
Henley, 23, 35
Herat, 200–3, 206, 214, 217–18, 220–2, 272
Herbert, Gabriel, 234
Herzfeld, Ernst, 211, 227
Hesketh, Peter, 230, 232
Heygate, John, 19, 21, 169
Hill, Derek, 5
Hilton, Eva, 113
Himalayas, 131, 237
Hitler, Adolf, 291–2, 295
Hoare, Katherine, Lady, 213, 215
Hoare, Sir Reginald, 213, 215
Hochberg, Lexel, Count, 303
Holden, Wanda, 118
Hongkong, 196
Honolulu, 284
Hore-Belisha, Leslie, 300
Hourmouzios, Mrs, 107, 116
Howard, Brian, 14, 15, 114
Howard, Francis, 53
Howard, Lura, 113–14
Hoyland, Consul and Mrs, 209–10
Hsinking, 257
Hügel, Lady Mary von, 100
Hungary, 293
Hyderabad, 160, 162

Ibn Battuta, 126
India, 120–1, 124–5, 127–9, 136, 140, 151–2, 156, 158, 163, 177–8, 188, 221, 224–5
Innsbruck, 46
Ireland, 293
Irkutsk, 247, 253–4
Irwin, Lady Dorothy, Baroness (later Countess of Halifax), 152, 155, 164
Irwin, Edward Wood, Baron (later 1st Earl of Halifax), 150, 152

Isfahan, 195, 206, 209–11, 214
Italy, 65, 67, 73, 121, 165, 246

Jacks, T. L., 195, 198, 208, 217
Jackson, Sir Francis, 134–5, 152
Jackson, Julia, Lady, 134–5, 152
Japan, 248, 252, 256, 269, 274, 276–7
Jask, 123–4
Jenkinson, Bobby, 47
Jerusalem, 124, 193
Jodhpur, 160
Jodhpur, Maharajah of, 148
Jong, Mrs Piet de, 67
Jordan, 124

Kabul, 198–9, 200, 202, 214–16, 218, 221–4
Kahn, Mrs Otto, 227, 235, 240, 242, 265, 275
Kala Nao, 201, 203–4
Kalamata, 84, 92
Kandahar, 199, 200, 203
Kandy, 121, 129
Kapurthala, Maharajah of, 172
Karachi, 120, 124, 152, 157, 159–61
Kashgar, 221
Kashmir, 221
Kauffer, E. McKnight, 177
Kavalla, 84
Kemsley, Edith, Lady, 290
Keppel, Alice, 5
Kerasia, 83
Khabarovsk, 251, 254
Khaipur, 160
Kharokh, 202
Kiev, 185–6, 239
King, Soltan, 270
Kinglake, Alexander William, 290
Kinross, Patrick Balfour, later 3rd Baron, 105, 116, 118–19, 293
Kirman, 212–13
Kish, 83
Knopf, Alfred, 108–10, 119
Knowle House, 98
Kobe, 252, 276–8
Korea, 252, 254, 257, 274
Kotzias, Mme, 79
Kovno, 288
Kushk, 200
Kutub Minar, 153

Lahore, 156, 158
Lamb, Henry, 105

Lang, Cosmo Gordon, Archbishop of Canterbury, 112
Leconfield, Charles Wyndham, 3rd Baron, 10–12
Leconfield, Constance Evelyn, Lady, 13
Lees-Milne, James, 303
Lelis, N., 233
Lenin, V. I., 179
Leningrad, 180, 184–6, 236–8, 246
Leslie, Shane, 165
Leverson, Ada (The Sphinx), 169
Lewisohn, Sam and Adolph, 228–9
Lhasa, 120, 135, 142, 144–5
Lidgie, 76
Lindsay, Lady Anne, 34
Lindsay, Elizabeth, Lady, 231
Lint, Van, 23
Littler-Powell, Mr and Mrs, 69
Liverpool, 294, 306
Lloyd George, 1st Baron, 107, 174
Lloyd George, David, 1st Earl, 178, 272
Locker Lampson, Bianca, 54, 55
Locker Lampson, Oliver, 54, 55
London, 28, 36, 38–9, 44, 53–5, 57–9, 96, 98, 104–6, 109, 113, 118, 131, 171, 175, 229, 291, 299
Loraine, Louise, Lady, 154, 174, 301
Loraine, Sir Percy, 154, 174, 294
Los Angeles, 285
Lubomirska, Princess, 302
Lubomirski, Prince Henryk, 255, 303
Luce, ('Loos') Clare, 240
Lutyens, Sir Edwin, 146, 149, 151–2, 155–6, 163–4, 166, 171, 177, 231, 233
Lygon, Hugh, 17, 32, 35, 38, 58, 109
Lygon, Lady Lettice, 40, 43

MacCarthy, Desmond, 96, 99, 106, 116
Macedonia, Metropolitan of, 77
Maclagan, Eric, 178
Macmillan, Harold, 102
Madras, 130, 155
Mahmud, 198, 208, 210
Maimena, 223
Mallet, Victor and Peggy, 208, 213
Malmsey, 62
Manchuquo, 252, 257
Manchuria, 2, 274
Maragha, 195, 197
Marlborough, 4, 283, 289, 304
Marseilles, 83, 85

Marunuma, 280, 283
Mary, Princess (Princess Royal), 11, 172
Mary, Queen, 12
Masaryk, Thomas, 239
Mavrogordato, John, 114–15
Maxse, Leo, 8
Mazar-i-Sherif, 199, 201, 216, 221, 222
Medlicott, Colonel H., 288
Melchett, Henry, 2nd Baron, 190, 191
Meletios IV, Patriarch of Alexandria, 67, 175
Meshed, 200, 202–3, 206, 216–17, 219–20, 294
Messel, Oliver, 5, 35, 54
Messel, Phoebe, 31
Messel, Rudolph, 10, 16, 19, 21, 25, 32
Mexico, 180
Mianeh, 197
Milan, 58, 63
Missolonghi, 51, 121
Mistra, 60, 62, 82, 84, 92–4
Mitford, Diana, *see* Guinness, Diana
Mitford, Nancy, 107, 115, 165, 207, 291
Mitford, Unity, 288, 291, 295
Mitylene, 63
Modis, G., 178
Mohammera, 220
Monsell, Joan Eyres, 243
Moore, Mrs William H., 213–14
Morland, Alice, 257, 276
Morland, Oscar, 257, 276
Morrel, Lady Ottoline, 42
Morton, H. V., 290
Moscow, 179–80, 183, 187, 215, 238, 240–2, 224, 246, 253–4, 264, 280
Mosley, Sir Oswald, 5
Mowat, R. B., 26
Mukden, 254, 257, 274, 276, 282
Mulholland, Alfred, 101
Munich, 294, 297
Murdoch, Ché, 53–4
Murghab, 223
Mussolini, Benito, 63, 66, 237

Nadjibullah, 127–9
Naples, 44, 122, 230
Nash, Paul, 99, 177
Neuilly, 292
New Delhi, 146, 150, 153, 155–6, 159, 161–4, 171, 177, 231

New York, 114, 116, 226–30, 234–5,
258, 264, 269, 275, 286–7
Newchurch Pendle, 1
Newton, Algernon, 177
Nicola, 81, 86, 88
Nicosia, 190
Nikko, 280
Nilgiri, Rajah of, 167
Novgorod, 183–4
Novo Sibirsk, 237, 245, 248, 253–4
Numata, 281, 283
Nuneham, 20
Nuremberg, 291

Odessa, 182, 186–7
Odom, William, 190, 227
Ogilvie-Grant, Mark, 36, 43, 83, 90, 92,
105, 154, 170, 190, 233, 294
Omar Khayyam, 196, 207, 210
Omsk, 247
Orbeli, Josef, 237
Overton House, 289–90, 293, 297
Ovey, Sir Esmond, 179–80, 288
Oxford, 1, 2, 4, 5, 23, 31, 42, 45, 53–6,
63–4, 108, 161–2
Oxus, 201, 216, 221, 223

Paget, Lady Muriel, 239–40
Pallis, A., 122
Paris, 33–4, 59, 94, 114, 187, 244, 274,
296, 304
Parsons, Lady Bridget, 55
Parsons, Desmond, 190, 226, 232, 237,
256–9, 262, 264, 277
Patey, George de, 101
Patras, 50–1, 87
Peking (Peiping), 226, 232, 248–9,
252–3, 255–6, 258–9, 267, 270, 277,
279
Persepolis, 195, 210–12, 214, 237
Persia, 6, 188–9, 191, 193–4, 197, 200,
203–4, 207, 209, 213, 215, 226, 230,
235, 242, 259, 261
Peshawar, 224
Peter Bonifacious, 78
Phari, 141, 143
Philadelphia, 232, 234
Phrantzes, General, 71, 88
Piraeus, 63, 72, 88
Poland, 293, 303
Ponsonby of Shulbrede, Arthur
Ponsonby, 1st Baron, 37, 112

Ponsonby, Elizabeth, 43
Ponsonby, Matthew, 26, 37, 39
Pope, Arthur Upham, 189, 213–14,
236, 265, 275
Port Said, 131
Porto Raphti, 71
Powell, E. W., 15
Price, G. Ward, 109, 119
Punjab, 158
Puri, 149, 166

Quetta, 204

Rajpipla, Maharajah of, 172
Rajputana, 161
Rampur, 150
Rampur, Nawab of, 148, 150, 154
Ramsbury, 283, 303
Rasputin, Gregory, 184
Ravenna, 44
Ravensdale, Irene, Baroness, 242
Reading, 30
Redesdale, Sydney, Baroness, 107
Reitlinger, Gerald, 83–4, 90, 263, 272,
277–8, 280, 282, 290
Rembrandt, 117
Rhodes, 44, 52
Rice, David Talbot, 16, 18–20, 29,
82–4, 90–2, 94, 174, 237
Richardson, A. E., 289
Richardson, Gladys Stuart, 60
Riga, 288
Robeson, F. E., 3, 7, 8, 10, 11, 13
Robinson, Alice, 2, 56
Robinson, Gladys, 58
Robinson, Norman, 2
Robinson, Phyllis, 58
Robinson, William, 2
Rochdale, 1
Rodd, Francis (later 2nd Baron
Rennell), 72
Rodd, Sir James Rennell (later 1st
Baron Rennell), 77, 122
Rodd, Lilias, Lady, 105, 111, 122
Rodd, Peter, 55, 59, 72–3, 111, 207
Rome, 46, 48–9, 63, 66, 70, 73, 77, 122,
301
Roosevelt, Kermit, 231
Ross, Sir F. Leith, 258
Rosse, Anne, Countess of, 258, 260, 264
Rosse, Michael Parsons, 6th Earl of, 41,
43, 55, 98, 107, 109, 117, 120–1,

131–5, 137, 140–4, 147, 149, 160,
170, 178–80, 182–3, 185–8, 258, 260,
262, 264, 277, 289, 293–4, 303
Rothenstein, Sir William, 14, 15
Rothermere, Harold Harmsworth,
Viscount, 168
Roublev, Andrei, 241
Roumania, 293
Rubens, Olive, 97, 111
Rufer, Peter, 19
Russell, Elizabeth, 39
Russell, Bertrand, 167, 176
Russia, 26, 29, 30, 33, 179, 182, 185–6,
188, 196, 211, 213, 237–8, 240–1,
268, 274, 288, 291, 303
Rutter, Frank, 165, 192, 193–4, 197

St Wolfgang, 96, 134, 172, 281
Salmond, Sir Geoffrey, 122
Salonika, 48, 75, 79, 81, 83, 91
Salzburg, 45, 46
Salzkammergut, 96, 282
Samarcand, 214–16, 223, 237, 254
Samnan, 219
San Francisco, 276, 284–5
Sandhurst, 28, 31
Sassoon, Siegfried, 114
Savage, Raymond, 38
Savernake Forest, 4, 5, 70, 72, 81,
95–6, 114, 188, 217, 226, 264, 281
Scarlett, Peter, 192–3, 288
Schroeder, Eric, 237, 286
Schurhof, George, 24, 103–4
Scone, Mungo, 19
Scotland, 83, 305
Scutari, 64
Seafield, Nina, Countess of, 98, 105,
112, 165, 169
Seisin, 257
Seistan, 204
Selchouk, 73
Shahi, 216, 219
Shiraz, 209–10, 234
Shoosmith, Mr and Mrs A. G., 159
Siberia, 189, 237, 239, 243, 246,
249–50, 253–4, 258, 280, 283
Siena, 48, 50
Sigiriya, 126
Sikkim, 120–1, 142, 144
Sinha, Aroon, 2nd Baron, 147
Sitwell, Georgia, 115, 206
Sitwell, Osbert, 96, 104

Sitwell, Sacheverell, 5, 115, 117, 206
Skeleri, Mme, 71
Slater, E. V., 7
Smyrna, 63–4, 67, 73, 76–7
Spain, 100, 109
Sparta, 51, 60–2, 67, 84, 94
Spencer, John, 22
Stalin, Josef, 238, 243
Stallybrass, W. S., 58
Stanley of Alderly, Edward, 6th Baron,
301
Steel, Flora Annie, 235
Stein, Sir Aurel, 188
Stokes, Adrian, 179
Stornoway, 305
Strachey, Julia, 37
Streit, Clarence, 293
Strzygowski, Josef, 188
Sukkur, 162
Sultaniya, 215, 217
Sutro, John, 84, 92, 98, 108, 111, 131,
293
Sutro, Mrs, 98, 103–9, 276
Sutton Courtenay, 20
Sverdlovsk, 245–6
Switzerland, 67
Sykes, Christopher, 188–9, 191–3,
195–8, 204, 210–11, 213–14, 224,
226, 234, 237, 243–4, 290, 294
Symonds Yat, 34

Tabriz, 195–7
Takoradi, 304
Tallents, Sir Stephen, 291, 293
Taylor, Geoffrey, 19
Teheran, 193, 194–5, 204–6, 209, 213,
215–16, 218, 220
Tehring, Jigmed, 145–6
Tehring, Mary, 145–6
Tennant, David, 115
Termez, 223
Tewkesbury, 8, 13, 25
Thame, 30, 31
Thring, Miss, 118
Thyateira, Archbishop Germanos,
Metropolitan of, 59
Tibet, 6, 120–1, 134–6, 143, 147, 153
Tientsin, 248, 252, 277
Tobruk, 122
Todd, L., 3
Tokyo, 277–8, 280, 282
Travancore, 121, 127–8

Trebizond, 81
Trieste, 26, 63
Tripolitza, 61
Tunisia, 293
Turkestan, 188, 205, 216, 218, 223, 243
Turkey, 76
Turner, J. M. W., 13, 16

Urbye, Mlles, 182, 185, 243

Van Gogh, Vincent, 117
Venice, 26, 145, 190, 227
Venizelos, Eleutherios, 84
Verchné Udinsk, 250
Vermeer, Jan, 117
Verona, 47
Vesci, Frances, Lady de, 43, 257, 260, 264
Vienna, 26, 29, 95–7, 103, 114
Villehardouin, Geoffroi de, 84
Vilna, 30
Vladimir, 185
Vladivostok, 237, 248, 252, 254–5, 257
Vogüé, C. J. M., Marquis de, 188

Waikiki, 284
Warburg, Frederic, 108, 114
Warsaw, 30, 288
Warwick, Charles Greville, 7th Earl of, 240
Washington, 231–2, 256, 282, 285
Waugh, Evelyn, 103–4, 116, 169, 290
Weir, J. L. R., 120–1, 144
Weir, Thyra, 121, 144
Wellesley, Lord Gerald, 289
Wembley, 2
Weymouth, Daphne, Viscountess, 118, 120

Weymouth, Henry Thynne, Viscount, 226
Whetham, John, 2
Whetham, Lucy Anne, 2
Whistler, James Abbott McNeil, 15
Whittall, Donald, 76
Whittemore, Thomas, 187
Wilhelm II, Kaiser, 112, 269
Wilson, Martin, 40
Wilson, Mona, 5
Windsor, 7, 22, 35, 126
Wishaw, manager of A.P.O.C., 211
Wolfe, General James, 2
Wong, Anna May, 276
Wortley, Edward Stuart, 112
Wright, Mrs, 98
Wyndham, Guy, 169, 303
Wyndham, Violet, 5, 169, 276, 303

Yaroslav, 185
Yatung, 136, 143
Yokohama, 282–3
York, 254
Yorke, Dorothy, 14, 43
Yorke, Gerald, 12
Yorke, Henry (Henry Green), 5, 7–14, 16, 22, 43, 53, 95–6, 104–5, 113–14, 119, 155, 159, 294–5
Yorke, Maud, 8, 9, 11–13, 40, 43, 119
Yorke, Vincent, 9
Young, G. M., 5, 177, 290, 292
Yusupov, Prince Felix, 97, 184

Zervos, Skevos, 44–5, 51, 59, 60, 66, 70, 73, 77, 81, 88, 122, 175
Zinfan, 197
Zoppot, 197